THE NEW

LEXINGTON
PRESS

HELPING TEACHERS TEACH WELL

HELPING TEACHERS
TEACH WELL

A New System for Measuring and
Improving Teaching Effectiveness
in Higher Education

Robert D. Pritchard, Margaret D. Watson, Karlease Kelly,

Anthony R. Paquin

THE NEW
LEXINGTON
PRESS

The New Lexington Press
San Francisco

For sales outside the United States, please contact your local Simon
& Schuster International Office.

The New Lexington Press Web address: http://www.newlex.com

Manufactured in the United States of America using Lyons Falls
D'Anthology paper, which is a special blend of nontree fibers and
totally chlorine-free wood pulp.

Library of Congress Cataloging-in-Publication Data

Helping teachers teach well: a new system for measuring and
  improving teaching effectiveness in higher education / by Robert D.
  Pritchard . . . [et al.].
      p.   cm.
    Includes bibliographical references and index.
    ISBN 0-7879-3965-X (hc : acid free)
    1. College teachers—Rating of—United States.   2. College
  teaching—United States—Evaluation.   I. Pritchard, Robert D.
  LB2333.H45   1997
  378.1'25—dc21   97-25642

FIRST EDITION

HB Printing 10 9 8 7 6 5 4 3 2 1

CONTENTS

PART ONE
Issues in Teaching Evaluation

PART TWO
Developing an Effective System

LIST OF TABLES AND FIGURES

TABLES

FIGURES

PREFACE

THIS BOOK IS ABOUT evaluating teaching in higher education. It describes ways to develop high-quality measures of teaching effectiveness to assess instructors and to help them improve their teaching. It is a scholarly book that reviews relevant literature, presents a new way to do teaching evaluation that is based on sound research principles, and carefully evaluates this new approach with empirical data. It is also an applied book, because it presents very specific information for designing and implementing teaching evaluation systems.

IMPORTANT FEATURES OF THE BOOK

This book has a number of important features.

- It presents a comprehensive review of the literature on teaching evaluation.
- It reviews the more general measurement and feedback literature from organizational psychology and human resource management.
- It lists the features for an ideal teaching evaluation system based on the integration of these different literatures.
- It presents the Productivity Measurement and Enhancement System (ProMES), a new approach to teaching evaluation and improvement that comes from organizational psychology. This approach has proven very successful at improving effectiveness in many organizational settings.
- It describes in detail how we used the ProMES approach with teaching evaluation in one higher education setting. It does so in enough detail that people can implement the system in their institutions. The book also provides sources that supply more detailed information about ProMES.
- It presents quantitative and qualitative results evaluating the ProMES teaching evaluation system's success.

- It discusses issues to consider in developing and implementing teaching evaluation systems in other institutions.

INTENDED AUDIENCE

This book is intended for several audiences. The first is faculty and administrators who are interested in doing teaching evaluation in their own institutions. They can view this book as a practical handbook on developing and implementing teaching evaluation systems. Such readers will be especially interested in what is known about teaching evaluation, what the features of an ideal teaching evaluation system are, and what issues need to be addressed to develop and maintain a good teaching evaluation system.

Another audience will be students and faculty interested in the scholarly, research-oriented treatment of the topic of teaching evaluation. Such readers will find the new approach to teaching evaluation and the research strategy used to evaluate this new approach particularly interesting.

A third audience consists of scholars who are interested in doing research on teaching. To evaluate the effects of different teaching strategies, one needs a good criterion measure. This book suggests a way to develop such a criterion measure and shows how to evaluate it.

Finally, scholars interested in the overall issue of feedback and performance in complex organizations will find the book useful. There is considerable material on this issue in general and on the use of ProMES in particular.

STRUCTURE OF THE BOOK

The book is organized into two major sections. The first part gives the project's background. The Introduction is an overview of the general issue of teaching evaluation. Chapter One reviews the literature on teaching evaluation and also brings in literatures from other areas. It concludes by listing characteristics that should be present in an ideal teaching evaluation system. Chapter Two describes the ProMES approach. This chapter concludes with a discussion of how the ProMES approach fits the list of ideal characteristics identified in Chapter One.

The second major section of the book includes Chapters Three through Six, which address the development and implementation of the evaluation system at the College of Veterinary Medicine at Texas A&M University. Chapter Three gives a detailed description of the steps involved in developing the ProMES system, especially the issues that arose at each step and the way we handled these issues. Chapter Four presents the quantitative and qualitative results of implementing Phase 1 of the system, which involved student ratings of classroom teaching effectiveness. Chapter Five describes the development of the second phase, which added peer evaluations and covered all aspects of teaching, not just classroom teaching. Chapter Six offers conclusions from this project. Chapter Seven raises a series of issues that must be considered when developing and implementing a teaching evaluation system in other settings. In this chapter, we attempt to share what we have learned with those who are considering starting a teaching evaluation system in their institutions.

ACKNOWLEDGMENTS

We would like to thank a number of people for their many contributions to this effort. Professor Donald Clark of the Texas A&M College of Veterinary Medicine (CVM) was the person who was initially enthusiastic about this project. He was a constant source of help, encouragement, and support throughout the effort. Dean John Shadduck of the CVM saw the potential for the project and supported it with CVM funds. He and his office were also a constant source of administrative support. Our special thanks go to Associate Dean William Banks.

The members of the CVM Teaching Excellence Committee—Donald Clark, Michael Tatum, Jeffrey Watkins, Bruce Simpson, Ralph Storts, Dub Ruoff, and Alice Wolf—put enormous amounts of time into designing the system, serving on department contingency committees, and helping to implement the system. We also thank all the CVM members of the department committees who helped design the contingencies.

The College of Liberal Arts under then Dean Daniel Fallon funded part of the project. Thomas Matthews and Mark Troy of the university's Measurement and Research Services helped again and again with the student ratings.

We would also like to thank other members of the research team. Noga Gottesfeld did the analyses comparing different composites in

Chapter Four. Arlette Decuir, Michael McCormick, Mark Stewart, Paul Bly, and Anne Sandow made helpful comments on earlier drafts.

Finally, we would like to thank Personnel Decisions, International, for supporting Robert Pritchard's research program. Their funds helped in the completion of this book.

August 1997   ROBERT D. PRITCHARD
                                           College Station, Texas
                                           MARGARET D. WATSON
                                           Philadelphia
                                           KARLEASE KELLY
                                           Washington, D.C.
                                           ANTHONY R. PAQUIN
                                           Chicago

THE AUTHORS

Robert D. Pritchard received his bachelor's degree in psychology from UCLA in 1966 and his Ph.D. in 1969 from the University of Minnesota, specializing in organizational psychology. He was a faculty member at Purdue University and the University of Houston. He has been professor of psychology and director of the Industrial and Organizational Psychology Program at Texas A&M University since 1988.

He has received several research awards, is a fellow in the American Psychological Association and in the American Psychological Society, and has been chairman of the Society of Organizational Behavior and president of the Houston Association of Industrial and Organizational Psychologists. He has been on the editorial boards of professional journals and has served on the Executive Committee of the Industrial and Organizational Psychology Division of the American Psychological Association. He was a member of the Commission on Incentives and Productivity for the state of Texas for five years.

His primary interest is in measuring and improving organizational productivity and effectiveness. He has worked on enhancing productivity and effectiveness with organizations in the United States and abroad and was a member of a National Research Council panel reporting on organizational productivity. He has published numerous articles and three recent books in this area, including R. D. Pritchard, 1990, *Measuring and improving organizational productivity: A practical guide,* New York: Praeger; R. D. Pritchard, U. E. Kleinbeck, and K. H. Schmidt, 1993, *Das Management-system PPM: Durch Mitarbeiterbeteiligung zu höherer Produktivität* (The Participative Productivity Management System: Employee participation for improved productivity), Munich, Germany: Verlag C. H. Beck; R. D. Pritchard, ed., 1995, *Productivity measurement and improvement: Organizational case studies,* New York: Praeger.

Margaret D. Watson received her bachelor's degree in psychology from Oklahoma State University in 1970, her master's degree in counseling psychology from the University of Houston in 1972, and her Ph.D. in industrial/organizational psychology from Texas A&M University in 1993. She is currently assistant professor of psychology at LaSalle University in Philadelphia, where she teaches graduate and undergraduate courses in statistics, research methods, and industrial/organizational psychology.

Although her research interests have included work in the area of productivity measurement and improvement, she is currently investigating issues surrounding the measurement of locus of control and its impact in organizational settings.

Karlease Kelly received her B.S. in social studies at Oklahoma Christian College in 1977 and her M.S. in counseling psychology at Texas A&M University in 1987. She expects to receive her Ph.D. in industrial and organizational psychology at Texas A&M University in 1998. She also completed the Organization Development Certificate Program at Georgetown University in 1997. She has done research on the link between the formation of identity and intimacy and has developed and managed managerial assessment centers. She was a member of Robert Pritchard's research team from 1992 to 1995. In her dissertation research, she is evaluating the use of ProMES as a strategic planning tool.

She is currently development specialist with the Office of Organization and Management Development at the Food Safety and Inspection Service, a USDA agency. She does training evaluation, assesses organization development projects, is developing a comprehensive development program for agency leaders and managers, and helps in strategic planning.

Anthony R. Paquin is presently completing a Ph.D. in industrial/organizational psychology at Texas A&M University. He received an M.S. in industrial/organizational psychology at San Diego State University and a B.A. in psychology from Assumption College in Worcester, Massachusetts. His professional career includes instructing developmentally delayed adults and special needs children and working as a mental health counselor. His main research interests include cross-cultural issues in organizational effectiveness and training. He is currently planning on pursuing an academic career.

INTRODUCTION:
MEASURING AND ENHANCING
TEACHING EFFECTIVENESS

THE OVERALL PURPOSE OF THIS BOOK is to address the important issue of evaluating teaching in institutions of higher education. We will describe what is known in this area and offer a new approach to doing evaluations and giving developmental feedback to improve teaching. We will also document the implementation of this new approach at a major university so that others can try it. Finally, we will discuss what we have learned about designing and implementing teaching evaluation systems to help others do such projects in their own institutions.

TEACHING EFFECTIVENESS

Teaching evaluation is the process of assessing instructors' effectiveness. The objective of teaching evaluation is to develop a valid, cost-effective way of measuring this so that instructors, administrators, and other constituencies (for example, state legislatures) accept the results of the evaluation process as accurately describing how well the teaching function is being done.

Classroom teaching is a major part of an instructor's function in higher education and is an essential component of any teaching evaluation system. Other important teaching tasks occur outside the classroom, however, and teaching evaluation must also include those responsibilities. For example, in graduate degree–granting institutions, faculty members devote a significant amount of time to guiding graduate student thesis and dissertation research. This advising process is part of the teaching function and therefore must be part of the evaluation system. Developing instructional materials, developing a curriculum, and working with students outside the classroom are also part of the teaching function.

THE IMPORTANCE OF TEACHING EVALUATION

For a number of reasons, evaluating teaching effectiveness in higher education is a matter of some importance. First, there is the issue of managing a key organizational function. A general principle of management says, "You cannot manage what you cannot measure." A function as important as teaching must be managed and thus measured well. Here, *management* means both evaluating an instructor's teaching accurately and giving instructors useful feedback to help them improve their teaching.

Second, what the organization measures communicates what that organization thinks is important (Tuttle, 1981). For example, research-oriented institutions measure research outputs very carefully. If they devote little effort to measuring teaching effectiveness, it communicates that teaching is less important than research.

Third, a good teaching evaluation system can assist in making promotion and tenure decisions. The more these critical personnel decisions are based on high-quality evaluations, the better the decisions will be and the more likely it is that they will be accepted.

A fourth issue that is currently receiving increased attention is posttenure review. Some have argued that posttenure reviews are important if the tenure system is to survive. Such reviews need good teaching evaluations.

Finally, if teaching effectiveness is to improve, it is essential that good measurement and feedback be available to help develop faculty teaching skills.

There is certainly no lack of evidence of the importance of teaching evaluation. There are well over a thousand published studies on the measurement of teaching effectiveness (Cashin, 1990) and many authors have argued for its importance (for example, Centra, 1980; Goodman, 1990; Marsh, 1987). At a more general level, there is increasing movement toward accountability. State governments, the federal government, and other national governments are requiring that agencies develop a method of evaluating their contributions. Universities are part of this general trend and are spending more effort on doing systematic evaluations of how well they are meeting their missions.

IMPORTANT ISSUES IN TEACHING EVALUATION

Before attempting to develop a teaching evaluation system, one must address a series of issues. If an existing system is being reevaluated, these issues should be reexamined. This constitutes the Preparation Phase. Next come the Design and Implementation Phases. Finally, in the Evaluation Phase the developed system must be assessed, and this assessment must be communicated before it becomes the permanent method of teaching evaluation. We will discuss important issues in each of these phases so as to orient the reader to some of the issues in this book.

The Preparation Phase

There are several background issues to consider before beginning to design a teaching evaluation system. One of the most important is understanding the *purpose* of the teaching evaluation system. Typically, there are three major purposes. The first is faculty evaluation. Most institutions want a system that assesses the teaching effectiveness of individual faculty. It is also desirable for this evaluation to be aggregated so that one can measure the teaching effectiveness of larger units, such as departments and colleges. A second purpose is to give feedback to individual faculty members so that they can improve their teaching. A third purpose is for research. This is by far the least common purpose, but it can be important. To do research on the effects of different teaching strategies, we need a good criterion of teaching effectiveness. To be maximally useful, such a measure must be comparable across different types of classes and teaching approaches. It is very important to make a clear determination of the program's purpose before starting. A teaching evaluation system whose only purpose is evaluation will be quite different than one that has all three purposes.

A teaching evaluation system cannot succeed without administrative support. It is important to know in advance what types of resources are needed and to obtain clear commitments from those who are going to provide this support.

An important issue related to support is how to help faculty improve their teaching once they are evaluated. Simply being told that one's teaching needs improvement is not enough. There must be mechanisms in place to help faculty improve, and these must be designed before the evaluation starts.

Instructors will be concerned about any system of teaching evaluation. This is especially true when a new system is installed or when an existing system is changed. Few of us like to be evaluated, so introducing such a system will create significant anxieties. It is important to understand what instructors' concerns are likely to be and to have plans for addressing them.

Instructors' acceptance of the teaching evaluation system is critical to its success. One of the best ways to maximize acceptance is by having faculty participate in the design and implementation of a system. Before involving faculty, however, one must understand how to incorporate this participation. Plus, one must realize that this participation will not necessarily lead to full acceptance.

The Design Phase

Once one has settled these and other preliminary issues, one can design the teaching evaluation system. We will discuss many design issues throughout the book and will touch on just a few right now.

It is of primary importance to develop a valid measure of teaching effectiveness. One must decide what good teaching is. The answer will not be obvious, but it must be addressed and agreed upon before any measurement can be done. Accomplishing this difficult task is essential to creating a good system.

A second issue deals with the selection of measures of teaching effectiveness. There is an enormous literature on this issue, and it contains some surprises. For example, measures of how much the student has learned are not a practical or particularly valid way of measuring the teaching effectiveness of individual instructors. Nor is having peers observe teaching a good method of evaluation. Student ratings of teaching can be biased in some ways, but the data suggest that they are not biased in the ways that instructors fear. Finally, the literature suggests that there is no one best way of measuring, because different approaches have advantages and disadvantages. By implication, an ideal system will combine different types of measures.

The idea of combining different measures presents new problems. If one uses multiple measures (for example, student ratings plus peer evaluations), how should one combine these measures? More important, how does one combine the measures from different types of courses taught to different types of students? For example, students typically give lower ratings to large undergraduate classes than to small graduate seminars. Should one take this into account? If so, how?

A teaching evaluation system must be able to fit multiple needs. Different types of courses have dissimilar purposes. A course covering large amounts of content differs from one in which integrating and generating new knowledge are the goals. Departments have varied missions. An applied discipline has a different teaching mission than a more academic discipline. The teaching evaluation system must be able to reflect these different purposes and missions while producing evaluations that are interpretable across these different teaching situations.

The Implementation Phase

Once designed, the system must be implemented. This must be done in a cost-effective way. There are a number of relevant issues here. Maintaining a teaching evaluation system can incur large direct costs and involve considerable work. To keep costs reasonable, one must know which features of a system are important and which are less important. For example, who should be evaluated and how often? Senior full professors who are good teachers probably do not have to be evaluated as often as young faculty members who are being considered for tenure.

A related issue is that some faculty members are concerned that they must undertake an increasing amount of administrative work; they evaluate each other, report or justify what they are doing, and make plans that are rarely implemented. To create more work for faculty by having them evaluate teaching can only be justified if it adds considerable value.

It is also important to realize that there is a trade-off between a system's accuracy and cost. It is not always wise to make a system more accurate. Beyond a certain point, this increase can be very costly and not worth the added effort.

Another critical aspect of implementation is whether faculty and administration accept the system. The most valid system is of little value if the users do not accept its results. This is a complex issue that must be considered carefully. Acceptance must be built into the system as it is designed and implemented, not added after it has been developed.

The Evaluation Phase

It is common for the work on a teaching evaluation system to stop once the system is implemented. We believe that any system must be carefully evaluated before its use becomes mandatory. Many issues need to be addressed in evaluating the system. In later chapters, for example, we discuss the reliability and validity of the measures; presence of bias; adequacy of methods to capture different teaching missions; perceived accuracy; and the fairness and acceptance of the system.

CONCLUSION

If you are reading this book, you already know the importance of teaching evaluation. At this point, we hope we have made you aware of some of the important issues that must be addressed when dealing with this complex topic. Our intention is to discuss all these concerns and others in the chapters to follow. We now turn to a review of the literature on teaching evaluation.

HELPING TEACHERS TEACH WELL

PART ONE

ISSUES IN TEACHING EVALUATION

I

SEARCHING FOR THE IDEAL

A Review of Teaching Evaluation Literature

WE WILL BEGIN this chapter by reviewing the traditional literature that focuses directly on teaching evaluation. The first section discusses introductory issues, such as the historical interest in evaluating teaching, the purpose of evaluating teaching, identification of effective teaching behaviors, and the use of quantitative versus qualitative measures. The next two sections review literature on evaluating teaching activities both inside and outside the classroom.

There is also significant literature, however, about evaluation in the workplace; many of the ideas in this literature have bearing on the measurement and feedback required for effective teaching evaluation. We will summarize this literature in a section and will explore these topics: having complete coverage, combining measures, and giving feedback.

Drawing on all these works, the chapter concludes with a compilation of characteristics for an ideal teaching evaluation system.

THE TEACHING EVALUATION LITERATURE

There has been an enormous amount of research on teaching evaluation. In 1990, it was estimated that there were more than 1,300 articles and books about student ratings of teaching, including such topics as methods of evaluation, reliability, validity, and sources of bias in evaluation methods (Cashin, 1990). The following sections review this research from postsecondary education settings.

Introductory Issues

In this first section, we review several issues that provide a background for the following discussion of the teaching evaluation literature. This review includes information on the historical interest in evaluating teaching, the different purposes that usually drive teaching evaluation systems, the techniques used to identify effective teaching behaviors and the behaviors these techniques have identified, and the use of quantitative versus qualitative evaluation systems.

HISTORICAL INTEREST IN EVALUATING TEACHING. Instructors have been evaluated since ancient times, when individuals first began to teach (Walden, 1909). Modern interest in evaluating teaching in higher education began in the United States during the early 1900s. For example, between 1900 and 1913, six studies evaluating college-level teaching were published (Morsh & Wilder, 1954). In the 1920s, students began to evaluate instructors at several prominent institutions, including Harvard, the University of Washington, Purdue University, and the University of Texas (Marsh, 1987). Remmers, who began his work at Purdue during this time, provided much of the foundation for modern research concerning student ratings of teaching (Marsh, 1987).

Over time, interest in evaluating teaching has increased and acceptance of the need to evaluate teaching has continued to grow. Programs to evaluate teaching using quantitative student ratings of faculty have become widespread (Astin & Lee, 1966; Centra, 1979; Doyle, 1983; Marsh, 1987). During the 1970s, the literature on teaching evaluation exploded, largely because the systematic collection of quantitative student ratings replaced the practice of gathering informal student opinions (Centra, 1979). More than half of the instructors surveyed at this time used course evaluations to diagnose deficiencies in their teaching methods and to plan improvements.

More recently, after institutional budgets shrank in the 1980s, instructor evaluations were seen as essential sources of information. Information from evaluations was used increasingly to make decisions about promotion, salary, tenure, and termination (Doyle, 1983). The current emphasis on quality in undergraduate education is likely to perpetuate and intensify the interest and need to evaluate teaching. One early researcher, Remmers, made a statement that is still true today: "Teachers at all levels of the educational ladder have no real choice as to whether they will be judged by those whom they teach. . . . The only real choice any teacher has is whether he wants to know what these judgments are and whether he wants to use this knowledge in his teaching procedures" (Remmers, 1950, p. 4).

PURPOSES OF EVALUATING TEACHING. There are two major reasons to evaluate teaching. First, evaluation provides diagnostic feedback that the instructor can use to improve teaching (Doyle, 1983). Second, evaluation can provide information to assist in making decisions about promotion, tenure, pay, and termination (Hoover, 1980; Seldin, 1989). Evaluations are also used for several less central purposes, such as helping students select courses (McKeachie, 1979) and providing a criterion for research on teaching (Doyle & Whitely, 1974; Gage, 1958; Werdell, 1967).

Different types of information are needed for each purpose. For example, to improve teaching, the evaluation must elicit specific information about particular teaching behaviors; instructors will need this information to identify strengths and weaknesses and to plan strategies for improvement (Abrami, Leventhal, & Kickens, 1981; Braskamp, Brandenburg, & Ory, 1984; Centra, 1979; Doyle, 1983). For example, questionnaires in which students rated items measuring the instructor's performance would provide this specific information; the mean item ratings would be fed back to the instructor. Feedback from individual items would indicate an instructor's strengths and weaknesses so that he or she could set priorities for improvement efforts. This type of specific or "formative" evaluation provides feedback that can be used to shape and guide efforts to improve teaching (Knapper, Geis, Pascal, & Shore, 1977).

In contrast, more global or "summative" information is best when the purpose is to make personnel decisions. One example of global information is the overall mean rating for all items on a student rating form averaged over all courses taught in the last three years. Another example is a measure that combines information from several sources, such as students and colleagues. A global measure is important, because decision makers need to combine all information about an individual's teaching in a single evaluation to make reliable personnel decisions.

IDENTIFICATION OF EFFECTIVE TEACHING BEHAVIORS. Before teaching can be evaluated, some determination must be made of what constitutes effective teaching. Four different approaches have been used to identify these behaviors: surveys of students, faculty, and alumni; summaries of previous studies; theories developed by teaching experts; and factors or constructs identified statistically as underlying existing rating instruments. In order to have a comprehensive understanding of effective teaching, one should examine information from each approach.

Surveys have been administered to students, faculty, and alumni—groups who are in a position to evaluate teaching. These surveys have identified the following behaviors as important for effective teaching: preparation for class, interest in the subject, ability to stimulate students, progressive attitude, interaction between the instructor and the students, organization, clarity, and enthusiasm (Drucker & Remmers, 1951; Hildebrand, Wilson, & Dienst, 1971).

Another approach used to identify the characteristics of effective teaching is to summarize previous research. Summaries of this type have identified the following characteristics as important for effective teaching: good communication, favorable attitude toward students, thorough knowledge of the subject, organization, enthusiasm, fairness in grading, flexibility, good speaking abilities, encouragement of critical thinking in students, clarity, understandability, preparation, and friendliness and openness toward students (Feldman, 1976b; Wortruba & Wright, 1975).

Researchers familiar with the issues involved in teaching are another source of information regarding effective teaching characteristics. Teaching experts have theorized that critical characteristics include rapport with students, course workload, feedback, course structure and organization, impact of the course, quality of group interaction, communication, classroom atmosphere conducive to learning, genuine interest in students, tolerance for others' views, encouragement of intellectual activities, and stimulation of students' interest (Doyle, 1983; Seldin, 1980).

Statistically examining the factors underlying rating instruments yields more information about effective teaching characteristics. For example, large samples of ratings are analyzed, using factor analysis techniques, to identify underlying dimensions. Some of the factors identified are organization, structure, clarity, teacher-student interaction or rapport, ability to communicate or lecture, course workload difficulty, grades and examinations, impact on students, instructor enthusiasm, and breadth of coverage (Centra, 1980; Marsh, 1984).

There is a good deal of overlap in the behaviors identified with the four approaches, but there are some differences as well. Table 1.1 summarizes the effective teaching behaviors identified by each approach. For example, at least three of the four sources agree that organization,

Table 1.1. Summary of Effective Teaching Behaviors.

Behavior	Surveys	Summaries	Theories	Statistically-Identified Factors
Organization	X	X	X	X
Group or individual rapport	X		X	X
Clarity	X		X	X
Enthusiasm	X	X		X
Communication	X	X	X	X
Flexibility	X	X	X	
Preparation	X	X		
Impact of the course			X	X
Stimulation of curiosity and motivation to learn	X		X	
Favorable attitude toward students		X	X	
Fairness in grades and exams	X	X	X	X
Encouragement of independent thinking		X	X	
Assignment of appropriate workload		X	X	X
Progressive attitude	X			
Knowledge of subject		X		
Atmosphere conducive to learning			X	

rapport, clarity, enthusiasm, communication, flexibility, fairness in grades and exams, and assigned workload are important elements of effective teaching. There is not complete agreement, however, on many specific characteristics that describe effective teaching. There are only three characteristics—organization, communication, and fairness in grades and exams—that all approaches include as a characteristic of effective teaching.

Examining this literature can yield two clear conclusions. First, a variety of behaviors must be included in a comprehensive evaluation of teaching. Second, it is worth considering the findings of all four areas when determining which teaching behaviors to evaluate.

USE OF QUANTITATIVE VERSUS QUALITATIVE MEASURES. Two basic types of information can be used to measure teaching effectiveness: qualitative and quantitative data. Qualitative information includes written evaluations, letters, and transcripts from structured discussions with individuals and groups. Because qualitative information is difficult to tabulate, combine, and norm, it is generally used to supplement quantitative data rather than being considered as primary data (Doyle, 1983).

In contrast, quantitative information, such as the responses of students or colleagues to a fixed rating scale, is easily tabulated, statistically analyzed, and normed. When quantitative ratings are provided, a large amount of information can be collected inexpensively and quickly. Quantitative data are also more precise than qualitative data. For these reasons, teaching evaluation systems typically rely on quantitative data and are supplemented with qualitative information. Because the bulk of the literature focuses on quantitative information, the remainder of this review focuses on quantitative information.

Evaluating Classroom Teaching

This section of the review covers literature about evaluations of instructors in the classroom. In a following section, we shall discuss evaluations of teaching activities that occur outside the classroom. In this first section, we discuss some issues associated with the types of information used to evaluate classroom teaching and then go through the various techniques in detail.

TYPES OF INFORMATION USED TO EVALUATE TEACHING. Information about classroom teaching can come from several sources, including students, peers, the instructor, and instructional consultants

(Centra, 1977). It is valuable to include information from a variety of sources in a teaching evaluation system for many reasons. First, no one method is ideal. Second, multiple sources of information reduce the amount of measurement error (Cashin, 1989). Third, because there is usually some overlap in the type of information obtained when data are collected from different sources, such agreement adds support for the quality of the measures. Fourth, each source adds unique information. For example, students have information about the type of rapport an instructor establishes with learners and the strategies used to motivate them. On the other hand, peers have a better sense of the subject matter knowledge necessary for effective teaching.

The following sections review each of the four possible sources and discusses them in terms of (1) the extent of their use, (2) reliability, (3) validity, and (4) susceptibility to bias. First, however, we will explain the meaning of the terms *reliability, validity,* and *bias,* because knowing how these terms are used in teaching evaluation is essential to understanding this literature.

Reliability

For a measuring instrument to be useful, it must be reliable. To claim that a test is reliable requires that results from the instrument demonstrate stability, repeatability, and consistency. There are three methods for assessing reliability: test-retest, internal consistency, and interrater reliability.

Test-retest reliability refers to the stability of ratings over time. Ratings are considered reliable to the extent that patterns of responses for the same individuals remain similar across repeated ratings, provided that teaching behaviors have not changed between measurements. To measure test-retest reliability, an instrument is administered to a group of raters. A specified time interval is then allowed to pass, and the same instrument is administered again. The correspondence between the ratings from the two time intervals is compared, yielding a measure of stability. *Internal consistency reliability* assesses the consistency across content or items. It measures the degree to which items tap the same construct or general idea, which in this case is teaching effectiveness. *Interrater reliability* examines agreement among raters. Ratings are considered reliable when different raters give a similar pattern of responses for the same instructor. In summary, a reliable instrument provides consistent information when used over time, when it measures one coherent construct, and when raters using the instrument are able to agree on judgments.

Generally, reliability is reported as a coefficient ranging in value between .0 and 1.0. The closer to 1.0, the more reliable the instrument. Internal consistency and interrater reliability estimates producing correlations below .70 are considered undesirable (Cashin, 1988). Test-retest reliabilities should exceed .80 in order for a test to be considered stable (Guion, 1965). For more information about the mathematical calculation of reliability coefficients, consult Carmines and Zeller (1979). Reliability is a necessary but insufficient condition for a good measure of teaching effectiveness.

Validity

In addition to being reliable, a useful instrument must be valid. That is, it must be a true measure of the construct it purports to measure. For teaching evaluation, validity indicates whether teaching effectiveness is actually being measured or whether some extraneous variables that do not specifically relate to teaching effectiveness are included in the measurement. Two approaches have been used to validate measures of teaching effectiveness: comparison to existing measures and external validity.

With the method of comparison to existing measures, results from a new measure are compared with a criterion or existing measure that is recognized through experience to be at least somewhat valid. For example, to validate a newly developed test of intelligence, one would compare the results of the new test with an existing measure that has proved accurate and useful over time. When a strong positive relationship exists between the measure and other indicators of effective teaching, it suggests that a measure of teaching effectiveness is valid.

External validity is demonstrated when the teaching skills being measured are the same or similar across several settings. This suggests that the trait being measured is general and underlying, rather than specific to a certain situation. In other words, external validity, which is also called *generalizability*, tells how well a sample of information represents the entirety of an instructor's teaching (Doyle, 1983).

Validity is typically expressed as a correlation coefficient ranging between −1.00 and +1.00. Validity coefficients between .20 and .49 suggest that the measure is practical and useful. Those between .50 and .70 indicate a measure that is very useful, although these coefficients are rarely found when one studies a complex variable. Correlations between .0 and .19 suggest a lack of validity, even when they are statistically significant (Cashin, 1988). Interpretation of validity coefficients is a complex matter, however, and simple rules of what constitutes good validity must be used with caution.

Bias

Bias occurs when variables that have nothing to do with teaching effectiveness spuriously inflate or deflate ratings (Marsh, 1987; Stumpf, Freedman, & Aguanno, 1979). When bias is present, measures of teaching are correlated with variables that should logically be unrelated to the construct of effective teaching. Therefore, bias decreases a measure's validity. For example, two variables that should theoretically be unrelated to teaching effectiveness are the student's gender and the instructor's gender. If student ratings were found to be related to the instructor's or student's gender, this would be evidence of bias. When bias occurs, there is usually some attempt to isolate it statistically so that it can be partialed out of the measurement.

The literature on teaching evaluation indicates that measures from different sources of information about teaching are associated with varying degrees of reliability, validity, and bias. To the degree that information about teaching effectiveness comes from sources that are reliable, valid, and free of bias, instructors can depend on it to guide improvement and administrators can use it confidently to make personnel decisions.

STUDENT LEARNING. Student learning is widely believed to be a good measure of teaching effectiveness (Duncan & Biddle, 1974). The logic is that students taught by more effective teachers should learn more than those taught by less effective teachers. Unfortunately, measures of student learning are not as ideal as they may first appear. Using such measures assumes that the amount of a student's knowledge at the end of the course is solely a function of the quality of instruction. Factors beyond the instructor's control can strongly affect the amount of material students learn, however. Examples include the initial level of student knowledge, student ability, and student motivation. Therefore, some consider student learning to be at best a crude index of the teaching effectiveness of individual instructors (for example, Abrami, D'Apollonia, & Cohen, 1990; Cohen, 1981).

A number of attempts have been made to overcome some of the difficulties associated with using student learning as a measure of teaching effectiveness. These include using pretests to measure the students' initial level of subject knowledge, as well as randomly assigning students to classes to reduce differences in ability and motivation (Marsh, 1987). However, these procedures are very time consuming and decrease the feasibility of using student learning as a measure of teaching effectiveness.

Extent of Use

Because of the difficulties associated with its measurement, student learning is rarely used to evaluate teaching effectiveness (Seldin, 1980). Aside from the problems discussed previously, there are other difficulties in using such measures for assessing individual instructors in higher education settings.

For example, for evaluation purposes, all faculty must be compared using the same "metric" or measuring stick. This would make it necessary to develop tests measuring student learning that are comparable or parallel across all courses. This is difficult enough to do for multiple sections of a single course. It would be virtually impossible to do across different courses. One solution would be to compare gain in knowledge across different courses. To be able to compare a gain in knowledge in one course with the gain in knowledge in another course, however, both the pretests and the final tests would have to be of the same difficulty level. Furthermore, every time an instructor updated or revised the course content, a new test would have to be developed, and it would have to be equal in difficulty to the old one. Therefore, although it is appealing in principle to use measures of student learning to evaluate teaching, such measures have enormous practical problems and are not commonly used.

Reliability

The reliability with which student learning is measured depends on the type of instrument used and the approach taken. Objectively scored teacher-designed tests or achievement tests are typically used to measure student learning. Objectively scored teacher-designed tests have internal consistency reliability coefficients that average near .70, whereas the coefficients for achievement tests typically average in the .90s (Doyle, 1983). Test-retest reliability for achievement tests that are constructed by testing companies ranges in the .80s or higher (Doyle, 1983). Therefore, student learning can be measured reliably.

Validity

One can demonstrate the validity of measures of student learning by using multisection courses with pre- and posttests. Measures of the gain in students' knowledge are related to other measures of teaching effectiveness. In studies using this design, student learning measures were positively correlated with student ratings of teaching (Cohen, 1981; Feldman, 1989). For example, correlations with overall student ratings ranged from .43 to .50 (Cohen, 1981). Correlations with specific dimensions of effective teaching averaged .31 (Feldman, 1989). These data provide some support for the validity of using student learning as an indicator of effective teaching in multisection courses.

Bias

The possibility of bias in measures of student learning is considerable. As discussed above, differing levels of initial knowledge and student ability, as well as the problems of developing tests of equal difficulty, are potential sources of this bias. Although it is theoretically possible to remove the majority of this bias, the amount of effort required is typically not practical.

Summary

Measures of student learning are widely accepted and can have high reliability and validity, at least in theory. There are problems, however, with using student learning to evaluate teaching. Particularly because of the difficulty of constructing parallel tests, measures of student learning are simply not practical for evaluating individual instructors in higher education.

We must make it clear, though, that we are not saying that measures of student learning are not practical in all settings. The point here is that they are not practical for evaluating individual instructors. Student learning measures can be quite useful in evaluating an entire teaching program. For example, it is probably quite useful for a law school to look at the percentage of their graduating students who pass the state bar examinations each year. In this case, because of the time and effort devoted to designing the test and the fact that each student takes the same test, problems associated with using student learning as a criterion for teaching effectiveness decrease significantly.

STUDENT RATINGS. Input from students is recognized as an essential component of a comprehensive system for evaluating teaching effectiveness (Abbott and others, 1990; Cohen, 1982; Harris, 1982). Quantitative student ratings are used more frequently in evaluating teaching than any other source (Braskamp, Caulley, & Costin, 1979; Centra, 1980; Dickinson, 1990; Seldin, 1978; Shapiro, 1990; Shingles, 1977). Typically, students evaluate teaching by using a questionnaire that lists particular instructor behaviors. Students anonymously rate the instructor by using a scale to provide a judgment or opinion about the instructor's behavior. These ratings are then averaged across student raters and a report is given to the instructor and administrators. In addition to the mean ratings and the overall mean rating, these reports frequently include measures of variability and other descriptive statistics on the ratings. It is also common for such quantitative rating systems to give the student the option to write qualitative comments and evaluations that are returned to the instructor.

Extent of Use

The vast majority of those who evaluate teaching use quantitative student ratings (Braskamp, Caulley, & Costin, 1979; Centra, 1980; Dickinson, 1990; Seldin, 1978; Shapiro, 1990; Shingles, 1977). For example, in one study that involved more than four hundred institutions, 53 percent used student ratings to evaluate teaching (Seldin, 1978). In a later survey, more than 80 percent of those universities surveyed used student ratings (Centra, 1980). It is therefore clear that student ratings are widely used.

Although most faculty accept the validity and utility of student ratings, some do not. Many recommend that student ratings be supplemented with other types of evaluations, such as peer reviews (Braskamp, Brandenburg, & Ory, 1984; Doyle, 1983; Knapper, Geis, Pascal, & Shore, 1977; Seldin, 1980).

Reliability

Student ratings tend to be consistent over time. The test-retest reliability coefficients of student ratings for time intervals of a few days to a few months range between the mid .60s and lower .80s (Doyle, 1975). Correlations between midsemester and end-of-semester ratings for teaching assistants tend to be higher, ranging between .70 and .87 (Costin, 1968). When end-of-course ratings are compared to ratings of the same instructor one year later, correlations are in the .80s (Guthrie, 1954; Overall & Marsh, 1980). These results suggest that student ratings have good test-retest reliability.

Student ratings have internal consistency reliabilities that range from the .70s to the .90s, which indicates a high degree of consistency (Doyle, 1975; Marsh, 1987). For example, Shingles (1977) reported internal consistency reliabilities of .79, .85, and .88 for three factors contained in a measure of teaching effectiveness. Runco and Thurston (1987) found coefficients of .73, .75, .85, and .90 for four composites measured by their student rating instrument. More recently, Hanges, Schneider, and Niles (1990) reported six internal consistency reliabilities in the .90s (.90, .92, .94, .94, .96, and .99) for factors of a measure of teaching effectiveness. Spencer and others found an average coefficient of .93 for sixteen different classes and an average of .85 for a smaller sample (Spencer, 1968; Spencer & Aleamoni, 1970). An internal consistency reliability of .90 was reported in a study examining the instructor's overall teaching skill (Stumpf, Freedman, & Aguanno, 1979). These findings show that student ratings have good internal consistency reliability, indicating that items from student rating instruments seem to be tapping one construct.

Student raters also show good agreement on evaluations of instructors. This measure, referred to as *interrater* or *interjudge reliability*, is the most frequently used measure of reliability (Cashin, 1988; Doyle & Crichton, 1978; Feldman, 1977, 1978; Kottke, 1984; Marsh, 1982, 1984, 1987). In this case, the raters are students in a particular class who provide judgments about instructor effectiveness. Ratings are considered reliable when students generally agree on ratings. As mentioned already, student ratings show good interrater reliability (Feldman, 1977).

For example, when ten to twenty students evaluate instructors, the average item reliability for the composite of the class ratings was .69 (Cashin, 1988). With twenty students for five items, the reliability ranges from .60 to .80 (Braskamp, Brandenburg, & Ory, 1984). When there are more than twenty student raters, the item reliability is higher, with the average reliability coefficient ranging between .70 and .90 (Feldman, 1977, 1978). It has been suggested that ratings from fewer than ten students are probably not reliable enough in an interrater sense to be used alone for faculty personnel decisions (Feldman, 1977). A solution to this is to combine data from several small classes (Cashin, 1990).

In summary, the data suggest that overall, student evaluations show good reliability, especially when the class size is greater than twenty. When class sizes are small, information from several classes should be considered when making personnel decisions. No matter what the class size, however, it is a much better policy to make any personnel decisions on the basis of ratings from multiple classes rather than from just one.

Validity

To be useful, measures must be valid as well as reliable. In this case, validity is the extent to which teaching effectiveness is actually being measured by student ratings. Because there is no single criterion for effective instruction against which student ratings can be compared, it is difficult to assess validity. Two approaches have been used to validate student ratings: external validity (also called generalizability) and comparison with other measures.

Generalizability. Using the first method, if student ratings are shown to be generalizable, this indicates that the evaluation data reflect a particular instructor's general teaching ability, as opposed to reflecting teaching ability for a particular course or a specific semester. Student ratings appear to demonstrate good generalizability, as illustrated by a study that examined the effects of two classes of variables: those associated with the instructor and those associated with the course (Marsh & Overall, 1981).

In this study, over one thousand students evaluated teaching effectiveness at the end of a course and again one year after their graduation. Analyses were performed to assess the effects of variables associated with the course, such as program level (graduate versus undergraduate), course type by content, items, time at which ratings were collected, and variables associated with the instructor. The student was used as the unit of analysis. An analysis of variance showed that the effect of a specific instructor's teaching explained 15.5 percent of the variance, whereas no other single effect accounted for more than 1.5 percent. Only two course-related factors showed statistically significant results: the effect of course type, which accounted for 1.5 percent of the variance, and the different evaluation items, which accounted for 0.2 percent of the variance. In sum, the only factor that accounted for a substantial amount of variance was the factor associated with the instructor. Another study examining the stability of ratings across persons and situations over thirteen semesters and six years yielded similar findings (Hanges, Schneider, & Niles, 1990).

Study findings suggest that student ratings do reflect an instructor's general teaching ability rather than teaching ability for a particular semester or a particular course. Also, student ratings seem to generalize across different semesters and different courses. These results provide some support for the validity of student ratings.

Comparison with Other Measures. The validity of student ratings is supported when a strong positive relationship exists between student ratings and other indicators of effective teaching. Research indicates that there is a fairly strong relationship between student ratings and other measures. For example, correlations between student ratings and measures of student learning range from .43 to .50 for overall teaching effectiveness (Blackburn & Clark, 1975; Cohen, 1981; Feldman, 1989; Marsh, Fleiner, & Thomas, 1975; Marsh & Overall, 1980). Studies comparing the relationship between student ratings and colleagues' ratings of teaching portfolios found correlations ranging from .48 to

.69 (Blackburn & Clark, 1975; Kulik & McKeachie, 1975). Pearson's product-moment correlation coefficient (r) between student ratings and instructor self-ratings ranged in the .30s and .40s ($r = .19$, Blackburn & Clark, 1975; $r = $ .30s and .40s, Braskamp, Caulley, & Costin, 1979; $r = $ .20, Centra, 1973b; $r = .48$, Doyle & Crichton, 1978; $r = .34$, Howard, Conway, & Maxwell, 1985; $r = .49$, Marsh, Overall, & Kessler, 1979; $r = .62$, Webb & Nolan, 1955).

When considering these findings, it is important to remember that for validity coefficients, values between .20 and .49 can be practical and useful, whereas those between .50 and .70 are very useful, though rarely found when studying a complex variable (Cashin, 1988). Therefore, the relationship between student ratings and other measures of teaching effectiveness, such as student learning, ratings by colleagues, and instructors' self-ratings support the validity of student ratings.

Bias

Many variables have been examined as possible sources of bias in student ratings and have been found to cause little or no effect on student ratings. Interestingly enough, some studies investigating bias in student ratings have actually supported their validity. A few variables clearly do bias student ratings, however.

In considering the issue of bias, one must interpret the findings carefully. Some of the concern and confusion about bias in student ratings has been due to faulty assumptions. For example, a positive correlation between two variables, such as class size and rapport with the instructor, does not automatically indicate bias. In fact, if a variable is highly correlated with a specific component of teaching to which it should be logically related, the validity of student ratings is actually supported.

One example of a correlation between variables that show support for the validity of student ratings rather than bias is the relationship between course difficulty and student ratings. Contrary to some faculty expectations, there is a moderately positive relationship between the difficulty of a course and the ratings that students give instructors. In other words, instructors who teach courses that students judge to be more difficult or demanding receive higher ratings than those who teach courses that students judge to be easy (Cashin & Slawson, 1977; Frey, Leonard, & Beatty, 1975; Marsh, 1984; Stumpf, Freedman, & Aguanno, 1979). Because it is logical to expect more learning to occur in difficult or challenging courses compared with easy ones, these results indirectly support the validity of student ratings rather than provide evidence that they are biased.

Variables That Do Not Cause Bias. The bulk of the evidence about bias in student ratings suggests that many variables suspected of causing bias do not affect student ratings (see Table 1.2). These uninfluential variables include instructor gender (Brandenburg, Slindle, & Batista, 1977; Brown, 1976; Marsh, 1987; McKeachie, 1979), student age (Centra, 1979; McKeachie, 1979; Menges, 1973), student gender (Basow & Howe, 1987; Braskamp, Brandenburg, & Ory, 1984; Centra & Creech, 1976; Marsh, 1984; Pohlman, 1972), student academic level, such as freshman, sophomore, and so forth (McKeachie, 1979; Menges, 1973), student personality (Braskamp, Brandenburg, & Ory, 1984; Doyle, 1983), and the time during the semester and time of day at which ratings are collected (Aleamoni, 1981; Cornwall, 1974; Feldman, 1979; Gillmore & Naccarato, 1975; Lunney, 1974; Mirus, 1973).

Variables That Cause Bias. Variables associated with the administration methods of rating forms show clear evidence that they cause bias in student ratings. Variables associated with inflated student ratings include lack of anonymity for raters, the instructor's presence while students do the ratings, and students' knowledge that evaluation results will be used to make personnel decisions (Braskamp, Brandenburg, & Ory, 1984; Cheong, 1979; Feldman, 1979; Marsh, 1984). Because none of these administration methods are logically related to teaching but are correlated with student ratings, they introduce bias into the ratings.

Variables for Which Bias Is Unclear. There is another class of variables in which the evidence concerning bias in student ratings is unclear. Therefore, bias cannot be ruled out for these variables. The variables include student interest in the course, instructor age and teaching experience, class size, course level, academic field of the course being evaluated, and grades received in that course. Each of these variables could be logically related to effective teaching, which suggests that they can legitimately influence student ratings. It is also possible, however, that each could be a source of bias.

For example, student interest in a course has been shown to be related to student ratings (Divoky & Rothermel, 1988; Marsh & Cooper, 1981; Moritsch & Suter, 1988; O'Hanlon & Mortensen, 1980; Ory, 1980). The correlation between class ratings and the average interest of students is low, ranging in the .10s and .20s (Gillmore, 1975; Gillmore & Naccarato, 1975). Logically, if the instructor stimulates

Table 1.2. Bias Found in Different Variables in Student Ratings.

Do Not Cause Bias	Cause Bias (All These Increase Ratings)	Results Unclear
Instructor gender	Lack of anonymity for raters	Student interest in the course
Student age	Instructor's presence during ratings	Instructor age and teaching experience
Student gender	Telling students ratings will be used for personnel decision	Class size
Student level (e.g., freshman, sophomore, etc.)		Course level
Student personality		Academic field of the course
Time during semester when ratings were done		Grades in the course
Time of day when ratings were done		

student interest, then that interest is attributable to teaching effective-ness; the relationship between interest and the ratings is therefore legit-imate. Some subjects are simply more interesting to students than others, though. If interest is a function of the subject matter being taught rather than the instructor, then student interest affects ratings independent of the quality of instruction; this makes it a source of bias. Therefore, when interest in a course is not related to the instructor, it acts as a source of bias in student ratings.

Two other variables that could be legitimately related to teaching effectiveness but could also be sources of bias are instructor age and teaching experience. A negative relationship was found between stu-dent ratings and instructor age (Horner, Murray, & Rushton, 1989; Marsh, 1986; Marsh & Overall, 1979a; Marsh, Overall, & Thomas, 1976; Rotton, 1990). In other words, older teachers receive lower rat-ings than younger ones. Similarly, a nonlinear relationship was found between teaching experience and student ratings (Feldman, 1983). In this study, the ratings of instructors increased gradually during the first ten years of teaching, but then began to decline, producing a curvilin-ear relationship between instructor experience and student ratings. In another study, although the differences were small, instructors with four to seven years of experience had the highest average ratings, fol-lowed by those with zero to three years of experience. Those with eight or more years of experience had the lowest ratings (Rabalais, 1977).

If the explanation for these findings is that an instructor becomes better as he or she gains more experience and then drops off over time because of a loss of interest in teaching or a failure to update skills, this supports the validity of student ratings. It is not clear, however, whether this explains why these relationships among student ratings, experience, and age exist. Therefore, it is not clear whether instructor age and teaching experience create bias or whether they are legiti-mately related to teaching effectiveness.

Class size may also cause bias in student ratings, although the evi-dence is unclear. There is a low negative relationship between class size and student ratings. The correlations from different studies range from −.09 to −.18 (Cashin & Slawson, 1977; Feldman, 1984). Classes of fewer than fifteen students and those with more than one hundred stu-dents receive the highest ratings (Centra & Creech, 1976). Class size is also moderately correlated with items that measure interaction and rapport with the instructor (Marsh, 1983). This suggests that higher ratings for very small and very large classes may occur because instruc-tion is more effective. Because there are no empirical studies to support this theory, however, the relationship between class size and student ratings is not fully understood.

Course level or type is another variable that may bias student ratings. Graduate classes generally receive higher ratings than undergraduate classes, and elective courses receive higher ratings than required ones (Aleamoni, 1981; Braskamp, Brandenburg, & Ory, 1984). It is not apparent, though, whether these types of courses receive higher ratings because they are associated with better teaching or because of some factor unrelated to the quality of instruction. A number of variables may interact to produce these results, such as class size, student interest, student ability, and student motivation. Therefore, it is unclear whether course level or type biases student ratings.

Academic field is another possible source of bias. Studies show that humanities courses receive higher ratings than courses in engineering, business, and physical sciences (Cashin & Clegg, 1987; Cashin, Noma, & Hana, 1987; Centra & Creech, 1976; Feldman, 1978). It is not obvious whether these variables are legitimately related to teaching effectiveness or whether they are sources of bias. Further research is required before it can be determined whether these variables bias student ratings of teaching.

It is also uncertain whether grades bias student ratings. This is an issue of considerable concern to some instructors. Students' anticipated grades and their actual grades in class are positively related to their evaluations of instructors (Feldman, 1976a; Marsh, 1984; Tatro, 1995). In other words, students who expect or receive higher grades tend to give higher ratings to instructors than students who expect or receive lower grades.

The correlations are low, however, generally ranging in the .10s and .20s (Gigliotti & Buchtel, 1990; Howard & Maxwell, 1980, 1982), and the relationship between grades and student ratings accounts for less than 10 percent of the variance in the ratings (Feldman, 1976a). One possible explanation for the relationship between student ratings and grades is that instructors may give students grades that are higher than students deserve, and students may reciprocate by giving instructors higher ratings than deserved. If this is the case, grades clearly bias ratings.

Another logical explanation, though, is that higher grades are due to greater student learning or interest in the course. To the extent that student learning or interest in the course is under the instructor's control, a positive correlation between grades and student ratings may support the validity of student ratings. In summary, the evidence neither establishes bias in student ratings of teaching due to student grades nor rules out this bias.

It is important to clarify a potential point of confusion. Earlier we pointed out that there was a positive correlation between course difficulty and ratings. Here we are addressing grades and ratings. The first set of findings correlates mean ratings across all students in the course with that course's difficulty level; thus, this is an analysis across courses based on average student ratings. The relationship between individual student ratings and their grades that we are now discussing deals with an analysis of a single course, based on individual students. The first analysis suggests that more demanding courses actually receive more favorable ratings. The second analysis suggests that students with higher grades give higher ratings.

Several studies have examined the overall degree of relationship between the combined effects of these potential sources of bias and student ratings (Marsh, 1987; Brandenburg, Slindle, & Batista, 1977; Brown, 1976; Burton, 1975; Centra & Creech, 1976; Stumpf, Freedman, & Aguanno, 1979). Factors such as whether the course was elective or required, student interest in the subject, class size, teaching experience, teaching load, and expected grade account for an average of 14 percent to 15 percent of the variance in student ratings. (Subject interest and expected grades had the strongest correlation with student ratings.) This implies that a small but meaningful proportion of the variance in student ratings is related to potentially biasing factors.

Summary

In general, student ratings are reliable and are significantly related to other criteria of effective teaching, such as student learning, instructor self-evaluation, and peer ratings. They also generalize across teaching situations. The cumulative nature of this evidence suggests that student ratings are a valid source of information about teaching.

There are a number of sources of potential bias in student ratings, but the evidence does not support potential bias for some of these variables. Several sources of known bias must be controlled or taken into account when student ratings are interpreted. Fortunately, one can control these fairly easily by doing the evaluation in a certain way.

Specifically, the ratings should be anonymous, the instructor should be out of the room, and all students should be consistently told whether the ratings can affect personnel decisions. There are some important variables in which bias is not clear. Overall, the combined effects of all sources of potential bias is fairly small. One way to interpret the findings here is that of all the factors that could influence student ratings, only about 15 percent of the factors could come from bias. This figure is a maximum because it includes factors that may not actually be biasing ratings.

PEER RATINGS. Peer ratings have the potential to provide unique information about teaching, because colleagues who rate teaching are experienced teachers themselves and should be familiar with the subject matter being taught (Cashin, 1990). Therefore, in addition to being able to make judgments about effective classroom teaching, colleagues can rate aspects of teaching that occur outside of the classroom, such as the quality of course syllabi, the course objectives, class assignments, and the coverage of course content.

Extent of Use

Surveys show that peer ratings are commonly used to assess teaching (Centra, 1977, 1980). In a survey of 670 liberal arts colleges, 42.7 percent of the institutions surveyed always used colleague opinions, 46.5 percent always used faculty committee evaluations, and 14.3 percent always used classroom visits (Seldin, 1980). The teaching portfolio approach in which peers examine documents and materials as evidence of teaching performance is increasingly recommended (Seldin, 1991).

One reason for the wide use of peer ratings is that faculty are perceived as better raters than students in judging some aspects of teaching, such as subject mastery and the content, organization, and objectives of a course (Miller, 1987; Seldin, 1980). Another reason is that peer ratings allow faculty members to take charge of their own evaluations (Seldin, 1991). In order for peer evaluation to work, faculty must trust and respect each other and be open to an honest exchange about strengths and weaknesses. It is recommended that raters have a substantial amount of teaching experience and be recognized as excellent teachers (Braskamp, Brandenburg, & Ory, 1984).

Reliability

The reliability of peer ratings depends on the method used to collect the evaluations. The critical distinction is whether or not peer ratings are based on classroom observation. Internal consistency coefficients for ratings that colleagues made by examining course material without observing a class range from the .60s to the .80s (Hildebrand, Wilson, & Dienst, 1971). Peer ratings based on classroom observation have fairly low interrater reliability (for example, $r = .26$, Centra, 1975), however, which indicates that there is very little agreement among the evaluators. In addition, reliability has been shown to vary across academic areas (Kremer, 1990). No information is available on test-retest reliability of peer ratings.

Validity and Bias

Peer ratings based on classroom observation have low correlations with other criteria of effective teaching, which also casts doubt on their validity. For example, colleague judgments made after observing in the classroom had low correlations with student ratings (Braskamp, Brandenburg, & Ory, 1984; Centra, 1975; Cohen & McKeachie, 1980; French-Lazovich, 1981). In addition, colleagues generally give their peers higher ratings than students do (Braskamp, Brandenburg, & Ory, 1984). Peer ratings based on classroom observation also had low correlations with measures of student learning (Morsh, Burgess, & Smith, 1956), with instructor self-ratings, and with the ratings of instructional consultants (Howard, Conway, & Maxwell, 1985).

Another concern about the validity of peer ratings based on classroom observation is that a visitor's presence may alter teaching performance, thereby threatening the validity of the ratings. If the observer influences typical teaching performance either positively or negatively, bias is introduced (Braskamp, Brandenburg, & Ory, 1984; Ward, Clark, & Harrison, 1981).

In addition to the problems with validity, classroom observation is costly in terms of time and effort. For example, it has been recommended that each instructor be observed three to four times in one semester in order to obtain reliable peer ratings (Braskamp, Brandenburg, & Ory, 1984). In conclusion, peer ratings based on classroom observation have questionable validity and present practical difficulties.

In contrast, when teachers evaluate their colleagues by reviewing and rating examples of teaching materials without visiting classrooms, the correlations between colleague judgments and other criteria of effective instruction are high. For example, this type of peer rating has high correlations with students' ratings ($r = .62$, Blackburn & Clark, 1975; Kulik & McKeachie, 1975; Maslow & Zimmerman, 1956) and with administrators' ratings ($r = .63$, Blackburn & Clark, 1975). Therefore, it appears that the data support the validity of this type of peer rating.

To be valid, the teaching materials that peers rate must represent an adequate sample of teaching behaviors. Typical elements for a teaching portfolio include a statement of individual teaching philosophy, a description of teaching responsibilities, syllabi for all courses presently taught, examples of examinations, copies of teaching materials (such as lecture notes or handouts for students), lists of assignments given to students, descriptions of steps taken to improve teaching, information about honors or recognition concerning teaching, and letters from current or former students regarding teaching. Several colleagues must review these materials in terms of how they relate to specific criteria for effective teaching, such as course planning and preparation, actual teaching, evaluating student learning, providing effective feedback to students, and continuing professional development (Edgerton, Hutchings, & Quinlan, 1991).

Summary

Because peer evaluation based on classroom observation lacks reliability and validity, it is considered a poor measure of teaching effectiveness. Rating colleagues' teaching by examining course and other teaching materials seems to be reliable and valid, however. Colleagues need access to a representative sample of instructional materials when making their evaluations. This type of peer evaluation allows faculty members to participate and takes advantage of their subject matter expertise.

INSTRUCTOR SELF-RATINGS. Another source of teaching evaluation is self-rating provided by the instructor. Instructors may evaluate their own teaching using a quantitative technique, such as rating themselves with an evaluation form similar to one that students use. They can also use a qualitative approach, such as keeping a journal to track the success of methods used in the classroom. Most research on self-evaluation is based on quantitative ratings. Generally, universities use self-evaluation to motivate instructors to improve their own teaching skills.

Extent of Use

Self-rating is not used in a formal evaluation system as frequently as student and peer ratings. Approximately one-third of the institutions surveyed reported that they used some form of self-rating (Centra, 1980; Seldin, 1978).

Reliability

The internal consistency reliability of quantitative self-rating ranges in the .70s and .80s (Marsh & Overall, 1979b). This method is therefore considered reliable enough to use in diagnosing and improving teaching (Doyle, 1983). There is no evidence about how stable self-evaluation is over time (Doyle, 1983). By definition, interjudge reliability cannot be determined, because the instructor is the only person who can do a self-rating.

Validity and Bias

There is mixed information about the correlations between self-rating and other criteria of teaching effectiveness. Self-rating is not correlated with factors that are identified as possible sources of bias, such as the instructor's age, gender, tenure status, teaching load, or years of teaching experience (Doyle & Webber, 1978; Marsh, 1987).

The pattern of correlations between self-rating and other criteria for effective teaching is not clear, however. For example, correlations between self-ratings and students' ratings range from .19 to .62 (r = .19 with global ratings, Blackburn & Clark, 1975; r = .20 with midterm ratings, Centra, 1973a; r = .48, Doyle & Crichton, 1978; r = .34 with presently enrolled students and r = .31 with former students, Howard, Conway, & Maxwell, 1985; r = .49, Marsh, Overall, & Kessler, 1979; r = .62, Webb & Nolan, 1955).

Self-ratings have moderate correlations with student learning (r = .30, Follman & Merica, 1973) and low correlations with administrators' ratings (r = .10, Blackburn & Clark, 1975). In addition, instructors tend to lower their self-ratings as they become familiar with the results of student ratings (Braskamp & Caulley, 1978; Centra, 1975). This suggests that self-evaluations may be inflated or biased. It is also important to note that administrators do not consider self-ratings valid (Centra, 1980) and that peers think they are untrustworthy. For these reasons, self-ratings are not recommended as the basis for personnel decisions.

Summary

Self-evaluation may be a useful way of improving teaching, although there has been little research on this issue. Some argue that self-evaluation may improve teaching because engaging in the process may lead to self-awareness, which can motivate the instructor to change ineffective teaching behaviors (Pambookian, 1973, 1974; Seldin, 1980). Because evidence indicates that self-evaluations may be inflated compared with other criteria of teaching effectiveness, they are not recommended for making personnel decisions.

INSTRUCTIONAL CONSULTING. Instructional consultants are infrequently used as a source of evaluating classroom teaching. The purpose of consultation is to help individual instructors improve teaching. Typically, the consultant videotapes classroom sessions and then reviews them in a counseling session with the instructor. The consultant gives feedback about teaching and helps the instructor plan a strategy for improvement.

Extent of Use

There is little documentation on the use of instructional consultants other than on an informal basis. A survey by Centra (1980) indicated that the videotaping service needed for this type of evaluation is available at about 50 percent of the institutions contacted. It was estimated that only about 5 percent of the faculty who have the videotaping service available actually use it, which indicates that teaching is not typically evaluated with this method.

Reliability

The information that exists about consultants' ratings suggests that they are reliable (Albanese, Schuldt, & Case, 1991). The reliability of ratings by instructional consultants ranges from .51 to .97, averaging about .76 for individual items (Marsh, 1987). More specifically, in one study, forty-nine raters used a sixty-item form to observe and evaluate fifty-four instructors three different times. Six to eight raters were present for each observation. In that study, the median reliability for the average rater response was .77 (Murray, 1983). Thus, compared with peer ratings of classroom teaching based on classroom observation, consultant's ratings demonstrate higher interrater reliability. This is probably because consultants receive training that allows them to avoid typical rating errors, which lower the reliability of ratings. No test-retest reliability data are available on consultants' ratings (Murray, 1983).

Validity and Bias

Ratings by instructional consultants correlate positively with measures of student learning (Dunkin & Barnes, 1986; Hines, Cruickshank, & Kennedy, 1982; Land, 1979) and student ratings of teaching (Land & Combs, 1981; Murray, 1976, 1983). In addition, student ratings of teaching could be predicted very accurately from observers' reports (Murray, 1983). This provides some support for the validity of consultants' ratings. There is no information in the literature about bias in ratings by consultants.

Summary

Consultants' ratings seem to have adequate reliability and validity. Because the process involves a great deal of time and expense, however, it is not practical to have consultants evaluate all instructors on a regular basis. It is more appropriate to have them coach individual instructors who need assistance in the classroom, which is typically how this service is used at present.

Evaluating Teaching Outside the Classroom

The information reviewed in this last section focused on evaluating classroom teaching. Instructors in higher education perform many teaching activities outside the classroom, as well. These activities include advising undergraduate students, supervising graduate students, developing curricular materials, and participating on various teaching-related committees. All of these teaching activities need to be included in a comprehensive teaching evaluation system. Very little research has been conducted on this type of evaluation. We now describe the research that is available.

ADVISING UNDERGRADUATES. Instructors routinely advise undergraduates both formally and informally. This function is rarely evaluated on a systematic basis (Seldin, 1980). One way to evaluate advising would be to survey students or peers about their experiences with each teacher's advising. They could rate advising on such dimensions as knowledge of relevant policies and procedures, availability for consultation, rapport with students, and quality of referral services (Centra, 1980; Seldin, 1980). To maximize the reliability and validity of such ratings, students should rate advisers approximately two weeks before the end of the term. This helps ensure that students have had enough exposure to their advisers to rate them accurately.

One study indicates that student ratings of advisers are reliable. Brock (1978) collected ratings from seven hundred students who rated seventy-eight faculty advisers. For ratings by ten students, corrected split-half reliability (a form of interjudge reliability) was .69. Student expectations, student gender, and year in school did not affect the ratings. These results imply that student ratings are fairly free of bias.

Nevertheless, more research is needed to draw firm conclusions about the reliability of student rating of advising.

SUPERVISING GRADUATE STUDENTS. Graduate student supervision can account for a significant portion of a faculty member's responsibilities in graduate degree–granting institutions. As with undergraduate advising, however, it is rarely evaluated on a systematic basis. One way to evaluate the supervision of graduate students is to consider the number of students supervised and the time required for each student to complete a degree (Knapper, Geis, Pascal, & Shore, 1977). Another approach is to collect feedback from students regarding the quality of their experience. Several sources provide examples of rating instruments (Braskamp, Brandenburg, & Ory, 1984; Centra, 1980), but there is no information about the reliability or validity of this type of evaluation.

DEVELOPING INSTRUCTIONAL MATERIALS. All instructors develop some form of instructional materials for their courses. Instructors sometimes spend considerable time designing, revising, and improving other professors' instructional materials, however. Although these materials are rarely systematically evaluated, some institutions have included instructional materials in their evaluations of teaching effectiveness. A survey reported that 20 percent "always used" colleagues' review of instructional material (Seldin, 1984).

Some guidelines for evaluating instructional materials have been recommended in the literature, particularly in publications concerning the use of teaching portfolios. For example, it is important to include a variety of materials, such as course syllabi, assignments, course objectives and content, exam questions, textbooks, handouts, readings, and lecture notes (Centra, 1980; Seldin, 1980, 1991). In addition, the materials may be reviewed across several dimensions, such as usefulness, innovativeness, appropriateness, and fairness. If instructional materials are developed for the instructor's own course, they should be evaluated in the previously discussed process of peer evaluation. If other people have developed the materials used in the course, the evaluations should be tailored to the purposes and special needs of that situation.

Conclusions from the Teaching Evaluation Literature

It is clear from this review that educational researchers regard evaluating instruction to be extremely important. Universities, researchers, and individual faculty members have maintained a consistently high level of interest in evaluating teaching, and they see evaluation as an accepted way to improve teaching and make personnel decisions. Additionally, although there is no clear definition of the characteristics that constitute effective teaching, there is a recognition that teaching consists of a combination of many related behaviors.

A variety of sources have been used to evaluate classroom teaching, including students, peers, instructors, and consultants. Measures associated with each of these sources vary in the degree of reliability and validity that they offer. Only two demonstrate the reliability and validity needed to evaluate teaching effectiveness on a regular basis: student ratings and peer ratings done without classroom observation.

Measures of student learning are not practical for evaluating individual instructors. Without an enormous amount of effort by faculty, such measures are not nearly as valid as faculty believe. Self-evaluations may be useful for improving teaching but are not considered valid enough to have a serious place in evaluating teaching. Use of instructional consultants can help improve teaching but is not practical for regular evaluation of all faculty.

Much less research has been conducted on the evaluation of teaching activities that occur outside the classroom. What has been done, however, suggests that the same two sources, students and peers, are adequate sources of such evaluations.

INFORMATION FROM OTHER LITERATURES

The previous section summarized the extensive literature on teaching evaluation. In discussing the measurement and improvement of teaching effectiveness, however, it is also useful to consider other literatures. Specifically, the topic of measuring and improving individual effectiveness in work settings has received considerable attention in the organizational psychology and organizational behavior areas. In fact, the authors of this book come from such a background and we undertook this entire effort because we believe that some of the ideas developed in organizational settings outside higher education could be useful in teaching evaluation and improvement.

This next section summarizes key issues from this body of literature while noting where the issues overlap with the traditional teaching evaluation literature. We will discuss having complete coverage, combining measures into an overall effectiveness index, and giving effective feedback.

Having Complete Coverage

A complete teaching evaluation system covers all types of teaching functions, including activities that occur inside and outside the classroom that affect teaching (Cashin, 1989; Miller, 1987; Seldin, 1980). In other words, a complete teaching evaluation system should cover the full range of teaching behaviors. Typically, however, only functions that are easy to measure are used in an evaluation system, whereas those that are difficult to measure are ignored. This can be very detrimental, because functions that are measured are usually given a higher priority than ones that are not measured.

The productivity and feedback literature supports the need to cover teaching behavior completely. This research indicates that functions that are measured are in fact given priority. These are thus the areas in which improvement occurs (Alluisi & Megis, 1983; Duerr, 1974; Mahoney, 1988; Mali, 1978; Peeples, 1978; Pritchard and others, 1988, 1989; Shetty & Buehler, 1985; Stein, 1986; Tuttle & Weaver, 1986).

Certain teaching evaluation systems tend to focus only on behavior within the classroom and are therefore not ideal. For example, student ratings, which are the source used most frequently to evaluate teaching, focus almost entirely on teaching behavior that occurs within the classroom. Peer ratings and feedback from instructional consultants based on classroom observation usually also concentrate on in-class behaviors. In contrast, peer evaluation of teaching portfolios can include the review of instructional activities that occur outside of class. In order to cover the range of teaching activities completely, some combination of information from various sources is therefore needed.

Combining Teaching Effectiveness Measures into an Overall Index

An overall quantitative index (or score) of teaching effectiveness that combines all the information about an instructor's teaching is generally valuable and occasionally essential. Such an index can give the instructor an overall impression of his or her teaching effectiveness and an idea of whether it is improving over time. When included with individual measures of specific teaching behaviors, this index makes an effective feedback package.

An index is also a valuable aid in personnel decisions (Abrami, Leventhal, & Kickens, 1981; Braskamp, Brandenburg, & Ory, 1984;

Cascio, 1987; Centra, 1979; Doyle, 1983). To determine raises, teaching awards, and promotions, administrators must rank applicants using some overall scale or standard. For example, in deciding which instructors will receive teaching awards, administrators must consider all the available information and place the applicants on a continuum from high to low. The instructors with the best credentials will receive awards. The decision makers must combine all the available information into an overall score, whether they make this explicit or not; otherwise, they cannot rank instructors. The issues are how well the evaluators do this combining and whether they make explicit the measures they considered and the way they have combined the information.

Another advantage of an overall index of teaching effectiveness is that it can be useful in interventions to improve teaching. For example, if instructors set teaching improvement goals, having a single index to use as the goal makes such an intervention much easier than having multiple measures with no overall index. Multiple measures must be combined in order to produce such an overall index. This is an area of some complexity, and such combinations must be done with care. The next section discusses some of the key issues to consider in making such combinations.

VARYING IMPORTANCE OF MEASURES. Typically, some aspects of teaching are considered more important than others. For example, presenting information in an organized manner and providing relevant research references are both aspects of effective teaching, but presenting information in an organized manner is generally more important. If the system is to be valid, these differences in importance need to be captured when effective teaching is measured.

If responses to items are averaged, differences in importance are lost (Cashin, 1990). The same problem occurs when we try to combine across sources of information (for example, student ratings and peer evaluations). Therefore, some method of weighting importance must be used so that measures can be combined into a single index in a way that preserves the differential importance of the components of the system. Determining a way to weight components may be the most important unresolved question in teaching evaluation research (Marsh, 1987).

One possibility is that the instructor or a faculty committee could weight the components or items differentially at the department level (Aleamoni, 1987; Cashin & Downey, 1992; Marsh, 1984, 1994). In some systems, people reflect differential importance by developing weights for each component with empirical techniques or with some process of making judgments (Schmidt & Kaplan, 1971; Sawyer, Pritchard, & Hedley-Goode, 1991).

It is important to note that when measures are combined into a decision such as tenure, dismissal, or a teaching award, the individual measures are being combined and weighted in some way. Only with this weighting can an overall decision be reached. The candidate usually does not know about the weighting system, however; frequently, it is not even explicit to the evaluator. Thus, the issue is not whether to weight; the issue is whether to make the weighting system explicit.

NONLINEARITIES. In most cases, techniques used to combine multiple measures make the assumption that there is a linear relationship between a measure and the total composite. When multiple measures are simply added or when they are multiplied by a weighting factor and then added, an assumption of linearity is being made. This process results in a composite measure. When such a composite is used to measure productivity, it assumes that performing at a higher level will always be beneficial, resulting in higher levels of effectiveness, no matter how well the activity is already being done.

When applied to teaching evaluation, the linearity assumption says that the more of a given teaching behavior the instructor performs, the better it always is. In many cases, this assumption of linearity does not hold, however. For example, consider a teacher's willingness to help students, which is one dimension of teaching effectiveness. If we assume that there is a linear relationship between the amount of help the instructor gives and the amount this aid contributes to overall teaching effectiveness, we would be saying that more would always be better. Yet, in reality, there is likely to be a level of courteousness and willingness to help students beyond which further increases would not meaningfully add to teaching effectiveness. In this example, we would say that a point of diminishing returns has been reached in a teacher's willingness to help students.

The issue of nonlinearity becomes further complicated when one considers the interaction between two or more dimensions of teaching. For example, it is important for an instructor to maintain a classroom atmosphere that supports learning. It is also important for the instructor to have mastery of the subject matter. Suppose that having subject mastery is considered more important than maintaining a supportive classroom atmosphere. Using the typical linear method of combining measures, subject mastery would have a greater weight than supportive classroom atmosphere. If the instructor's subject mastery is already high and the classroom atmosphere is poor, however, it would be more beneficial for the instructor to concentrate on improving classroom atmosphere than to continue improving subject mastery. Because of nonlinearities such as this, the importance of a particular factor in teaching must be considered relative to how well the other factors are already being performed.

The point of all this is that the issue of nonlinearities must be considered in a measurement system so as to produce optimal validity. Such nonlinearities are very common, with the vast majority of measures reflecting this nonlinear quality (Pritchard, 1995). Considering these nonlinearities also significantly affects the decisions one makes about measurements (Pritchard & Roth, 1991; Sawyer, Pritchard, & Hedley-Goode, 1991). Thus, the issue of nonlinearities should be considered in teaching evaluations. Pritchard and others (1989) have developed a solution to the nonlinearity problem. This approach is used in the teaching evaluation system described in this book. We will describe it somewhat in Chapter Two and in more detail in Chapter Three.

DIRECTLY COMPARING DIFFERENT CLASSES. When measures are combined, the resultant teaching evaluation scores should allow for comparisons across different types of classes. For example, the system should allow evaluators to compare instructors who teach graduate classes with those who teach undergraduate classes. The problem is that in most settings, different levels of classes receive different ratings; graduate classes receive substantially higher ones. Thus, if an instructor teaches predominantly graduate classes, his or her ratings will tend to be higher than an instructor of equal ability who teaches undergraduate classes. A valid teaching evaluation system should take this into consideration, especially when the evaluation information will be used for personnel decisions (Abrami, Leventhal, & Kickens, 1981; Braskamp, Brandenburg, & Ory, 1984; Centra, 1979; Doyle, 1983).

COMBINING MEASURES FROM DIFFERENT SOURCES. As mentioned earlier, information about teaching is usually gathered from several sources, including students and peers. If an overall index is to be explicitly developed, there must be a way to combine measures from different sources. For example, student ratings could be combined with peer evaluations to obtain an overall index of teaching. In addition, when an evaluation system combines such different measures into a single index, it should do so in a way that preserves the differential importance between types of measures.

Giving Feedback

One objective of evaluating teaching effectiveness is to improve teaching. Typically, this is accomplished by providing feedback to the instructors who have been evaluated. For example, instructors may receive students' mean ratings for items on an evaluation form. There is a large body of literature about using feedback to help individuals improve their performance in work settings and the relationship between feedback and improvement. Although there are certainly many cases in which feedback does not improve performance (Kluger & DeNisi, 1996), in most cases the effect is positive (Ammons, 1956; Annett, 1969; Bilodeau & Bilodeau, 1961; Cusella, 1987; Ilgen, Fisher, & Taylor, 1979; Kluger & DeNisi, 1996; Nadler, 1979; Wilke, 1970). The positive effect of feedback on performance has proven difficult to document in teaching situations, however.

In following sections, we will first review the literature on the effects of evaluation feedback on teaching performance. We will then summarize the best forms of feedback to give in this type of setting, according to the more general feedback literature.

EFFECTIVENESS OF FEEDBACK FROM STUDENT RATINGS. A number of studies have investigated the effects that feedback from student ratings have had on teaching. In general, the findings indicate that such feedback causes some improvement in instruction (Marsh & Roche, 1993). Several meta-analyses have been conducted to review the effects of feedback on the quality of teaching (Cohen, 1980; Menges & Brinko, 1986). In these studies, feedback was presented in the form of normative comparisons with colleagues.

For example, an individual instructor received mean ratings at midterm for himself or herself and those of colleagues on all or similar courses. At the end of the semester, students reevaluated these teachers. Typically, the end-of-term student ratings for teachers who had received feedback was more than one-third of a standard deviation higher (an effect size of approximately 0.3) than for those who had not received feedback. According to Cohen (1977), an effect size of 0.2 is small, 0.5 is medium, and 0.8 is large. Thus, an effect size of 0.3 is rather small. Large effect sizes emerged when a teacher both received feedback and consulted with a teaching expert. The two studies concluded that instructors required more than a simple normative comparison with colleagues in order to use feedback from student ratings to improve their instruction significantly.

It should be noted that some methodological problems with these studies may have affected the results. First, nearly all the studies included in the two meta-analyses measured the change in ratings from midterm to the end of the semester. There may not have been enough time for instructors to make the alterations in teaching behaviors suggested by the feedback. Second, most of these studies used instructors who volunteered to participate in the program. Volunteers may have been more motivated to use the feedback than instructors who did not volunteer. Third, the studies did not examine the reward structure at the teachers' universities. If studies are done at institutions that primarily base promotions and salaries on factors other than teaching, such as research, then the effects of feedback may be artificially limited (Stevens, 1987).

More recently, L'Hommedieu, Menges, and Brinko (1990) conducted a meta-analysis using twenty-eight studies with feedback from student ratings. The studies used control groups and the researchers were able to separate the effects of feedback from the effects of consultants' training. The researchers drew conclusions that matched previous findings, as their average effect size was 0.34. Again, the improvement is meaningful, but small.

It is worthwhile to compare these effects to those in other settings in which researchers have studied the effects of feedback on performance improvements. Guzzo, Jette, and Katzell (1985) reviewed this literature and found that the mean effect size for using feedback to improve productivity was 0.35. Thus, the effect size in such settings is essentially the same as in the teaching setting.

Besides problems with methodology, a lack of instructor knowledge of how to use feedback may also explain the insignificant effects that feedback had on teaching in these studies. Stevens (1987) argues that feedback will have little effect unless instructors know how to interpret and apply the feedback they receive. Other researchers say that knowing how to modify performance is a critical factor in improvement based on feedback (Canelos, 1985; Cohen, 1980; Ilgen, Fisher, & Taylor, 1979).

No research has examined the effects of having students give repeated feedback over a long period of time with a true experimental design (Marsh, 1987). Although such a study would make an important contribution to an understanding of the effects of feedback, it may not be practical or possible.

CRITERIA FOR GOOD FEEDBACK. In the literature on teaching, there is not much information about the elements of good feedback. Fortunately, these issues are discussed more extensively in literature about organizational productivity. The criteria are general and apply equally well to teaching feedback. The important elements of effective feedback include control over the measures, the ability to compare units, timeliness, specificity and completeness, knowledge of what will be measured, and acceptance.

Control over Measures

If the purpose of measuring behavior is to improve performance, feedback should be limited to aspects of work that personnel can control. Therefore, the elements of teaching measured should be under the instructor's control. If feedback is given using measures over which instructors have little control, the feedback has less power to motivate. This can be explained in terms of expectancy theory, which maintains that a lack of control over the measures reduces the relationship between effort and performance, which weakens motivation to improve (Campbell & Pritchard, 1976). Therefore, when performance evaluation includes measures that are not under the control of the person being measured, the effects of feedback diminish.

Comparative Data

Feedback should include not only how the instructor scored on each factor but also information on how positive that score is. For example, giving an instructor mean student ratings is helpful, but the instructor also needs to know how good this rating is compared with some reliable factor. In other words, compared with expectations, are the ratings average, above average, or exceptional? Without this type of information, the feedback is incomplete (Campbell, 1977; Cashin, 1990; Pritchard and others, 1988).

The most typical way to provide this comparison is to supply the ratings that other instructors receive. With normative feedback such as this, teachers can see how well their ratings compare with others in their peer group. Such systems have considerable disadvantages, however. How well a specific instructor does becomes a function of how well his or her colleagues teach. If they are relatively poor teachers, he or she looks good. If they are good teachers, the reverse is true.

Another problem is the use of such normative information over time. If everyone's teaching is improving, the definition of good teaching keeps changing in a normative feedback system. Thus, a good teacher whose colleagues keep improving their teaching looks over time as if he or she is doing a poorer job of teaching.

An approach that avoids these problems and still allows the instructor to understand how well he or she is doing is to use a comparison with fixed standards of performance. Here, a designation is made of what constitutes excellent, good, fair, and poor teaching. This can be done with mean student ratings, peer evaluations, and so forth. This standard is then compared with an individual instructor's teaching evaluation.

Timeliness

Feedback should be provided on a timely basis (Coburn, 1984; Pritchard & Montagno, 1978; Pritchard, Montagno, & Moore, 1978). Research has shown that feedback leads to improvement most frequently when it is provided as soon as possible after the performance occurred (Ammons, 1956; Annett, 1969; Ilgen, Fisher, & Taylor, 1979; Nadler, 1979). If too much time passes between collecting the evaluation data and giving feedback, the feedback ceases to be meaningful. It has also been argued that feedback should occur on a regular and predictable schedule to be most effective (Ilgen, Fisher, & Taylor, 1979).

Specificity and Completeness

Feedback must also be specific and complete. If it is too general, the instructor may know how he or she is doing but not know enough about what to improve. Specificity must be integrated into the feedback system's design. Instructors must be asked what level of detail would be most useful in the feedback they receive.

In addition, effective feedback should provide information about all the different components of effective teaching, not just some of them. For example, simply giving instructors feedback on classroom teaching usually overlooks important teaching activities, such as advising and working with students on projects outside of class.

Knowledge of What Will Be Measured

Another important aspect of good feedback is that the recipients should know in advance what is going to be measured and how it will be measured (Miller, 1974; Seldin, 1980). Such knowledge helps instructors understand and use their teaching evaluation feedback. For a teaching assessment system to be effective, all instructors should also know how the ratings are going to be combined and used.

Acceptance

The best measurement and feedback system will be largely useless if it is not accepted by those being evaluated (Pritchard, 1995). To gain such acceptance, the system must be seen as valid, fair, and sensitive to the needs of those being evaluated. The system must be designed with great care to ensure that it has these characteristics. Another critical way to promote acceptance is through participation. Specifically, the instructors who are going to be evaluated should participate heavily in developing the system. Such participation fosters ownership, understanding, and interest (Weiss, 1984).

THE IDEAL TEACHING EVALUATION SYSTEM

As a conclusion for this chapter reviewing the literature, it is appropriate to summarize what we have discussed about designing the ideal teaching evaluation system. Most of the following points come directly from the literature we have reviewed. A few come from our own experience in measurement and feedback systems (for example, Pritchard, 1990, 1995). These ideal aspects fall into the categories of (1) overall structure, (2) measures to use, (3) measurement characteristics, and (4) feedback characteristics.

Overall Structure

1. The objectives of the teaching evaluation system must be clear and publicly stated. Typically, these objectives are to evaluate instructors and to give instructors information so that they can improve their teaching.

2. The evaluation system should be based on quantitative information. With quantitative data, institutions can make personnel decisions and the instructor can unambiguously assess his or her performance. Qualitative information can and should be added, especially to help the instructor make changes, but quantitative information is essential.

3. The evaluation system must give an overall index of teaching effectiveness, as well as information on specific aspects of teaching. The composite index is essential for the university to evaluate an instructor's teaching and for the faculty member to receive an overall

performance assessment. Information about the specific, more detailed aspects of teaching is needed to help the instructor improve.

4. The evaluation system must capture teaching policy accurately. This means that it identifies all important aspects of teaching and assesses the relative importance of these different factors. Instructors and the administration should agree on these value judgments.

5. Both instructors and the administration must understand the system and accept it as accurate and useful.

6. The system must be cost effective to develop and maintain. Of special importance here is the time required to conduct an evaluation once the system is in place. When the system includes peer evaluations, considerable resistance is to be expected, because the evaluation process is likely to be very time consuming for the faculty doing the peer evaluations.

7. The system should be developed with significant and meaningful instructor participation.

8. If it is important to evaluate how well instructors teach, it is also important to assess how well the evaluation system is working. The first part of such an evaluation should be done as each step in the evaluation system is completed. These steps include determining the evaluation's purpose, choosing evaluation methods, constructing or selecting instruments, collecting and reporting the data, and maintaining and refining the system. Then, once the evaluation and feedback system is in place, it should receive a formal overall evaluation and then be reviewed periodically to ensure that it is still meeting the needs of those involved.

Measures to Use

1. Teaching is multidimensional. Thus, the system must measure a variety of teaching behaviors.

2. Critical teaching behaviors must be identified before the measurement system is developed. If the system is to evaluate the important parts of teaching and be accepted by instructors and administrators, they must agree on what behaviors constitute effective teaching and what must be measured to assess these behaviors.

3. To give a complete assessment of teaching contribution, the evaluation must include all aspects of teaching, not just classroom instruction.

4. Because there is no one perfect measure of teaching effectiveness, multiple complementary measures should be used.

5. Student ratings are a practical and valid source of instructor evaluation and should be part of the system.

6. To improve the validity of the overall measurement system and promote acceptance by those skeptical of student ratings, the system needs to supplement these ratings with other measures. The best supplement is peer evaluations made after a review of teaching materials but not based on classroom observation.

7. To avoid bias in student ratings, the instructor should be absent from the classroom when the ratings are done, the ratings should be anonymous, and all students should be told that their ratings can have effects on personnel decisions.

8. Instructors should only be measured on factors over which they have control.

Measurement Characteristics

1. The measurement system must show three types of reliability: internal consistency, interjudge, and test-retest reliability.

2. The system must be valid. To be valid, it must be complete, use scales that are carefully developed and clear to the users, and be as free from bias as possible.

3. The system should be able to account for differential importance of teaching factors.

4. The system should be able to account for nonlinearities.

5. The system should allow for direct comparisons across different types of classes. For example, it should allow for comparing instructors in graduate classes with those in undergraduate classes, even though the latter typically receive lower student ratings.

6. The system must be flexible enough to allow for different teaching missions. Not all academic departments have the same teaching objectives and the teaching evaluation system should reflect this. For example, a class or teaching unit whose role is to transmit content knowledge has a different mission than one which attempts to train students to solve problems in actual situations using that content knowledge. The teaching evaluation system should not place the same importance on all teaching factors if departmental missions are different.

7. The system should be sensitive to the importance of teaching in the instructor's overall work. In most settings, instructors are expected to perform research and service to the university, as well as to teach. For some, teaching is by far the most important part of the job. For others, it is least important. The system should capture this difference

in some way, especially when personnel decisions are to be made on the basis of the teaching evaluations. Sensitivity to this issue should also be reflected in the amount of effort devoted to the teaching evaluation. For someone whose primary responsibility is teaching, a more detailed evaluation is needed than for one who does very little teaching.

Feedback Characteristics

1. Faculty should know what is going to be measured, how it is going to be measured, how the measures are to be combined, and how the information is to be used.

2. Measurement and the resulting feedback should occur on a regular, predictable basis.

3. The feedback should be given in a timely manner—as soon after the evaluation as is practical.

4. The feedback should include not only how the instructor scored on each factor but also how good that level of performance is. This is best done by comparison with agreed-upon performance standards rather than by normative comparisons with other instructors.

5. The feedback should help improve teaching performance. It should communicate the differential importance of the various aspects of teaching, communicate the existing nonlinearities, and allow for the identification of priorities for improving teaching.

2

PRODUCTIVITY MEASUREMENT
AND ENHANCEMENT

A New System

AS NOTED IN THE INTRODUCTION, this book describes a new method of measuring and improving teaching evaluation. The method is based on an approach used to measure and improve productivity in organizations. As we will discuss below, the method has worked quite well in the organizational setting. An overriding question guiding this research was whether this approach could be adapted to teaching evaluation and improvement. With the literature and the list of factors for an ideal teaching evaluation system in mind, we now describe this approach.

This chapter will first summarize the approach, and then compare it to the list of ideal characteristics for a teaching evaluation system. The final section of this chapter describes how the basic approach has been used in other settings and what the results there have been.

A SUMMARY OF PROMES

The basic approach is called the Productivity Measurement and Enhancement System, or ProMES. It is described most fully in Pritchard (1990, 1995). The four steps of ProMES are (1) identifying salient objectives, (2) developing indicators of these objectives, (3) establishing contingencies, and (4) putting the system together to provide feedback.

To illustrate these four steps clearly, we will use an extended hypothetical example based on the type of teaching effectiveness measurement system implemented in the first phase of this research project. We will limit the discussion to classroom teaching and assume that the basic measurement data will come from student ratings of teaching effectiveness. Later chapters will describe ways of including other aspects of teaching and evaluation of teaching in the system.

Step 1: Identify Objectives

An instructor is expected to perform a set of activities while teaching. We call these activities *objectives*. Because performance is a function of how well these objectives have been met, the first step in developing the teaching measurement system is to identify the teaching objectives.

To identify them and to conduct the other steps in developing the system, we use a representative committee, called a *design committee*, which makes decisions through group consensus. A design committee for an academic department would be composed of teaching faculty chosen to represent the different types of teaching done in that department (for example, graduate, undergraduate, lecture, laboratory, and so forth).

The design committee would develop the objectives by answering the question "What are the important things an instructor must do in classroom teaching?" They would discuss this issue and through a process of consensus develop a list of these objectives. Assume that the committee developed a list of objectives that included the following:

1. The instructor presented appropriate material in an organized fashion.
2. The instructor evaluated students fairly.

In an actual application, more than two objectives would certainly be identified. Typically, there are five to ten such objectives. This subset of two will suffice, however, for explaining how the system works.

Step 2: Develop Indicators

Once the objectives are determined, the next step is to develop indicators of these objectives. An *indicator* is a measure of how well the instructors are achieving the objective in question. To identify the indicators, the faculty design committee is asked to think of things that show how well the objectives are being accomplished. In our abbreviated example, the measurement will be based only on student ratings, so the indicators would be items on a student rating questionnaire. After the questionnaire items (that is, indicators) are discussed and refined, the objectives and indicators might look like this:

- Objective 1: The instructor presented appropriate material in an organized fashion.

  Indicator A: The instructor was well organized.

  Indicator B: The amount of material that the instructor presented or assigned was appropriate.

- Objective 2: The instructor evaluated students fairly.

  Indicator A: The instructor's examination questions were reasonable in difficulty.

  Indicator B: The instructor's examination questions were graded fairly.

Thus, for Objective 1, Indicator A, the item on the student evaluation questionnaire would be: "The instructor was well organized." The students would rate how well this indicator described the individual instructor.

Once the list of indicators has been completed to the design committee's satisfaction, the next step is to obtain formal approval of the objectives and indicators, first from the faculty and then from the administration, typically the dean's office. These are important steps in the process; in this phase, the system's accuracy and completeness are checked. By going through these approval steps, faculty and administration have the opportunity to suggest revisions to the system. This process of review and ultimately approval is important not only so that people will accept the system but also so that all agree that the system indeed represents teaching standards, or "policy."

Step 3: Establish Contingencies

The student rating form developed in the first two steps of our approach is not particularly different from a traditional student evaluation form. The real difference between our approach and more traditional methods is the next step—developing contingencies. The term *contingencies* refers to functions that describe the relationship between how well the instructor is rated on an item and how much that level of performance affects overall teaching effectiveness. The term *contingency* should not be confused with behaviorists' use of the term. We use it to mean that the level of an indicator's contribution to teaching effectiveness is *contingent* or dependent on the amount of that indicator. Specifically, a contingency is the relationship between the amount of the indicator and the effectiveness of that amount.

A contingency can best be explained by an example. The top half of Figure 2.1 shows the general form of a contingency. The horizontal axis is the amount of the indicator, which ranges from the worst possible to the best possible level. In our example, the horizontal axis is the mean rating on one of the items from the student rating questionnaire (that is, the mean rating for the item that the students gave that instructor for the semester). Assume that a five-point rating scale is being used with a low of 1 and a high of 5. The worst possible rating an instructor could receive would be a mean of 1.0. The best possible rating would be a mean of 5.0.

On the vertical axis of the figure are the effectiveness values of the indicator's various levels. *Effectiveness* is defined as the contribution to the teaching effort that the indicator's level would make. The axis ranges from 0, which is minimum effectiveness, to 200, which is maximum effectiveness. The axis also has an *expected level* (an effectiveness value of 100), which is defined as the point at which performance is neither particularly good or bad. One can think of a contingency as a type of utility function relating the level of the rating to the utility (effectiveness) of that rating.

To develop contingencies, the design committee goes through a series of formally defined steps. We will describe these steps more fully in Chapter Three. The basic idea, however, is to use group discussion and consensus to go through a process that results in the development of these contingencies.

An example of a completed contingency appears in the bottom half of Figure 2.1. The item (indicator) is "The instructor was well organized." The figure shows that the design committee believed that a mean rating of 3.0 corresponds to a value of 100 effectiveness points; in other words, the design committee believed that a rating of 3.0 was the expected level. This rating is neither especially good or bad. It simply defines the score expected from an instructor in that setting. The contingency also shows that the minimum indicator score of 1.0 would

Figure 2.1. ProMES Contingencies.

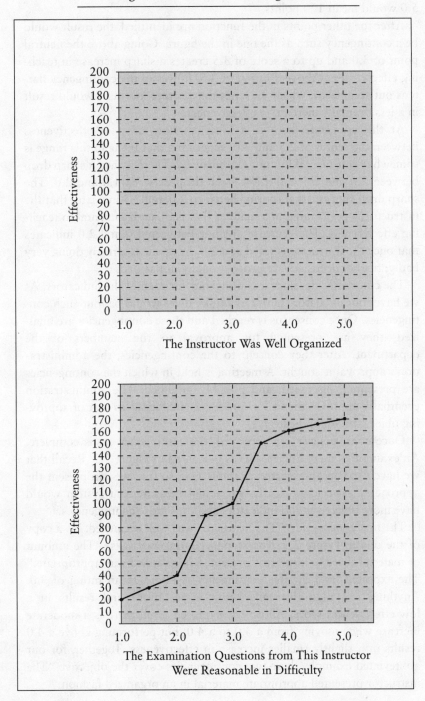

The Instructor Was Well Organized

The Examination Questions from This Instructor
Were Reasonable in Difficulty

correspond to an effectiveness level of 20 points, whereas a mean of 5.0 would mean 170 points.

After the other points in the function are identified, the result would be a contingency such as the one in the figure. Going above the neutral point of 3.0 and up to a score of 3.5 creates a sharp increase in teaching effectiveness. Above a rating of 3.5, however, the contingency flattens out somewhat, which indicates that further increases would result in a less dramatic increase in effectiveness.

At the low end, there is a fairly shallow drop in effectiveness between the scores of 2.5 and 3.0, suggesting that being in this range is somewhat detrimental but not extremely so. There is then a sharp drop between 2.0 and 2.5 and a less steep drop between 1.0 and 2.0. The sharp drop suggests that scoring between 2.0 and 2.5 indicates that the instructor is performing in a manner that is quite detrimental to teaching effectiveness. The decrease in slope between 1.0 and 2.0 indicates that once the instructor is rated at a 2.0, he or she is already doing very badly; further decreases are proportionally not as bad.

The committee develops a contingency for each of the indicators. As we have four indicators in our example, there would be four such contingencies. Once consensus is reached and these contingencies are finalized, they are presented for approval to the members of the department. After they consent to the contingencies, the administration's approval is sought. A meeting is held in which the contingencies are presented, discussed, and possibly modified. The administration eventually approves them. The process is analogous to that of approving objectives and indicators.

Once contingencies are approved, the contingency set is complete. An example of a contingency set is presented in Figure 2.2. Recall that we have used an abbreviated example here so that we can present the approach's basic logic clearly. An actual measurement system would have more objectives and indicators and thus more contingencies.

The first contingency, "The instructor was well organized," is a copy of the one in Figure 2.1. The second contingency says, "The amount of material that the instructor presented or assigned was appropriate." The expected level for this contingency is also a mean rating of 3.0. Anything less than this falls below expectations and results in a low effectiveness score. Above the expected level, there is a moderate increase when moving from a 3.0 to a 4.0, but performing above a 4.0 results in a slightly smaller increase in effectiveness. Together, for our abbreviated example, these two contingencies cover the objective "The instructor presented appropriate material in an organized fashion."

The second objective refers to the fairness with which the instructor evaluated students. The first indicator, "The instructor's examination questions were reasonable in difficulty," is a fairly flat contingency. Performance below the expected level of 3.0 does not result in a large loss of effectiveness points. Similarly, performing above the expected level does not result in a substantial gain in effectiveness. The final indicator, "The examination questions from this instructor were graded fairly," is fairly flat above the expected level of 3.5, but is fairly steep below the expected level. This indicates that performing below the expected level in terms of grading students fairly is quite detrimental to teacher effectiveness, but that grading students fairly more frequently than expected does not increase effectiveness.

Three things are particularly noteworthy about the contingencies. First, the overall slope of the function expresses the indicator's relative importance. A steep slope implies that changes in the indicator (mean student rating for that item) cause large variations in effectiveness; a less steep slope implies that changes in the indicator create less variation in effectiveness.

Second, the relationship between the mean student rating and the effectiveness of that level is not always linear. As such, contingencies can be and usually are nonlinear. As we shall discuss below, this nonlinearity is necessary to reflect the realities of the teaching function accurately.

It is important to recognize what these first two properties of the contingencies do. Many performance measurement systems, even if they attempt to measure all important aspects of the individual's performance and combine them into a single index, do so by adding the measures somehow (Landy & Farr, 1980; Nagle, 1953). This amounts to assuming that all of the individual's functions are equally important. Clearly, this does not reflect reality. The instructor's different tasks are not equally important.

One way of incorporating differential importance into a measurement system is to measure each aspect of the work and then to weight each measure by its importance (Cawunder & Tasker, 1981). We feel that this weighting method is flawed because, as we discussed in Chapter One, it assumes a linear relationship between the amount of a measure and its effectiveness. That is, to improve a given amount at the low end of the measure is as good as improving that same amount at the high end.

We have found that this is often not the case. It would be very common, for example, for improvements in the middle range of an

Figure 2.2. Sample Contingencies.

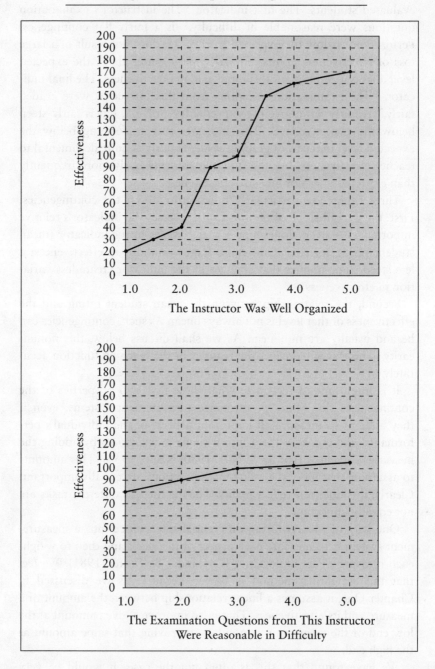

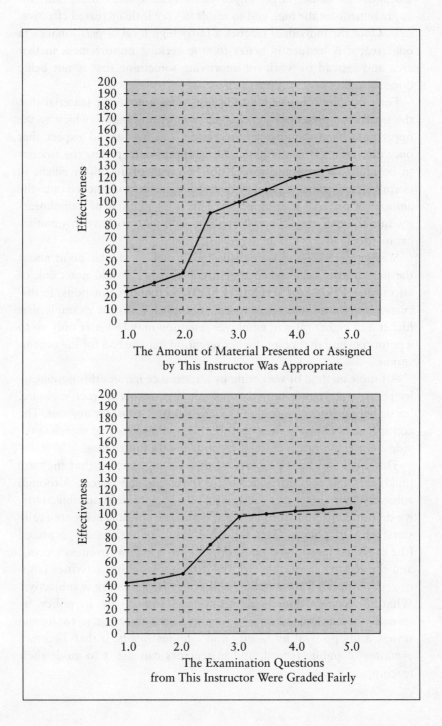

indicator to cause large improvements in effectiveness, but for improvements at the high end to result in very little increased effectiveness. Once the individual reaches a fairly high level of performance in one area, it is frequently better to stop seeking improvement in that area and instead to work on improving something that is not being done as well.

For example, consider the indicator "The amount of material that the instructor presented or assigned was appropriate," which is the upper-right-hand contingency in Figure 2.2. We would expect that once the amount of material was fairly appropriate, raising the amount to be highly appropriate would not be much of an improvement in overall effectiveness. A point of diminishing returns is reached once the amount of material is appropriate. This is an example of a nonlinearity. In our experience, the vast majority of indicators have this nonlinear quality.

Seashore (1972) and Campbell (1977) make a similar point about the nonlinearity issue when they argue that we should not think of effectiveness measures in terms of linear, continuous functions. In discussing organizational effectiveness, Campbell gives the example that higher and higher rates of employee retention may be better only up to a point. Beyond that point, higher retention may be bad for the organization.

A simple method of weighting by importance ignores this nonlinearity because no matter how the individual performs on each measure, his or her performance is always weighted by a constant amount. The contingencies in our system capture this nonlinearity and thereby provide a more accurate picture of the individual's functioning.

The third and final property of the contingencies is that they are judgments and thus introduce subjectivity into the system. Although subjectivity is sometimes viewed as less acceptable than objectivity, we do not consider this to be a problem. The contingencies are really statements of policy. They say what levels of ratings are expected (the expected level), how good other levels are (effectiveness scores), and the relative importance of the different teaching activities (contingency slopes). This is policy, and policy by its nature is subjective. What the system does is to reduce the subjectivity in policy by formally discussing it, quantifying it, and subjecting it to formal review and approval by faculty and administrators. It then becomes a matter of public record, and instructors can use it to guide their teaching.

Step 4: Put the System Together

The last step is to provide the instructors with feedback from the system. This would be accomplished by first collecting the indicator data in the form of student ratings and calculating the mean rating for each indicator. These means are the indicator values. In our abbreviated example, there would be four such means for a given instructor in a class. Then, based on the contingencies, effectiveness scores would be calculated for each indicator value. An illustration of this can be seen in the hypothetical feedback report found in Table 2.1. For example, suppose the instructor had a score of 3.21 on the indicator "The instructor was well organized." The 3.21 corresponds to an effectiveness value of 122 on the vertical (effectiveness) axis of the contingency. Continuing this process would give an effectiveness value for each indicator, as the table shows.

Once the effectiveness values are determined, they can be averaged to determine overall effectiveness for each objective. The total effectiveness of the first objective, "The instructor presented appropriate material in an organized fashion," would be the average of the two indicators for that objective; with a score of 122 for being well

Table 2.1.   Sample Feedback Report: Part One.

BASIC FEEDBACK INFORMATION

TEACHING EFFECTIVENESS REPORT FOR: M. Smith, Anatomy 391.
BASIC EFFECTIVENESS DATA FOR: Spring 1996.

Objectives and Indicators	Indicator Data	Effectiveness Score
Presented appropriate material in organized fashion		
Instructor well organized	3.21	122
Material appropriate	4.23	121
Average effectiveness: 122		
Evaluated student fairly		
Exams reasonably difficult	3.21	101
Exams graded fairly	2.83	83
Average effectiveness: 92		
Average overall effectiveness score:	**107**	

Table 2.2.   Sample Feedback Report: Part Two.

FEEDBACK REPORT PRIORITY INFORMATION

TEACHING EFFECTIVENESS REPORT FOR: M. Smith, Anatomy 391.
Potential effectiveness gains for the next period.

Objectives and Indicators	From Indicator Data	To Indicator Data	Effectiveness Gain
Presented appropriate material in organized fashion			
Instructor well organized	3.21	3.46	25
Material appropriate	4.23	4.48	2
Evaluated student fairly			
Exams reasonably difficult	3.21	3.46	1
Exams graded fairly	2.83	3.08	13

organized and 121 for presenting an appropriate amount of material, the average would be 122.

Next, the instructor's overall performance can be calculated by averaging the effectiveness scores for each objective. In the example, this average overall effectiveness score is 107. Being able simply to average effectiveness scores is one of the system's major advantages. Because the contingencies already reflect the relative importance and nonlinearity of the indicators, a simple averaging reflects the overall effectiveness of the instructor.

These effectiveness scores also have a distinct meaning. A score of 100 means that the individual is meeting expectations, performing at a level that is neither particularly good or bad. As the score moves above 100, the instructor is exceeding expectations. The higher the score, the more expectations are being exceeded. When the score falls below 100, the individual is not meeting expectations.

A second part of the feedback report is shown in Table 2.2. This is the identification of priorities for making improvements. Even if a person is highly motivated to make improvements, it is frequently difficult to know where to focus these improvement efforts (for example, Earley, Connolly, & Ekegren, 1989). ProMES offers a way to identify priorities. Recall that in the contingencies, an effectiveness score is associated with *each* value of an indicator. As the contingencies in Figure 2.2 show, it would be quite easy to note the effectiveness score for the current level of an indicator and then to calculate the change in effectiveness that would occur if the person improved on that indicator by any specified amount.

For example, suppose the instructor's rating on "Exams graded fairly" were 2.83. If the instructor increased his rating on this factor by .25, for example, the rating would go from 2.83 to 3.08. Using the contingency, it is easy to calculate the change in effectiveness from a rating of 2.83 on this item to a rating of 3.08. In this example, 2.83 has an effectiveness score of 83 and 3.08 has an effectiveness score of 96, so the gain in effectiveness is 13 points. The possible gain in effectiveness can be calculated for each indicator and reported to the instructor.

An example is shown in Table 2.2, which is also part of the feedback report. The current semester rating for each indicator is shown in the "From Indicator Data" column, the amount of change that would reflect an increase of one interval on the indicator is shown in the column labeled "To Indicator Data," and the change in the effectiveness score appears in the last column.

These effectiveness gain scores identify the impact that making improvements has on each of the indicators on the person's overall teaching effectiveness. This indicates what the *priorities* should be for improving overall teaching effectiveness. Because the gain scores are based on the contingencies, they are based on policy to which all have agreed.

In this example, Table 2.2 indicates that the instructor should first consider ways to increase the degree of organization, because that is where the most gain in effectiveness (25) could be made. After the teacher considers possible strategies for increasing that indicator, the next priority would be to work on fairness of examination grading with its potential effectiveness gain of 13. It is clear, however, that very little can be gained from trying to improve appropriateness of material (a gain of 2) or difficulty of examination questions (a gain of 1).

A feedback report containing the information shown in the abbreviated example in Tables 2.1 and 2.2 would be generated for each course that an instructor taught. In addition, each instructor would receive a report that contained the average overall effectiveness score for each course and an average overall effectiveness score across all courses that semester.

In the typical application of ProMES, a formal feedback meeting occurs between the individual or group and his or her supervisor to review the feedback report. They talk about how well the individual did overall for the period and then focus on the specific indicators. For those that improved, they discuss what they did to cause the improvements and how those improvements can be sustained. For indicators that decreased, they discuss what caused this decrease and how they could improve the situation. The instructor would be expected to study the feedback report and make changes based on that information. A formal meeting with the instructor's supervisor (the department head) to review the report would be optional.

We will discuss several other features in the system when we give a more detailed presentation in Chapter Three of how we actually implemented the system in our project. This summary is sufficient, however, to present an overview and to be able to assess how the system compares with the list of ideal features for a teaching evaluation system.

COMPARISON OF THE SYSTEM WITH IDEAL CHARACTERISTICS

At the end of Chapter One, we listed a series of criteria for an ideal teaching evaluation system. We shall now review these characteristics and assess the degree to which the ProMES system meets these criteria. In order to make this section clear, we will first briefly preview our teaching evaluation project.

The project took place in the College of Veterinary Medicine at Texas A&M University and involved five academic departments in which instructors taught courses at undergraduate, graduate, and professional (Doctor of Veterinary Medicine) levels. The first phase of the project was to develop and implement the student evaluation portion of the evaluation system. Thus, objectives, indicators, and contingencies were developed, the system was implemented, and instructors received their feedback reports over several years. The second phase of the project covered aspects of teaching outside the classroom and used peer evaluation of teaching activities that occurred inside and outside the classroom. Objectives, indicators, and contingencies were developed and approved, but this second phase was not actually implemented. The following discussion restates the ideal criteria for such a system and details how ProMES matches up with these characteristics.

Overall Structure

1. *The objectives of the teaching evaluation system must be clear and publicly stated.* This is not a specific characteristic of ProMES but one that should be true of any approach. In this project, we formally identified and communicated our objectives to all. We will discuss these objectives in Chapter Three.

2. *The evaluation system should be based on quantitative information.* The system meets this criterion, because the feedback reports are quantitative in nature. In addition, qualitative information is added to the system when the students write comments on the back of the student evaluation form. The peer evaluations elicit additional qualitative information.

3. *The evaluation system must give an overall index of teaching effectiveness, as well as information on specific aspects of teaching.* The system meets this criterion in that the ProMES overall effectiveness score is an overall index that can be used for evaluation. For classroom teaching, the mean across courses gives the overall index for the semester. Examining this mean over time shows how well the instructor is doing over an extended period.

The effectiveness scores for the individual indicators give the instructor information on how well he or she is doing with specific aspects of teaching. In addition, in the final system, the peer evaluation component could be combined with the student evaluations into a single score reflecting the overall effectiveness of an individual's teaching activities. The specifics of how this was done in this project will be described later.

4. *The evaluation system must capture teaching policy accurately.* The system does this by starting with overall teaching objectives and then identifying what will be measured through the indicators. The contingencies determine the relative importance of each indicator and show how different scores on the indicators match up with departmental expectations. Faculty committees develop these aspects of the system and college administrators approve them. Once this is done, college policy is established and presented in a communicable form.

5. *Both instructors and the administration must understand the system and accept it as accurate and useful.* One of the strengths of our approach is that both faculty and administration are actively involved in designing it at each stage of development. Based on our experience in other types of organizations, this helps them considerably to accept the system. The level of participation should also make the system easy to understand, because faculty will be familiar with each step.

6. *The system must be cost effective to develop and maintain.* Our system is costly to develop in the sense that a significant amount of faculty time is needed to develop the objectives, indicators, and contingencies. Once developed, it must be periodically evaluated to ensure that it is current. Once in place, however, the system is no more difficult to operate than any evaluation system using student ratings. Whether the

system is in fact cost effective is one of the questions we assessed in this project.

7. *The system should be developed with significant and meaningful instructor participation.* For the most part, it is instructors who develop the system's components. A committee with representatives from several departments identifies objectives and indicators. Faculty and students then give input on these measures. Once these tasks have been accomplished, all department members must approve the contingencies.

8. *If it is important to evaluate how well instructors teach, it is also important to assess how well the evaluation system is working.* Although this is not a formal part of the ProMES process, considerable effort was made to assess this teaching evaluation system. We will discuss the approach and results in later chapters.

What Measures to Use

1. *Teaching is multidimensional. Thus, the system must measure a variety of teaching behaviors.* The system does this by carefully identifying all the salient aspects of teaching and measuring them with the different indicators.

2. *Critical teaching behaviors must be identified before the measurement system is developed.* System development begins with the identification of teaching objectives. Once identified, these critical teaching behaviors guide the remaining development of the measurement system.

3. *To give a complete assessment of teaching, the evaluation must include all aspects of teaching, not just classroom instruction.* As discussed above, the system also includes other aspects of teaching, such as advising, working with students on individual projects, curriculum development, and so forth.

4. *Because there is no one perfect measure of teaching effectiveness, multiple, complementary measures should be used.* Our plan for this project was to combine student ratings with peer evaluations and then to integrate the two components. We will present a way to accomplish this, even though we did not implement the peer evaluation component.

5. *Student ratings are a practical and valid source of instructor evaluation and should be part of the system.* The system used in this project included student ratings.

6. *To improve the validity of the overall measurement system and promote acceptance by those skeptical of student ratings, the system needs to supplement these ratings with other measures. The best sup-*

plement is peer evaluations made after a review of teaching materials but not based on classroom observation. Peer evaluations were designed in the second phase of the project. We will describe the specifics of this aspect below.

7. *To avoid bias in student ratings, the instructor should be absent from the classroom when the ratings are done, the ratings should be anonymous, and all students should be told that their ratings can have effects on personnel decisions.* In this project, we ensured this setting for the student ratings.

8. *Instructors should only be measured on factors over which they have control.* When we designed the measures for both student and peer evaluation systems in this project, we made a concerted effort to meet this criterion.

Measurement Characteristics

1. *The measurement system must show three types of reliability: internal consistency, interjudge, and test-retest reliability.* The reliability of the student rating system was assessed, as we will describe later.

2. *The system must be valid. To be valid, it must be complete, use scales that are carefully developed and clear to the users, and be as free from bias as possible.* Carefully developing the objectives for effective teaching and including all aspects of teaching in the system ensure completeness. We gave considerable care to developing and pretesting the scales to maximize clarity, as we will discuss in later sections when we address other validity data. Validity also means accounting for differential importance, nonlinearities, and differences in types of classes. We discuss these topics next.

3. *The system should be able to account for differential importance of teaching factors.* Because of the contingencies, the system meets this criterion. Differential importance is contained in the overall slopes of the contingencies. This means that teaching factors may receive different weights. For example, a factor such as knowledge of course material can have a different weight than the factor of assigning appropriate readings.

4. *The system should be able to account for nonlinearities.* The contingencies clearly allow the system to meet this criterion. Accommodating nonlinearity should enhance both actual and perceived validity.

5. *The system should allow for direct comparisons across different types of classes. For example, it should allow for comparing instructors*

in graduate classes with those in undergraduate classes, even though the latter typically receive lower student ratings. One of the system's major strengths is its ability to do this. Different sets of contingencies can be developed for various types of classes. For example, we might expect different contingencies for graduate seminars, large lecture professional classes, laboratory classes, and undergraduate classes. The sets of contingencies would have different expected levels of performance.

Recall that the expected level in ProMES is a student rating of 100 on the Effectiveness scale of a contingency. Recall further that by policy, scoring at this point is considered as meeting expectations and is viewed as neither especially good or bad. The expected level for a course in which higher student ratings are expected should be set higher than one in which lower ratings are expected. For example, graduate seminars are typically rated higher than undergraduate classes. If departmental policy suggests that graduate courses receive higher ratings, which is typical in many settings, the typical expected level for a graduate course might be 3.5, whereas the typical expected level for an undergraduate course would be 3.0. This compensates for the differences in ratings for the two courses, because a disparity in the expected levels compensates for the expected difference in ratings. Although the same level of quality in teaching receives a different student rating, it gets a similar ProMES effectiveness score.

This ability to develop tailored contingency sets for different types of courses allows for a direct comparison of the scores from various courses. The overall effectiveness scores will reflect how well the instructor scored relative to agreed-upon departmental expectations. This makes it possible to determine an average overall effectiveness score for all the courses an instructor teaches and to compare that score directly with another instructor's score, regardless of the mix of courses taught. This greatly simplifies the evaluation process.

6. *The system must be flexible enough to allow for different teaching missions.* Contingencies also allow various evaluation systems for dissimilar courses. For example, encouraging students to develop their own ideas would be more important in a graduate seminar than in a first-year undergraduate class. Different sets of contingencies for the various types of classes would capture such diversity in mission. If encouraging students is an important factor in that type of class, its contingency has a steep slope. If encouraging students is less important in another type of class, that indicator has a less steep slope.

This feature of ProMES also allows departments to assign different weights to the same teaching factor when they design their contingencies. The list of measures will be the same for all departments, but individual departments can choose to weight the measures in a way that captures their own policy and mission.

7. *The system should be sensitive to the importance of teaching in the instructor's overall work.* As part of the feedback from the system, especially the feedback reports given to department heads and deans, the system identifies the percentage of a faculty member's overall role that is teaching related. If this varies from faculty member to faculty member, as it did in this project, this helps interpret the teaching evaluation data relative to other evaluation factors, such as research and service. In addition, for this project the amount of detail in the evaluation of a faculty member varied according to the need for feedback and evaluation. For example, there was less need for frequent and extensive evaluation of senior full professors than for untenured assistant professors.

Feedback Characteristics

1. *Faculty should know what is going to be measured, how it is going to be measured, how the measures are to be combined, and how the information is to be used.* The system meets this criterion, because faculty members know beforehand about the evaluation factors and contingencies used in the student evaluations and peer evaluations. Furthermore, faculty, department heads, and college administrators will have agreed upon all these factors and contingencies. Thus, faculty will know exactly what is going to be measured and how (the indicators) and how the measures will be combined (the contingencies). Finally, when faculty members are introduced to the project, they will learn who has access to the feedback information and how it will be used.

2. *Measurement and the resulting feedback should occur on a regular, predictable basis.* The system meets this criterion in that each semester the instructor receives a feedback report showing his or her performance as rated by the students. In our project, the design further called for a regularly scheduled peer evaluation. We also planned for this system to include an integrated evaluation that combined the student and peer evaluation into an overall evaluation.

3. *The feedback should be given in a timely manner—as soon after the evaluation as is practical.* In our project, the students rated instructors at the end of the semester. The plan was for feedback reports based on these student ratings to have been distributed soon afterward.

4. *The feedback should include not only how the instructor scored on each factor but also how good that level of performance is.* One of the problems with most student or peer evaluation systems is that instructors and administrators receive feedback on the ratings but do not know how to interpret these values. That is, they do not know how good the ratings are.

As discussed in the last chapter, one solution is to compare the instructor's scores with normative data. This, however, ignores the overall effectiveness level of the instructors who comprise the normative sample. If the comparison instructors are quite good, a good teacher will look only average. Furthermore, if instructors attempt to improve their teaching and their scores increase over time, the overall average increases. This makes it very difficult to interpret how an individual instructor is doing.

The approach of the ProMES system is different. The overall effectiveness scores reflect teaching performance relative to standards that faculty and administrators have reviewed and approved. Thus, the overall effectiveness scores do indeed reflect how good the teaching performance is. If the score is over 100, it exceeds expectations. The more it is above 100, the more it exceeds expectations. If it is below 100, it falls below expectations.

5. *The feedback should help improve teaching performance. It should communicate the differential importance of the various aspects of teaching, communicate the existing nonlinearities, and allow for the identification of priorities for improving teaching.* Clearly, the system will communicate differential importance and nonlinearities, which should help improve teaching. The system also gives a precise set of priorities that instructors can use to improve teaching. Because the contingencies are nonlinear, an equal increase in the indicator score for a given indicator will *not* cause an equal increase in effectiveness. In other words, a given improvement in ratings results in different changes in effectiveness, depending on how well the instructor is already performing that behavior. (Table 2.2 illustrates this feature.) Because this priority information is included as part of the feedback report, instructors will be able to make better decisions about how to improve their teaching.

Conclusions from Comparison with Ideal Characteristics

This comparison of the characteristics of an ideal teaching evaluation system to the ProMES system used in our project shows that the ProMES system meets most of these criteria or has the potential to do so. The results of the project, which we discuss in later chapters, will indicate how well these characteristics were actually met.

PREVIOUS APPLICATIONS OF PROMES

Approximately ninety organizational units have used ProMES. These units exist in eight countries (the United States, the Netherlands, Germany, Australia, Switzerland, Hungary, France, and Sweden). Eight different research groups have conducted evaluations with ProMES. A sampling of projects appears in Figure 2.3, where we have broken them down according to manufacturing, service, and white-collar or professional settings. The country where the project was done is also shown.

Considerable data about ProMES's effects on productivity are now available. An extended discussion of the method of analysis and the resulting findings appears in the concluding chapter of Pritchard (1995). The typical design of a ProMES project develops the system in one or more units of an organization. After this development, there is a baseline period in which indicator data are collected but not fed back to the unit personnel. Then feedback starts with its corresponding feedback meetings. In addition, there are typically comparison units in which available measures of important aspects of the work are collected throughout the baseline and feedback periods. The most important criterion for the ProMES groups is the average overall effectiveness score that comes from the feedback report. It is the average of the effectiveness scores for each indicator and appears at the bottom of Table 2.1.

Although, as mentioned above, ProMES has been used in approximately ninety units, some of the projects under way do not yet have sufficient data to analyze. Some projects were done a while ago and the data are not available. Other projects were discontinued because of organizational changes that occurred before ProMES feedback could be elicited. At this time, however, we have sufficient data for analysis from twenty-three ProMES projects (not counting ours). Those projects have lasted from nine months to several years; most have lasted at least eighteen months.

The change in productivity from the baseline period to the feedback period is quite compelling. When averaged across the twenty-three units, productivity started out just slightly above the expected level. When the first period of feedback began, there was an immediate and substantial improvement. Then productivity continued to improve

Figure 2.3.   Examples of Where ProMES Has Been Used.

Manufacturing Settings
- Assembly-line manufacturing of batteries (United States)
- Assembly-line manufacturing of consumer products (United States)
- Chemical processing (Netherlands)
- High-tech team manufacturing of electrical components (Germany)
- Manual assembly of electrical components (Germany)
- Textile manufacturing (United States)
- Steel manufacturing (Netherlands)
- Team-based manufacturing of printed circuit boards (United States)
- Team-based manufacturing of paper (Netherlands)
- Manufacture of outdoor equipment (United States)
- Team-based manufacturing of cardboard boxes (Netherlands)
- Food (confectionery) manufacturing (Hungary)

Service Settings
- Sales and repair of office machinery (United States)
- Repair of complex communication and navigation equipment (United States)
- Various departments in a large warehouse (United States)
- Police department (Netherlands)
- Computer repair (Australia)
- Commercial painters (Germany)
- Bank (Netherlands)
- Oil distribution (Netherlands)
- Government social services (Sweden)
- Residential care of mental patients (United States)
- Dock workers (Australia)
- In-house corporate library research unit (United States)
- Bar in restaurant (United States)
- Photocopier maintenance mechanics (Netherlands)

White-Collar or Professional Settings
- Life insurance agents and their managers (United States)
- Organizational consultants (United States)
- Professional school training (Netherlands)
- Counseling services (Switzerland)
- Intensive care ward (Netherlands)
- Top management of government research laboratory (United States)
- Top management of consulting firm (United States)
- Top management of rubber manufacturing (Germany)

substantially throughout the project. Data from the comparison groups indicated no overall change in productivity over the same time periods.

The effect sizes for the change from the baseline to the feedback period ranged from −0.6 to +5.0, with a mean effect size of 2.0. This means that on average, productivity after ProMES feedback is 2.0 standard deviations higher than productivity during baseline. As we noted in Chapter One, an effect size of 0.2 is considered small, 0.5 is medium, and 0.8 is large (Cohen, 1977). Clearly, our mean effect size of 2.0 is very strong. This effect size is also much larger than the 0.3 to 0.4 effect size found in the teaching effectiveness literature and the feedback literature.

In addition to improving productivity, the research program has also aimed to enhance job satisfaction, reduce stress, and enable people to develop their potentials fully. In the original ProMES study (Pritchard and others, 1988, 1989), it was found that in the five organizational units doing ProMES, job satisfaction increased, morale increased, and the clarity of how people were being evaluated improved. Other variables such as turnover intentions and individual role clarity did not improve, but they did not worsen either. Przygodda (1994) found that attitudes improved and stress decreased in two ProMES groups in a German manufacturing setting. Kenneth Malm (personal communication, October 1995) found that the ProMES development process alone decreased stress for six groups of Swedish Federal Social Insurance personnel. These studies suggest that ProMES is effective at addressing problems in the social structure of organizations in addition to improving productivity.

This chapter has provided a brief review of the ProMES system, indicated how well ProMES compares to an ideal evaluation system, and presented information on previous applications of the system. All of this information has been rather general, however, so we now turn to a more detailed description of the system and how to use it to evaluate teaching. Individuals interested in applying for ProMES in their own settings should find this information quite useful.

PART TWO

DEVELOPING AN EFFECTIVE SYSTEM

3

PHASE ONE

Implementing a Student Evaluation System

THIS CHAPTER DESCRIBES the process used to develop the first phase of the teacher evaluation system. It begins with a description of the project setting and the history that led to our involvement with this organization. It then describes the steps we took to develop and implement the teaching evaluation system. Chapter Two presented a brief description of this process, along with an abbreviated example. This chapter provides a more detailed description of the actual steps taken, beginning with the development of objectives and indicators and ending with the process of implementing and using the feedback reports.

Recall that the ProMES process has four steps: Identify Objectives, Develop Indicators, Establish Contingencies, and Put the System Together. The most complete description of how to do the steps in ProMES appears in Pritchard (1990).

This chapter begins with the history of the project and then describes the specific steps involved in completing each portion of the process (for example, developing objectives, developing indicators, and so forth). Following each of these sections (except the section on Step 1) is a discussion of the reactions and concerns faculty expressed during that stage of development and the ways in which we addressed those responses.

HISTORICAL BACKGROUND OF THE PROJECT

The first events leading to this project occurred in 1989. The ProMES research group, headed by Robert Pritchard, had been working in the area of productivity and effectiveness improvement for some time; Pritchard had worked specifically with ProMES for six years. One of the important questions guiding us as a research team was to what extent the positive results found with ProMES generalize to other types of organizations and jobs. Being academics, we had discussed applying ProMES to the postsecondary setting.

Fortunately, an opportunity to test ProMES in an academic setting presented itself in our own backyard, Texas A&M University. The College of Veterinary Medicine (CVM) wanted to find a better way of evaluating faculty. The CVM was composed of five departments and had approximately 150 full-time faculty. At that time, the CVM used qualitative evaluations by students that focused as much on the curriculum as on the instructor's effectiveness. It was difficult to summarize these qualitative evaluations and, as a result, it was hard to recognize and reward good teaching.

We discussed the potential advantages of a ProMES-based teaching evaluation system with Professor Donald Clark, who was a member of the Teaching Excellence Committee (TEC) at the CVM. Clark reacted positively and suggested that he and Pritchard present the idea to the dean. The dean responded positively as well and encouraged us to prepare a written funding proposal. In addition, we presented our ideas to the TEC and the dean's advisory committee. Not only did both groups support the proposal but the entire TEC agreed to serve as the design team for the first part of the project. They also became coauthors of the research proposal.

The proposal was approved and work began in 1990. The project had three objectives. The first was to develop a teaching evaluation system that accurately evaluated the teaching effectiveness of the CVM faculty. The second was to design an evaluation system that provided high-quality feedback, which would enable faculty to improve their teaching. The third was to implement a system that could serve as the basis for future scholarly research on teaching.

The work was to proceed in two distinct phases. Phase 1 was to develop a ProMES-based evaluation of classroom teaching based on student ratings. Phase 2 was to evaluate the aspects of teaching that occurred outside the classroom and to use peers as the source of those evaluations.

As a final step in the approval of the project, we made a presentation to the CVM faculty. We discussed the project's objectives, stated what steps we would take and why, and summarized the advantages and disadvantages. A lively discussion ensued. Below, we present the important issues that arose. At the end of the meeting, the faculty approved the project.

Although it was important to our research team to develop as good a teaching evaluation system as we could for the CVM, we also had another reason for undertaking the project. Specifically, we wanted to test the applicability of ProMES in such a setting. Even though it had shown good results elsewhere, it had not been evaluated in an academic environment. We designed the project so that it would answer the following specific research questions:

1. Can the ProMES system be developed successfully in this environment?
2. Is the resulting system a valid measure of teaching effectiveness?
3. Will teaching effectiveness improve with feedback from the system?
4. Do faculty and administrators see the resulting system as valuable?
5. Is the new system better than traditional systems that provide measurement and feedback on teaching effectiveness?

FACULTY REACTIONS BEFORE THE DEVELOPMENT OF OBJECTIVES AND INDICATORS

This section discusses how the faculty reacted to the proposed system before we began the first steps in ProMES. Many of these responses came from the collegewide faculty meeting in which we explained the project. Some came from our discussions with faculty after this meeting and in other settings. We are presenting these reactions and the way we responded to them because we expect that most, if not all, of these reactions will arise in any attempt to do teaching evaluation. Thus, our experience with them may be useful to those considering such a project.

Reactions to Being Evaluated

Before the project was under way, the faculty had mixed feelings about having instruction evaluated. The majority favored the idea, but a distinct and vocal minority did not. They were skeptical about our developing a formal teaching evaluation process. They revealed these feelings in a survey that the TEC conducted approximately one year before the start of the project. The TEC did this survey to gather faculty reactions to the idea of being evaluated.

ANXIETY ABOUT BEING EVALUATED. One faculty concern related to the general anxiety associated with being evaluated and how favorable that evaluation would be. We pointed out that the college administration was already evaluating faculty. Thus, it was not a matter of whether faculty would be evaluated but rather what inputs into and knowledge of the system faculty members would have. The existing evaluation process had little faculty input or control. We noted that in the new system, faculty would develop objectives, indicators, and contingencies. This system would allow faculty, not students or administrators, to set policy about teaching standards. In fact, faculty department representatives would initiate all decisions about the system. In addition, we said that because this system clarified teaching policy, instructors would clearly understand the dimensions and rating processes that would be used to evaluate their teaching.

We further explained that this system was quite different from the traditional evaluation approach, which uses overall mean ratings as a standard for comparing individual instructors. This method is not appropriate for a variety of reasons that we have discussed previously. For example, if the department already does a good job of teaching, some of the faculty will receive average and below average ratings, when in fact their teaching is actually quite good. In contrast, when objectives, indicators, and contingencies are used, the system compares each instructor's performance to a predetermined and agreed-upon standard of excellence. Thus, everyone in the department or college could potentially meet or exceed the expectations or standards set for teaching.

Although these arguments had some effect on faculty attitudes, some concerns remained. Once instructors received feedback, however, much of their anxiety dissipated, probably because they could actually see their results. Nevertheless, a few faculty felt uncomfortable about being evaluated even after receiving their feedback.

CONCERN THAT STUDENTS ARE UNQUALIFIED TO RATE. Approximately one-quarter of faculty responding to the survey conducted before the project began reported that they did not believe students could evaluate teaching. They believed that students were not qualified or knowledgeable enough about the subject matter to rate teaching. We addressed this issue by explaining that although students do have a limited knowledge of particular subjects, they certainly have an important viewpoint after being exposed to the instructor day after day. It is therefore valuable to gather their input. In fact, there are some aspects of teaching, such as rapport, that only students can rate. We also explained that student ratings would not be the only component of the system. To balance input from students, the final system would also include ratings from colleagues who had adequate subject matter knowledge.

CONCERNS OVER STUDENT FAIRNESS. Another faculty concern was that students would not rate the instructor fairly. For example, some instructors thought students would not provide ratings on teaching skills but would instead base ratings on whether or not they liked the course topic or personally liked the instructor. This would make ratings higher for popular courses and instructors and lower for unpopular courses and instructors, regardless of instructors' teaching skills.

We handled this issue in two ways. First, we explained to the faculty that the rating instrument would focus on teaching behaviors rather than on course characteristics. To the extent that the instructor's effective teaching behaviors increased his or her popularity, popular teachers would receive higher ratings. We further explained that it would be unlikely for a popular instructor with ineffective teaching behaviors to receive high ratings using our rating instrument. Whether the system would eliminate this potential problem remained an empirical question, however. Thus, we used a second approach. During the first two years the system was in use, we conducted a study to determine whether students gave unduly negative ratings to faculty members. The results indicated that very few students gave extremely negative ratings to faculty for any reason. The details of this analysis will appear in Chapter Four. Some faculty members expressed a related concern that a few students could band together and give such low ratings to an instructor that they would unduly bring down the overall class mean rating.

Because of these concerns, faculty members suggested that the system use median ratings instead of mean student ratings to compute effectiveness scores. It is a well-known statistical fact (Gravetter & Wallnau, 1988; Heiman, 1992) that the mean is more susceptible to the effects of extreme scores than the median. Thus, we conducted an analysis to determine how much of a problem this could be.

We used three separate hypothetical distributions. The first, with a sample size of 120, was designed to represent a professional (DVM) class. The second distribution, with a sample size of 50, was designed to represent an undergraduate class. The third, with a sample size of 10, was designed to represent a graduate seminar. Each distribution was composed of average student ratings ranging from 1 to 5 with the means of each distribution set as described below.

We assumed that the typical distribution of student ratings would be negatively skewed, with more high scores than low scores, and that the mean of each distribution would conform to what the teaching literature suggested (Aleamoni, 1981; Braskamp, Brandenburg, & Ory, 1984). Thus, we assumed that the small distribution (representing the graduate seminar) would have the highest mean; we therefore set the original mean for that distribution at 4.2 on a five-point scale. We believed that the distribution of fifty would be the next most positive grouping as it represented an undergraduate class, so we set the original mean at 4.0. The professional class (DVM) was expected to be the most critical and thus the least positive. Thus, we set its original mean at 3.8.

Once we established the original distributions, we began shifting individual scores to assess the impact on the final results. We believed it unlikely that a student who would normally have rated a teacher at a very high level (that is, 5) could be convinced to shift an evaluation to a very low score (that is, 1) without a valid reason. We therefore thought that only students whose responses were originally in the middle range or lower (2s, 3s, and 4s) would shift their evaluations to extremely low scores (1s). With this in mind, we began by shifting those scores.

As we made these shifts, we observed the effect on both the mean and the median. Results indicated that in all three distributions, approximately one-fifth of the class would have to give extremely low scores to create a significant shift in the mean rating (a change of 0.25 points in the mean rating was defined as a significant shift). We believed it unlikely that this high a percentage of students could be persuaded to give negative ratings to an instructor unless there was some valid reason for doing so.

In terms of what effect shifting scores would have on the median, 50 percent of the class had to give extremely low scores to shift the median, thus demonstrating that the median is more resistant to extreme scores than the mean. Because we believed it unlikely that 20 percent of the class would shift their scores to extremely low scores, though, and because the mean is a more stable measure than the median (Gravetter & Wallnau, 1988; Heiman, 1992), it remained the preferred measure of central tendency. We concluded that the system results should be based on mean rather than median student ratings.

We presented the results of these analyses to the faculty. They agreed that it would be highly unlikely for 20 percent of the class to band together intentionally to give the instructor artificially low ratings. Because of these analyses, concerns about this type of student bias seemed to disappear.

Desire for Measures of Student Learning

In one department, faculty members expressed the opinion that the ultimate criterion of teaching effectiveness was whether students learned. The group that held this view wanted to include measures of changes in student learning as a component in the teaching evaluation system. As Chapter One makes clear, there are great difficulties in using student learning as a measure of teaching effectiveness.

We explained to these faculty members that to use student learning, one must first measure all variables related to learning that are not under the instructor's control. Then, one must control these measures statistically through the use of covariant analyses. Doing so allows one to determine whether the learning that occurred actually resulted from the teacher's effectiveness rather than the student's motivation level, prior interest in the subject, ability, and so forth. This method could not be used in this setting because no valid measures of confounding variables were available.

We also told faculty that to measure student learning, one must assess student knowledge levels both before and after one presents the material. This would mean constructing tests comparing knowledge before and after the course. These tests would need to have similar difficulty levels. In addition, every time a change was made in the course content, the pre- and posttests would have to be rewritten. Otherwise, data could not be interpreted correctly across instructors.

Because of the difficulty and time involved in constructing these measures, we recommended that measures of student learning not be included in the teaching evaluation system. Once these difficulties were explained, most faculty members were satisfied and opted to exclude student learning as part of the measurement system.

Resistance to Assessing with a Single Number

Although many faculty members liked the idea of a single index that reflected overall teaching effectiveness, some felt it was not possible to reduce multifaceted teaching skills and abilities to one number. In response to this, we explained that administrators were already, in effect, forming judgments about teaching to make personnel decisions and that this meant combining all the available information into a single binary or rank-ordered number. For example, department heads decided on pay raises for individual faculty members and promotion and tenure committees made choices about tenure after reviewing an instructor's dossier. Thus, the complex information was ultimately reduced to a single index. With existing procedures, however, there were no clear guidelines on what was considered, what was more important, or how the information would be combined to make these decisions.

We told faculty members that in contrast to the existing approach, the proposed system would provide a clear, communicable method for combining the information. The effectiveness points for each indicator would be combined to produce an average overall effectiveness score. Therefore, the average overall effectiveness score captured some of the richness provided in the indicator data. Using this score to make global judgments would also ensure that the teaching standards set by faculty were incorporated into decisions. In addition, scores on each indicator would guide instructors in their improvement efforts. With contingencies developed at the department level, the system would provide much richer data than the typical evaluation system. Therefore, beyond providing one number, the system's flexible design would allow it to provide data that could represent complex teaching behavior better than typical evaluations could. When global judgments were needed, the number used would derive from data representing the many facets of teaching behavior.

Most faculty accepted this explanation. Those with the original concerns still felt that rich qualitative information was necessary, but they also saw the merits of the approach used here.

Concerns About System Validity

Some faculty were concerned about whether or not the system would be valid, given that ProMES had never been applied in an academic setting. We argued that we could only resolve this issue by implementing the system and collecting the information necessary to determine validity. The college's faculty were in the hard sciences and were used to clear evaluation criteria. In their experience, one validated a new measuring instrument by comparing it with those already established. We explained to them that no such definitive criterion existed for teaching evaluation. If it did, the CVM would use it and this project would be pointless.

We explained to them that to validate an instrument that measured something as nebulous as teaching effectiveness required a series of data sources. Only a combination of information collected over time could offer cumulative evidence for the validity of a teaching evaluation process. We then described to them the steps we planned to use to validate the approach and assured them that these results would be available before a final decision was made to use the system. This alleviated their concerns to some degree. These validation procedures and the results are discussed in Chapter Four.

Decision to Establish a Trial Period

Because of the various concerns expressed by faculty about the effort, it was decided that for the initial phase of the project, the assessment would only be used by instructors to improve teaching and not for evaluation purposes by the dean's office. Complete details of this initial trial period are provided later in this chapter.

STEP 1: IDENTIFY OBJECTIVES

We identified objectives by using a *design committee* that made decisions through group consensus. As described earlier, the design committee was an existing CVM group, the Teaching Excellence Committee (TEC). Because this group included faculty members from different CVM departments, and because it was expected that much of the system would be consistent across departments, this seemed like a perfect solution.

To help the design committee in its task, we also attended design committee meetings to act as ProMES facilitators. Using our experience with ProMES, we helped the faculty complete the steps in the process. Our role was to be experts not in teaching evaluation but in a process that would ideally help the design committee develop a sound measurement and feedback system.

The design committee met once a week for approximately an hour and a half. During their first meeting, they became familiar with the project and the steps involved. Then the design committee began to develop a list of objectives by answering the question "What are the important things an instructor must do in classroom teaching?" All suggestions were recorded on a blackboard so that all committee members could see and respond to them. Between the meetings, a typed list of suggested objectives was circulated to members to stimulate their thinking for the next committee meeting. The committee discussed each of the suggested objectives until a consensus was reached.

To help ensure that the design committee had not missed any important aspects of teaching, the research team conducted a literature search to determine what major goals or objectives of teaching other researchers had suggested. It was found that (1) all seven of the objectives that the TEC selected were among the important teaching characteristics identified in the literature (listed in Chapter One) and (2) the literature did not suggest any major objectives that the design committee had overlooked.

After three meetings that each lasted one and a half hours, the committee agreed on the list of objectives. Overall, the process of developing objectives was quite smooth and congenial. Also, the TEC members had a sense that the objectives covered the important components of classroom teaching that students could observe. Here are the seven objectives:

1. The instructor presented appropriate material in an organized fashion.
2. The instructor demonstrated subject mastery.
3. The instructor communicated effectively.
4. The instructor promoted critical thinking and problem solving.
5. The instructor motivated students to learn.
6. The instructor exhibited a positive attitude toward students.
7. The instructor evaluated students fairly.

STEP 2: DEVELOP INDICATORS

Once the TEC determined the objectives, the next step was to develop *indicators* for these objectives. Because this portion of the project included only student ratings of teaching, the indicators were all items on a student rating questionnaire. We helped the design committee determine indicators by asking them to identify (1) the behaviors a teacher would use in the classroom to accomplish each of the objectives and (2) the questions to be asked of students to determine if the behaviors were being performed.

To develop indicators and to build on the teaching evaluation literature, we obtained copies of existing student rating questionnaires. We reviewed the questionnaires and developed lists of items that could be used to measure each of the seven objectives. We presented these lists to the TEC members, who modified them for the purpose at hand.

Again, the committee used a consensus process to ensure that they developed the best list of indicators. All suggestions were recorded on a blackboard so that committee members could see and respond to them, and a typed list of suggested indicators was circulated to members between meetings to stimulate their thinking for the next committee meeting. They finally chose seventeen indicators, which appear in Figure 3.1 along with the seven corresponding objectives.

Developing indicators was more difficult than developing objectives, requiring six meetings of one and a half hours each. During these meetings, there was some disagreement about the specific wording of some indicators and about whether certain behaviors were important enough to be included in the system. The committee members knew they needed to include all the important aspects of classroom teaching that students could observe, but they also knew that the questionnaire needed to be fairly short. The general feeling was that twenty or more items would make the questionnaire too long for students to complete. Although there was considerable dissension, consensus was finally achieved.

Evaluation of the Objectives and Indicators

Once the design committee completed the list of indicators, the system needed to be evaluated by students and faculty and approved by the college administration. Students evaluated the system in two separate phases. First, eighteen individual students were interviewed to determine whether the items were understandable and clear. They were also asked to explain the meaning of each item. We have regularly had users explain the meaning of items in a pretest, because mismatches between explanations and intents quickly reveal problems. The results of this pretest indicated that the wording on three items was unclear. The TEC made changes in the items based on these suggestions.

Next, representative groups of students reviewed the items to ensure that they could be answered easily and accurately. In addition, the student groups were asked if they would be able to rate the teaching effectiveness of each instructor who taught them, even those in team-taught courses. A total of 186 professional, undergraduate, and graduate students provided feedback on the items. Although the students recommended changes in the wording of a few indicators, they suggested that the items were essentially clear, understandable, and easy to answer. We presented the data from this review to the TEC, which made some additional revisions in the items.

Next, the entire CVM faculty had the opportunity to review and comment on the objectives and indicators. This review was to serve two distinct purposes. First, it would help ensure that the system was as clear and complete as possible. Second, it provided an opportunity

Figure 3.1. Seven Objectives and Seventeen Indicators.

- Objective 1: The instructor presented appropriate material in an organized fashion.

  Indicator A: The instructor was well organized.

  Indicator B: The amount of material that the instructor presented or assigned was appropriate.

- Objective 2: The instructor demonstrated subject mastery.

  Indicator A: The instructor appeared to have a thorough knowledge of the subject.

  Indicator B: Information and references provided by this instructor were relevant.

- Objective 3: The instructor communicated effectively.

  Indicator A: The instructor spoke clearly and was easily understood.

  Indicator B: The instructor emphasized major points.

  Indicator C: Concepts were presented in a manner that aided my understanding.

- Objective 4: The instructor promoted critical thinking and problem solving.

  Indicator A: The instructor's examination questions required me to do more than recall factual information.

  Indicator B: The instructor helped me integrate facts, develop conclusions, and arrive at solutions.

  Indicator C: The instructor raised challenging questions or problems for consideration.

- Objective 5: The instructor motivated students to learn.

  Indicator A: The instructor created and maintained an atmosphere that facilitated learning.

  Indicator B: The instructor stimulated my interest in the subject.

- Objective 6: The instructor exhibited a positive attitude toward students.

  Indicator A: The instructor was courteous and easy to approach.

  Indicator B: The instructor was willing to help students outside of class.

- Objective 7: The instructor evaluated students fairly.

  Indicator A: The instructor's examination questions covered the important concepts presented in the course.

  Indicator B: The instructor's examination questions were reasonable in difficulty.

  Indicator C: The instructor's examination questions were graded fairly.

for the faculty to help develop the system, thus increasing the probability that they would accept it.

To obtain this faculty input, we prepared a questionnaire that showed the objectives and indicators and that asked for an overall judgment of their accuracy, completeness, and clarity. (A copy of this questionnaire appears in Appendix A.) In addition, we requested comments on each of the items.

Of approximately 150 faculty members, 41 (27 percent) responded to the survey. Of those responding, 88 percent agreed that the questions were clear and understandable, 81 percent felt that feedback from the items would aid the teacher in improving classroom teaching, and 83 percent thought the feedback would be useful to administrators.

In addition, 73 percent of the respondents felt that the instrument covered all important aspects of classroom teaching. Those who disagreed with this statement suggested adding seven additional aspects of teaching to the system. Of these suggestions, only one—the need to evaluate the quality of instructional aids—was mentioned by more than two people.

The TEC reviewed these suggestions and, after much discussion, decided not to include any of the proposed changes in the system. The TEC felt that there were no concerns expressed by a meaningful number of faculty members and that the only suggestion with a moderate amount of faculty support (that is, evaluating instructional aids) was already covered by the objective on communicating effectively.

Once these reviews were completed, we presented the objectives and indicators to the college administration (that is, the dean, his staff, and the department heads) for approval. This review was conducted in a joint meeting between college administration, the five department heads, the design committee (the TEC), and the research staff facilitators. After a discussion, the objectives and indicators were approved unanimously with only one minor modification. This approval process was another attempt to ensure that the system was comprehensive and accurate and that college administrators accepted it.

Response Anchors

The final step in establishing the objectives and indicators was for the design committee to determine what response anchors to use on the student rating form. The types of response formats usually employed in student rating forms fall into three basic categories (Bass, Cascio, & O'Connor, 1974; Cliff, 1959; Shaw & Wright, 1967; Spector, 1976):

evaluative responses (for example, excellent, above average, average, below average, and poor); descriptions of the extent to which the student agrees or disagrees with the statement (for example, strongly agree, agree, neither agree nor disagree, disagree, and strongly disagree); and descriptions of the extent to which the instructor demonstrated the described behavior (for example, almost always, very often, regularly, infrequently, and almost never).

A review of these three formats (Spector, 1976) suggested that the frequency of behavior format would probably be the best choice for a student rating form. We felt it was inappropriate to ask students to judge how well an instructor performed a given behavior; instead, we believed students should simply indicate how often the professor performed the behavior, and faculty should then evaluate the behavior and determine its usefulness. This would be accomplished by applying the contingencies and generating an effectiveness score for that behavior (or indicator). In addition, the committee felt that the agree-disagree format would provide information that would be hard to quantify; having students indicate the frequency of an instructor behavior would provide better, more interpretable data than asking them to "agree" or "disagree" regarding the behavior. Consistent with this position, the committee decided to tentatively select the frequency of behavior format and test it through a variety of methods.

It was decided that the scale should include five anchors; in other words, there would be a five-point scale. The design committee felt that five was the maximum number of discriminations that students could make accurately.

The next major decision to be made dealt with the words that should be used to describe each of these five anchors. Selecting the words that would most precisely capture the frequency with which instructors performed various behaviors was somewhat difficult. For example, should the top anchor be "always" or "almost always"? Should the middle anchor be "regularly" or "sometimes"? In order to get some guidance in this process, we gathered suggestions for anchors from commercially available student rating forms and from other faculty members. We worked with ten undergraduate students to construct and evaluate several possible scales. All the people who evaluated the various scales were asked to (1) rate an instructor using two indicators and each anchor scale and (2) determine which scale allowed them to describe the instructor's behavior most accurately. The consensus was that the anchors "almost always," "very often," "regularly," "infrequently," and "almost never" were the most descriptive and precise.

In order to verify that the frequency of behavior format was most appropriate, we asked twelve CVM students to compare both the frequency of behavior and degree of agreement response anchors for clarity and ease of answering. They each received two lists, both containing a subset of indicators. One subset listed anchors ranging from "strongly agree" to "strongly disagree," in a typical five-point format. The other subset listed the frequency alternatives "almost always," "very often," "regularly," "infrequently," and "almost never." The students preferred the frequency of behavior anchors, because that format required them to think carefully about their answers. They also found it more quantifiable and objective. Based on this feedback, the design committee adopted the frequency of behavior format.

Pilot Test

After choosing the response format, we tested the actual student evaluation questionnaire with a representative sample of classes. This pilot test was designed to assess administrative procedures and to provide data for an item analysis.

Using the proposed instrument, 379 students evaluated seven instructors. The seven instructors were selected because they taught a representative sample of classes, including two undergraduate classes, two graduate classes, and three professional classes. Students were asked to rate these instructors. They were also to indicate whether they agreed that the instrument instructions and items were clear and whether the response choices (that is, anchors) allowed them to describe the instructor's teaching activities accurately.

The indicator (that is, item) means ranged from a low of 2.86 to a high of 5.00, indicating that the students evaluated the teaching behaviors described by the indicators differently. Also, the students evaluated instructors differently, as the overall means for the instructors ranged from a low of 3.54 to a high of 4.76.

In addition, the students agreed that the instructions were clear (94 percent either agreed or strongly agreed), and that the seventeen items were clear (93 percent either agreed or strongly agreed). A lower percentage of students agreed that the anchors allowed them to describe teaching behaviors accurately (66 percent agreed or strongly agreed), with 16 percent neither agreeing nor disagreeing, and 18 percent disagreeing or strongly disagreeing with the choice of anchors. Most of those who disagreed with the choice of anchors recommended that slightly different words be used as the anchors (for example, "would prefer often to regularly," "would prefer a category of sometimes," "should have a choice for always and never"). There was no general consensus among the comments made by those who disagreed with the original choice of anchors, however, so the TEC decided to keep the anchors as they were originally designed.

The pilot also provided data for reliability and item analyses. The instrument's internal consistency reliability was .93, indicating that the seventeen items were tapping one basic underlying construct. The item-total correlations were high (ranging from .57 to .82), with only one exception.

That one exception (a correlation of .23) was for the item "The instructor's examination questions required me to do more than recall factual information." When the TEC reviewed this information, it seemed clear that the item described one of the most important teaching behaviors in the instrument. Furthermore, according to members of the TEC, most CVM faculty members were not performing this behavior very well at the time.

Therefore, it was no surprise that this item did not correlate highly with the other items. Instead of seeing this low correlation as evidence of a poorly constructed item, the TEC saw this correlation as confirmation that the item was measuring a very important aspect of teaching that had been long overlooked in the CVM. Thus, the decision was made to retain this item as it was originally written.

Based on these pilot results, the TEC determined that the instrument was acceptable and ready to use.

FACULTY REACTIONS TO THE DEVELOPMENT OF OBJECTIVES AND INDICATORS

After the instrument was ready for use, it was shared with faculty. Their reactions ranged from quite positive to somewhat skeptical. Those who were less positive expressed a variety of concerns, including how the system would be administered, what impact environmental factors might have on the ratings, whether some faculty members would be able to subvert the system by "teaching to the instrument," and whether the system could be adapted if teaching policy changed. Finally, some faculty members were concerned about some of the objectives and indicators. Each of these issues is addressed in the paragraphs that follow.

Administering the System

A number of concerns arose related to the administration of the evaluation form. One was a concern for standardized administration procedures. At one point, it appeared that there would be no centralized process for distributing and collecting the rating forms. It was recognized that without a centralized administration process, departments would be likely to distribute and collect the rating forms in different manners, leading to problems with interpreting results. For example, if instructions were read to one group of students that differed from what another group was told, results might not be comparable. Eventually, when the system was implemented, a standardized process was designed, instructions were written, and the rating forms were distributed and collected through the dean's office.

Another concern related to the administration of the rating forms had to do with the amount of class time lost to teaching while students completed the forms. There was initially some uncertainty about how much time it would take to administer the form. Results from the pilot test indicated, however, that it took approximately fifteen to twenty minutes to read the instructions, have students complete the forms, and collect the forms. The design team felt that this was a reasonable amount of time and that it would not significantly detract from teaching.

Faculty also worried about how it would be for students in team-taught courses to complete the same form over and over for each instructor. It was thought that this might tire students, causing them not to give careful ratings. Once it was determined that the administration time for one form was fifteen to twenty minutes, it was felt that this risk was worth taking, given the importance of the data collected.

Similarly, design committee members raised the concern that students might not take the form seriously, thinking that their input would not be used. To address this issue, it was suggested to the dean that the importance of student ratings be emphasized in the orientation sessions provided to new students and in meetings between the administration and existing classes. It was also suggested that a statement explaining the ratings' importance be added to the instructions for administering the rating form. In all cases, students were to fill out the forms anonymously with the instructor absent from the room, and a clear statement was to be made that student ratings played a part in personnel decisions.

The design committee also had to decide whether the forms should be completed during the semester or at the semester's end. Because many of the professional classes were taught by teams of instructors (some of whom finished teaching very early in the semester), some design team members felt that the forms should be completed as soon as each instructor finished his or her series of lectures. These committee members felt that this was the only way to ensure that students in a team-taught course could record the behaviors of each instructor accurately.

To address this concern, the committee took two steps. First, there was a careful review of the logistics involved in administering ratings immediately after each instructor finished teaching; this process was found to be rather problematic. Second, there was a review of the literature, which indicated that ratings conducted one year or longer after the completion of a course were quite consistent with ratings taken at the end of the course (Guthrie, 1954; Marsh & Overall, 1981; Overall & Marsh, 1980). This suggested that students have the ability to retain information regarding the teaching skills of their instructors. Consequently, the committee decided to collect all instructor ratings at the end of the semester.

There was some disagreement, however, over whether these end-of-semester ratings should be collected prior to the final exam or after the course was completed. Again, a review of the logistics suggested that completing the forms before the final exam would be preferable, because collecting the forms after the course was completed presented the problem of gathering students together. If students knew about grades, it might also cause some contamination of the ratings.

After some discussion and consultation of the teaching evaluation literature, the committee decided that the best time to administer the rating forms would be one or two weeks before the final examination. This would allow ample time for students to form an opinion about the instructor's behavior. It would also allow for timely feedback to the faculty who were being rated, because feedback could theoretically be provided within the first few weeks of the following semester.

Minimizing Environmental Effects on Ratings

There was some concern that instructor ratings would be affected negatively when room conditions distracted from the learning environment. For example, it was felt that students would "take it out on the instructor" if the room were too cold or if the lighting were poor. The committee felt that the system might need some way of accounting for the room conditions.

We pointed out, however, that the questions on the evaluation form centered on teaching behaviors. Therefore, it would be unlikely for students to confuse instructor behaviors with room conditions. In addition, we noted that the individuals most concerned with the effectiveness scores generated by the system—the instructor and the department head—would be familiar with problems associated with the room and would thus be able to make allowances in interpreting results under these conditions.

"Teaching to the Instrument"

Some faculty brought up the issue of instructors' modifying their behavior to manipulate the system. In other words, individuals might "teach to the instrument," or perform in such a way that they would ensure high ratings. We pointed out that even though this might at first seem dishonest or unfair, it would actually be beneficial, because the instrument was designed to capture the behaviors that led to effective teaching. Thus, an increase in evaluation scores would actually indicate an increase in teaching effectiveness. In other words, "teaching to the test" would only be a problem if the instrument were found to be invalid (that is, if higher scores did not indicate higher teaching effectiveness).

Adapting to Changes in Teaching Policy

As the project progressed, there was a movement in the college to consider making major changes to existing teaching processes. Instead of using the didactic approach, the college was considering a problem-based approach. This created some concern over how such a change might affect the teaching evaluation system. We explained that if such a change were made, the system could be modified to incorporate additional objectives and indicators and to eliminate ones that were deemed unnecessary. In short, the system was flexible enough to incorporate any future changes in teaching policy.

Approving Objectives and Indicators

Although we had solicited approval of the objectives and indicators by sending the questionnaire to all faculty members, very few responded (only 41 out of approximately 150, or 27 percent). Given that fact, we decided to conduct meetings in each department after developing objectives and indicators.

We held these meetings for two purposes. First, they allowed the design team and research facilitators to present the objectives and indicators to faculty who had not responded to the questionnaire. Second, they provided a vehicle for selecting department members to be involved in the next phase of the project, the development of contingencies. The plan was to develop contingencies separately in each department, thus allowing each department to have the contingencies reflect its unique policies. To do this, the plan called for a committee from each department to develop that department's contingencies. The department committee would include faculty from the department along with the person from that department who had been on the TEC design committee.

A representative from the design team conducted each meeting, although at least one of the research facilitators was also present. We explained the system and answered questions. In most cases, these meetings were well attended.

Although the faculty had been asked for their input on objectives and indicators approximately three months before the meetings, some reacted with surprise, saying that they were unaware of the effort. These individuals, although few in number, were quite vocal in expressing concern about the system. Many of the concerns that had been raised and addressed earlier came up again. Some expressed a general anxiety about being evaluated. Some were concerned about the system's validity. There were questions about the wording of items and the acceptability of having students evaluate teaching.

We addressed these concerns by listening, pointing out that faculty in fact did have input into the development of objectives and indicators, explaining where the items came from, and indicating that data on the performance of the system would be tracked to review system validity. With regard to item wording, the design team reviewed comments collected at department meetings. Because there were no consistent recommendations, the design team decided to retain all items with no changes.

STEP 3: ESTABLISH CONTINGENCIES

The next step in the ProMES process is to develop contingencies. Contingencies were to be developed in each department separately.

In order for the members of the TEC to understand contingencies fully, however, we decided to train the members of this committee in contingencies by having them go through the process on a pilot basis.

We held several meetings with them to create this set of simulated contingencies. This was useful to both the faculty members and us. It gave us some practice with facilitating the development of contingencies in a setting that allowed for experimentation. It also familiarized the committee members with the process of contingency development, enabling them to go to the contingency committees in their own departments with a good knowledge of the process.

Unlike with our perception of objectives and indicators, we felt that the contingencies would probably not be the same across departments. Because contingencies capture teaching policy, we expected policy differences across the different departments. For example, an instructor in a basic science department such as anatomy might rely more heavily on lecturing and presenting facts, whereas an instructor teaching a more process-oriented subject (such as those in the clinical departments in which students work with actual animals) might require the students to integrate disparate information and solve problems. Consequently, the importance of these indicators (and therefore the slopes of the contingencies) would be quite different for courses in these two departments.

Because of these expected policy differences, we convened a separate contingency design committee in each of the five academic departments. In general, each committee was composed of four to five senior faculty members representing the undergraduate, graduate, and professional programs within each department. In some cases, the faculty elected the representatives; in other cases, the department head appointed them. In all cases, one of the members of the department committees had been a member of the original collegewide ProMES design team that developed objectives and indicators. Once the department design committees were selected, they developed contingencies as described below.

Determining the Number of Contingency Sets

In developing the contingencies, the team first determined the type of class for which they would develop the contingency set. It was expected that the different levels of classes (that is, undergraduate, graduate, and professional classes) might require different sets of contingencies. This situation is analogous to the need for different contingencies between departments. Just as we expected different teaching behaviors to have varied effectiveness values between departments, we also expected different teaching behaviors to have varied effectiveness values for different levels of classes. For example, it might be very important that the instructor be extremely organized and easy to understand when presenting information to undergraduates, because undergraduates do not have a strong conceptual background for the topics presented. Graduate students, on the other hand, are expected to have a strong conceptual background in many of the topics presented in the graduate curriculum. Consequently, it might be less important that the instructor be extremely organized but more important that he or she raise challenging questions or problems for discussion. Based on this reasoning, the indicators were expected to have different levels of importance and thus different contingencies.

To make this decision, each contingency committee considered the courses offered by their department, including undergraduate, graduate, and professional levels. Most department contingency committees decided to begin the process by developing contingencies for the large professional lecture classes, because this was where the bulk of their teaching occurred.

Choosing Contingency Values

The next part of developing ProMES contingencies is to define the maximum and minimum values that the indicators could have. Because each of the indicators in this research was an item on a student rating questionnaire, the anchors on the scale determined both the maximum and the minimum score that an instructor could receive. A five-point frequency of behavior scale was used, so the maximum that an individual could receive would be a score of 5.0, which would indicate that the instructor was perceived by all students as "almost always" having demonstrated the behavior in question. The minimum score that an instructor could receive would be a score of 1.0, which would show that every student perceived the instructor as "almost never" having demonstrated the indicated behavior.

The steps in contingency development are summarized in Table 3.1, the ProMES Contingency Worksheet. The values in this example come from actual contingencies for one department's large professional lec-

Table 3.1. ProMES Contingency Worksheet.

Indicator	Maximum Value	Minimum Value	Expected Value	Maximum Rank	Maximum Effectiveness	Minimum Rank	Minimum Effectiveness
1. Concepts aided understanding	5.0	1.0	3.0	1	200	2	25
2. Helped integrate facts, solutions	5.0	1.0	3.0	2	195	3	90
3. Raised challenging questions	5.0	1.0	2.75	3	140	4	95
4. Exams graded fairly	5.0	1.0	4.0	4	102	1	0

ture courses. In the example, we will use only four contingencies for simplicity, but each step was done for all seventeen indicators. The table shows the four indicators in the first column. The second and third columns show the maximum and minimum values for each indicator, 5.0 and 1.0 in every case.

Determining Expected Levels

The next step in contingency development was to determine the expected level for each indicator. The expected level is the mean rating that is considered neither good nor bad. In other words, it is the rating that the design committee considered as just meeting expectations for that department. The design committee discussed this issue and, through consensus, decided on the expected level for each indicator.

In the example in Table 3.1, the expected level for the first indicator was determined to be 3.0. Thus, an instructor with a mean rating of 3.0 on "Concepts were presented in a manner that aided my understanding" met but did not exceed the department's expectation on that teaching factor. A rating below 3.0 on that item fell below expectations, whereas a rating above 3.0 exceeded expectations.

The fourth indicator, which is about whether examination questions were graded fairly, has an expected level of 4.0. This expected level is higher because the design committee believed that expectations for grading examinations fairly should be quite high. That is, to meet departmental expectations, an instructor should do this task quite well. To exceed expectations, the instructor should receive a mean rating higher than 4.0. Anything below 4.0 would fall below expectations.

The lowest expected level is 2.75, for the third indicator in the table, which deals with raising challenging questions. The design committee felt that this aspect of teaching was more difficult in a large lecture class.

Determining Effectiveness Levels

The committee then established the effectiveness levels of the maximum and minimum indicators. The first step was to list the maximum values possible for each of the indicators. Because there were seventeen indicators, there were seventeen maximums.

The design committee then ranked these maximums in terms of the contribution each made to the instructor's overall effectiveness. That is, the maximum most important to teaching effectiveness received a rank of 1, the next most important maximum received a rank of 2, and so on until all the maximums were ranked. The design committee discussed this until consensus was reached. The ranking of the maximums appears in the fifth column of Table 3.1.

Once the maximums were ranked, the committee determined actual effectiveness scores. To do this, they gave the maximum with the highest rank an effectiveness value of 200. They evaluated the other maximums relative to this. To do this, they then considered the indicator maximum with a rank of 2. The committee was asked to consider how close this maximum was to the one ranked highest and to express this relation in a percentage. For example, if they thought the second maximum was only half as important as that ranked first, they would give it an effectiveness score halfway between the expected level (100) and the maximum (200); it would have a value of 150. If they thought it was 90 percent as important as the one ranked first, they would give it 90 percent of the possible effectiveness points above the expected level, or a value of 190. The committee made this decision for each of the maximums.

In Table 3.1, for the instructor to help students integrate facts, develop conclusions, and arrive at solutions was seen as nearly as important (maximum = 195) as presenting concepts in a manner that aided understanding (maximum = 200). The maximum score for grading examination questions fairly was only slightly above the expected level (maximum = 102), however.

The committee undertook an analogous process for the minimum values of each indicator. They ranked the minimums in terms of the worst thing an instructor could do and determined effectiveness scores. This was done by first taking the minimum that was ranked number 1 and giving it the lowest effectiveness score (usually somewhere near 0). All other minimums received effectiveness scores that were relative to this.

Plotting and Completing Contingencies

At this point in the process, the expected level, the effectiveness score for the maximum indicator value, and the effectiveness score for the minimum indicator value have all been determined for each of the contingencies. These three points can then be plotted on a contingency graph such as that in Figure 3.2, the graph for the first indicator in Table 3.1. As the table indicates, the expected level for this indicator with its predefined effectiveness score of 100 has been determined to be an indicator value of 3.0. The contingency committee assigned an effectiveness score of 25 to the minimum indicator value of 1.0 and an effectiveness score of 200 to the maximum indicator value of 5.0. In essence, the contingency worksheet identifies three points on the contingency, which are plotted on graphs such as that in Figure 3.2.

We then showed these figures to the design committee. After they reviewed them for accuracy, the next step was to determine the other points between the minimum and the expected level and the expected level and the maximum. We asked the committee if an improvement of a given amount from the minimum through the expected level always produced the same amount of gain in effectiveness, or if this changed at some point. Put another way, was there a straight line from the minimum to the expected level, or was there an inflection point?

One example of this type of nonlinearity is diminishing returns. An example of this occurs in Figure 3.3, which shows the final contingencies developed for the four indicators used in this extended example. In the lower right quadrant, note that the contingency starts to level out as the value of the indicator becomes larger, indicating diminishing returns. Specifically, the contingency shows that the effectiveness scores for the mean rating values of 2.0, 3.0, and 4.0 are 30, 90, and 100, respectively. Thus, the effectiveness score gain from a mean rating of 2.0 to a mean rating of 3.0 is 60 points, but the gain from a mean rating of 3.0 to a mean rating of 4.0 is only 10 points. Clearly, this illustrates diminishing returns.

It takes a bit of explaining to communicate the idea of possible nonlinearities. Once the design team understands the concept, however, the members can make these judgments readily. In fact, many people have reported to us that the nonlinearities offer the first opportunity they have had to represent policy accurately.

What helped as we completed contingencies was to use an overhead projector, transparencies of blank contingency forms, and an erasable marker. These tools allowed the committee members to make suggestions about the shape of contingencies and actually to see what effect each suggestion would have. In addition, this process gave us a written record of the committee's decisions. We then graphed these transparencies using a computer graphics package and circulated them to the committee members between meetings. This exchange of information greatly facilitated the development process, because committee members were able to review their decisions and make plans for their next committee meeting.

Figure 3.2. Plotting Maximum, Minimum, and Expected Effectiveness Values.

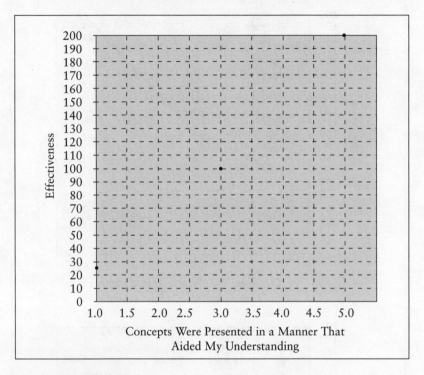

Interpreting Contingencies

One can learn much from examining the contingencies. As we discussed earlier, contingencies capture what is expected. Because the expected levels can vary, and usually do, the contingencies reveal that there are different expectations for various aspects of teaching. In the example, the expectations for grading fairly are much higher than those for raising challenging questions.

The overall slope reflects this differential importance. A quick glance at Figure 3.3 reveals that the indicator in the upper left quadrant is the most important, the one in the lower left is the least important, and the other two are in between and roughly equal to each other. In other words, of the four teaching factors in the example, the most important thing the instructor must do is to present material in a way that students understand. The least important task is to raise challenging questions and problems. Helping to integrate material and grading fairly are of medium importance.

Figure 3.3.   Sample Contingencies: Part One.

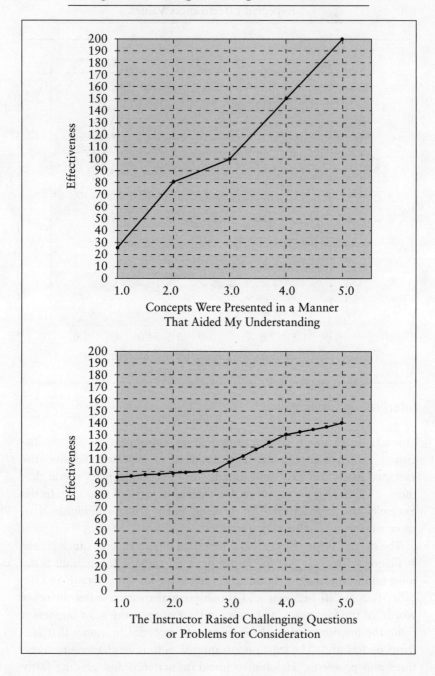

Concepts Were Presented in a Manner
That Aided My Understanding

The Instructor Raised Challenging Questions
or Problems for Consideration

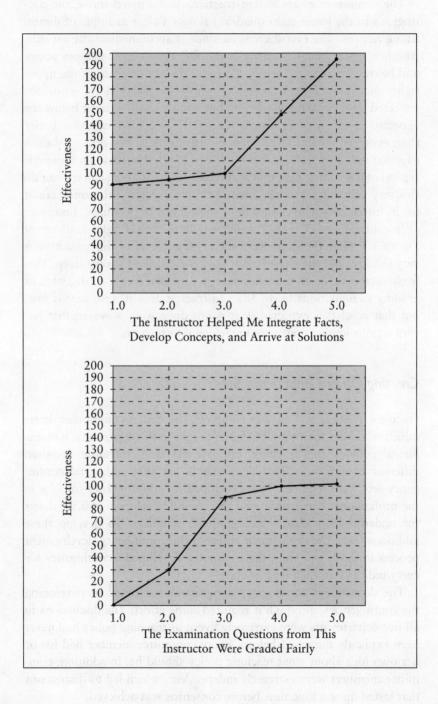

The nonlinearities are also instructive. As discussed above, the contingency in the lower right quadrant shows a clear example of diminishing returns. The ever-decreasing slope is an immediate cue for this. Another aspect of nonlinearity is the differences in the slopes above and below the expected levels. Consider the contingency in the upper right quadrant. This contingency shows a steep slope from the expected level up to the maximum but a fairly shallow slope below the expected level. In other words, doing this teaching behavior better than expected creates large gains in effectiveness, but doing it below expectations does not cause large losses in effectiveness. This slope is typical of a teaching task that is difficult to do. If an instructor can do this very valuable task well, he or she should receive substantial credit for it. Instructors who cannot do it should not be penalized, however.

In contrast, consider the contingency in the lower right quadrant of Figure 3.3. Here the slope from the expected level to the maximum is very shallow, but the slope below the expected level is very steep. This is characteristic of an indicator that is considered easy to do, such as grading examinations fairly. If an instructor does it well, that is fine, but that is what is expected. If it is not done well, however, that has very serious implications about teaching effectiveness.

Creating Other Contingency Sets

Once the contingency set was complete, the design committees determined whether other types of classes taught in the department had different policies for teaching effectiveness and therefore required different contingencies. Two departments felt that additional contingency sets were required. One developed an additional set for labs in the professional curriculum, and the second developed additional sets for undergraduate classes and graduate seminars. To develop these additional sets, the department repeated the contingency development process for each set. Thus, the committee developed a contingency for every indicator in each type of class.

The department contingency committees succeeded in developing the contingencies, although it required some effort. The discussions in all five departments were extremely lively, as teaching policy had never been explicitly discussed before. Every committee member had his or her own idea about what teaching policy should be. In addition, committee members were extremely independent, which led to discussions that lasted quite a long time before consensus was achieved.

Three departments were able to achieve consensus on their contingency sets within six to ten hours. Two departments, however, spent approximately twenty hours discussing their first contingency sets. For the departments that developed a second or third set of contingencies, the total development process for the multiple sets was slightly longer. These departments took their original contingency sets and adapted them according to their expectations for the different classes. Those departments needed three to five more hours to develop each additional set.

After each department completed contingency sets, the other members of the department and the department head reviewed the contingencies in department meetings. Members of the contingency committee made the presentations and answered questions. In these meetings, there were some disagreements about committee decisions, although most of these concerns were rather minor. To resolve the disputes, the contingencies were altered to reflect a consensus within each department.

Next, the college administration reviewed all of the sets from every department. This review process was similar to the review of objectives and indicators and provided an opportunity for the administrators to ensure that policy had been captured accurately. To obtain the administration's approval, the design committees presented the contingencies to the associate dean for academic affairs, who approved them without modification. This approval process completed the development of contingencies.

FACULTY REACTIONS TO THE CONTINGENCY DEVELOPMENT PROCESS

When the contingency committees began working on developing contingencies, several members expressed some concerns. These concerns fell into two different categories: general concerns about the indicators and specific concerns about departmental issues.

Response to the Indicators

The most common issue that arose during contingency development was that committee members wanted to modify indicators. Some members wished to change the wording of indicators. Others wanted to add or subtract indicators. The research team explained that, unlike contingencies, the indicators were for collegewide application. Therefore, a collegewide committee dealing with teaching policy, such as the TEC, would be the only group authorized to change the indicators. Individuals who had strong feelings about changing the indicators were asked to consult their department representative on the TEC so that their concerns could be considered. In the end, no indicators were changed.

Departmental Concerns

During the process of developing contingencies, some issues unique to departments arose. In one case, the committee representing one of the two clinical departments proposed that they be allowed to develop contingencies jointly with the other clinical department, because their courses and teaching methods were similar. Representatives from the second clinical department disagreed because they thought their courses, policies, and styles were different enough to develop contingencies separately. This meant that representatives from each department developed their own set of contingencies.

In a second case, members of a department committee were very uncomfortable with the idea that they had the responsibility of developing contingencies reflecting the department's policy about teaching. They were not certain they knew what the policy was or what it should be. Even though these individuals completed one set of contingencies, they were unsure of that set's validity. When they discussed this concern with us, it was clear that they did not want anyone else to determine these policies (especially not the college administrators), but they were concerned about establishing policy for the entire department. We explained that the representatives from each of the five departments were in similar situations, as teaching policy had never been made clear in this way. The majority of department representatives understood that they were pioneering a process to develop and clarify policy through consensus. They were also reminded that the entire department would review and approve the policies reflected in the contingencies before they were finalized. Although these points did not completely eliminate committee members' concerns, they seemed to reduce them.

In a third case, one department head asked why there were straight lines between contingency points. He noted that this was not the case with biological data, which typically has curved lines between points. We explained that the contingency committee had the option of drawing any shape they felt was representative of policy. The shapes that appeared were based on discussion and consensus.

STEP 4: PUT THE SYSTEM TOGETHER

The final step in developing the new approach was to design the feedback system and produce feedback reports using that system. The TEC made decisions about this phase, because it was important that the feedback reports be consistent across the entire college.

After reviewing the feedback reports developed for prior ProMES projects, the TEC decided to use the previous report format. This format included a variety of information, which will be briefly described below, along with a discussion of the actual feedback reports.

Generating Feedback Reports

The system generated a feedback report for each course taught by an instructor. To create these reports, we first collected the indicator data in the form of student ratings and then calculated the mean rating for each indicator. These means are the indicator values.

Then, based on the contingencies, we calculated effectiveness scores for each indicator value. This is illustrated in Table 3.2, which is the first page of an abbreviated feedback report. The table is based on the contingencies shown in Figure 3.4.

The feedback report lists the objectives and indicators. For the first indicator, "The instructor was well organized," the mean rating by the students in that class was 3.21. The 3.21 corresponds to an effectiveness value of 122 on the vertical (effectiveness) axis of the contingencies shown in Figure 3.4. Continuing this process would give an effectiveness value for each indicator. Once an effectiveness score is determined for each indicator, those effectiveness scores are averaged to provide several average effectiveness scores. First, an average effectiveness score is developed for each objective. In Table 3.2 there are two objectives; therefore, we have to average effectiveness scores. For the objective "The instructor presented appropriate material in an organized fashion," the average effectiveness score is 122. For the objective "The instructor evaluated students fairly," the average effectiveness score is 107. The overall average effectiveness score is also shown at the bottom of Table 3.2. This is the average effectiveness score across all the indicators.

In addition to the effectiveness scores, the feedback report also presents a percentage of maximum score for each indicator. The percentage of maximum score is another type of overall score. Based on

Table 3.2.   Sample Feedback Report: Part One.

BASIC FEEDBACK INFORMATION

TEACHING EFFECTIVENESS REPORT FOR: M. Smith, Anatomy 391.
BASIC EFFECTIVENESS DATA FOR: Spring 1996.

Objectives and Indicators	*Indicator Data*	*Effectiveness Score*	*Percentage of Maximum*
Presented appropriate material in organized fashion			
Instructor well organized	3.21	122	70
Material appropriate	4.23	121	91
Average effectiveness: 122			
Evaluated student fairly			
Exams reasonably difficult	3.21	101	84
Exams graded fairly	2.83	83	65
Average effectiveness: 92			

Average overall effectiveness score: 107
Overall percentage of maximum: 78 percent

---

effectiveness scores, it is a ratio comparing how well the person performed with the maximum possible performance. The closer the instructor is to performing at the highest possible level on an indicator, the higher his or her percentage of maximum score will be.

The formula used to compute the percentage of maximum score is as follows: subtract the minimum indicator effectiveness score from the person's actual indicator effectiveness score. Then divide this value by the difference between the maximum indicator effectiveness score possible and the minimum indicator effectiveness score possible.

For example, assume that an individual instructor had an effectiveness score of 101 on the indicator "The examination questions from this instructor were reasonable in difficulty." By referring to the contingency for this indicator in the contingencies shown in Figure 3.4, we determine that the minimum effectiveness score for this indicator is 80 and the maximum effectiveness score is 105. Consequently, the instructor could only have scored between 80 and 105, for a total range of 25 points. Because the instructor scored 21 points into this range (a score of 101), his or her percentage of maximum score will be (101 – 80)/(105 – 80) = 21/25 = 84 percent.

Table 3.2 illustrates the percentage of maximum score that corresponds to each indicator value. On the indicator "The instructor was well organized," the mean student rating is 3.21 and the effectiveness score is 122. Using the percentage of maximum formula suggested above, the percentage of maximum score for this indicator would be 70. This suggests that the instructor is performing at a reasonably high level, having scored 70 percent of the possible effectiveness points. The report also includes an overall percentage of maximum score, shown at the bottom of Table 3.2. The overall percentage of maximum score is the average percentage of maximum across all the indicators.

The percentage of maximum is another type of overall index of teaching effectiveness. It has a distinct advantage in this setting. Because each department developed different contingencies and the same departments developed unique contingency sets for various types of courses, the overall effectiveness scores from the different departments and from the different types of courses are not directly comparable. For example, three of the departments developed contingencies for their large lecture DVM courses that produced essentially the same overall effectiveness scores for the same mean student ratings. One department had lower expected levels, however, producing somewhat higher overall effectiveness scores. Another department used higher expected levels, which produced lower overall effectiveness scores. Thus, to compare instructors from different departments, the dean could not use the overall effectiveness scores, because they were not directly comparable. A similar situation occurred in comparing the overall effectiveness scores from different types of classes, for example, a large lecture DVM course and a small graduate seminar.

Using percentage of maximum allows for this direct comparison. Because the instructors' scores are compared to the maximum possible for each contingency set, the interpretation is the same no matter what contingency set is being used. Thus, a percentage of maximum of 90 percent means the same regardless of department or course type.

The second section of the feedback report appears in Table 3.3. This table indicates what the priorities should be for improving teaching for the upcoming semester. As described in Chapter Two, one can estimate potential improvements in teaching by increasing each indicator value an equal amount and calculating the resultant increase in effectiveness. Because the contingencies are nonlinear, an equal increase in the indicator score for each indicator will not cause an equal increase in

Figure 3.4.   Sample Contingencies: Part Two.

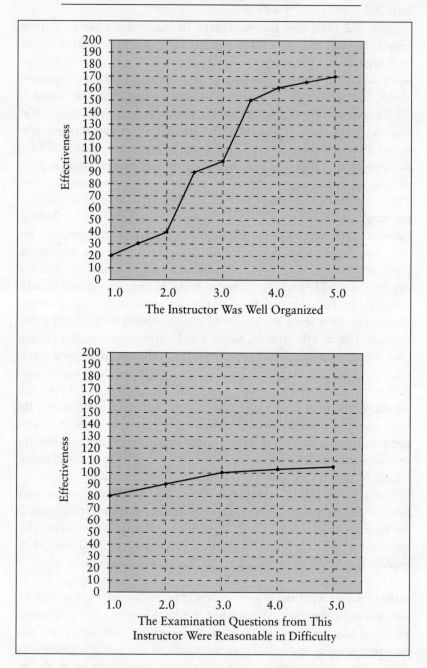

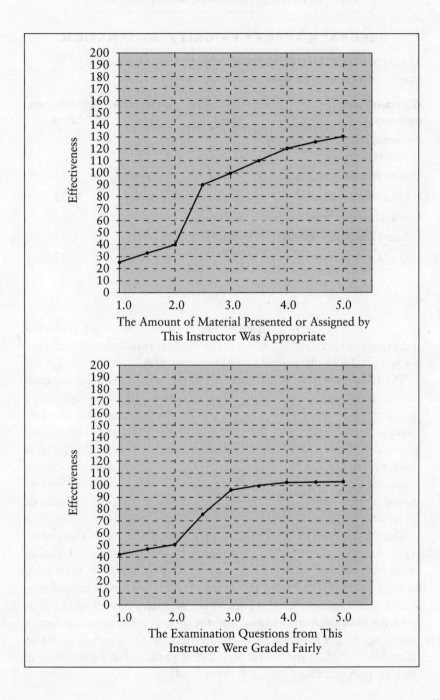

Table 3.3. Sample Feedback Report: Part Two.

FEEDBACK REPORT PRIORITY INFORMATION

TEACHING EFFECTIVENESS REPORT FOR: M. Smith, Anatomy 391.
Potential effectiveness gains for next period.

Objectives and Indicators	From Indicator Data	To Indicator Data	Effectiveness Gain
Presented appropriate material in organized fashion			
Instructor well organized	3.21	3.46	25
Material appropriate	4.23	4.48	2
Evaluated student fairly			
Exams reasonably difficult	3.21	3.46	1
Exams graded fairly	2.83	3.08	13

effectiveness. In other words, improving some indicators will provide a large jump in effectiveness, whereas the same increase in another indicator will produce only a small jump in effectiveness.

The table shows the values received in the current semester for each indicator. It also shows how those indicator values change when increased by a uniform amount, as well as the potential gain in effectiveness corresponding to that increase in the indicator scores. This example indicates that if the instructor wants to have the greatest impact on his or her teaching effectiveness, he or she should focus on becoming more organized (Indicator A). A 0.25 increase in performance on this indicator would produce an increase in effectiveness of 25 points.

The third section of the feedback report (see Table 3.4) is a summary report for all classes taught that semester by that instructor. The mean of all the average effectiveness scores and percentage of maximum scores are calculated for all the classes taught that semester and presented in this section of the report. Other summary reports were calculated for each department head and the dean. The department head's report aggregates the indicator, effectiveness, and percentage of maximum data for all of the instructors in that particular department. The dean's report includes data for the entire college.

Table 3.4.   Sample Feedback Report: Part Three.

SUMMARY FEEDBACK REPORT

TEACHING EFFECTIVENESS REPORT FOR: M. Smith.
SUMMARY DATA FOR: Spring 1996.

Name	*Department*	*Class*	*Average Effectiveness Score*	*Percentage of Maximum*
Smith, M.	VTAN	VTAN391	107	78
Smith, M.	VTAN	VTAN913	125	89

Average overall effectiveness score: 116
Percentage of maximum: 84 percent

All reports were generated by a computer program written for this project. This program took the mean student ratings for each instructor (calculated from Scantron sheets completed by students) and computed effectiveness scores, percentage of maximum scores, and priorities for improving teaching. The program then generated feedback reports for each instructor for every class taught. It also generated the summary reports described above for (1) each instructor (across all classes taught by the instructor during the semester), (2) each department (across all instructors and all classes taught by the department during the semester), and (3) the dean (across all instructors and all classes taught within the college).

Training College Personnel to Use the Feedback Reports

Although we had explained the overall system to faculty and administrators on several occasions, we felt it necessary to provide additional training once the actual feedback reports were prepared. We developed a manual to help faculty and department heads use the feedback report, and we gave this manual to each faculty member and administrator. We also met with each department head to deliver the first set of feedback forms. During the meeting, we showed department heads how to interpret the data on the forms for individuals, programs, and the department.

FACULTY REACTIONS TO THE SYSTEM'S IMPLEMENTATION

As we began implementing the system, a number of problems arose to which many faculty members had strong reactions. These issues included problems with the actual administration of the system, the decision to establish the system as a method for evaluating faculty for promotion and tenure, the perception that the system was overly focused on negative feedback, and the availability of resources to assist faculty in improving their teaching. Each of these issues is discussed in the following paragraphs.

Administering the System

One of the major issues that arose when we implemented the feedback system concerned the administration of the student rating forms. The design team recommended that the rating forms be administered centrally to avoid inconsistencies that might invalidate results. Once the system had been approved at all levels, we asked the dean to identify an individual who would be responsible for coordinating the teaching evaluation administration. He designated an administrative assistant who had a good reputation for attending to details and following through on complex projects. This individual was trained to use the computer program which had been developed to produce feedback for instructors.

During the first round of data collection, the staff member had some difficulties administering the forms in all of the classes. Some of the instructors forgot that the forms were to be administered at that class meeting, some did not allow much time for students to complete the forms, and some did not want the forms to be administered.

Because of this confusion, an individual with more authority was asked to administer the project. We gave this person a list of tasks outlining the processes required to generate the forms and obtain the feedback reports. We met with the individual and a new staff member to explain the process. The new staff member was trained to use the computer program.

Despite this explanation and training, problems continued to occur during the administration of the rating forms. In one case, the department received the forms from the individual so late that they administered them in the new semester. Once again, we met with the individual in charge to answer questions and to make procedures clear. Problems with the administration process continued, although each time they seemed to be slightly different.

Some of the problems that occurred were beyond the control of the individual in charge. One such problem was related to the scanning of the rating forms. This was done by a service department on campus not associated with any particular college. Scanning operators familiar with the process left, and new personnel made mistakes that delayed the feedback reports. There were also some minor problems with the computer program, which members of the research team addressed. It was expected that at some point, the individual in charge would be able to develop enough experience with the system to handle unforeseen problems successfully. We thought that the administration process would eventually become routine. In fact, this occurred in time.

Although there were many significant concerns about the administration of the system, the final concern had to do with a fairly simple administrative problem: Which contingency set should be applied to instructors teaching interdisciplinary courses? It was recommended that the contingency set of the department in which the course was being offered be applied, regardless of the departmental home of the faculty member teaching it.

Establishing the Use of the System as Policy

Besides administrative issues, the other major issue that arose during implementation had to do with developing collegewide teaching policy. These policy concerns included a number of issues.

The most pervasive issue had to do with the discomfort many faculty felt about being evaluated. To address these concerns, the college initially implemented the system only on a partial basis. The dean recognized that the faculty had many questions, some uncertainty, and considerable anxiety. Therefore, at his request, only the instructors who were rated and their respective department heads received the early cycles of feedback. The data provided to the dean's office were identified by department only, omitting individual names. This approach was meant to alleviate some of the faculty's concerns by allowing individuals to get a sample of the system and by letting us fine-tune it before the college formally adopted it.

During this trial period, we collected data about reliability and validity (to be discussed in Chapter Four) and reported these data in collegewide meetings to the faculty. We held at least one such meeting during each of the first two semesters in which the system was in use.

For example, after two rounds of administration, we presented data showing the gains in effectiveness scores and the instrument's reliability. We answered questions about the system. In addition, we showed the variability among contingencies to illustrate that different departments set different teaching policies. These data showed that the project was yielding the expected results.

In general, the system was taken very seriously during the trial period. In fact, some departments used the data in promotion and tenure committees for decision making. Because the use of the system had not yet been established as official policy, however, individual faculty members supplied the data used in the promotion and tenure process on a voluntary basis.

The length of the trial period was not initially specified. After four semesters, however, it was clear that the data provided in the feedback reports were useful and that most people seemed to consider system feedback to be valid and reliable. Therefore, the executive committee formally moved to adopt the system. With this adoption, the system became collegewide policy.

Another policy issue related to whom should be evaluated. Some thought that each instructor should be evaluated every time they taught a course or section of a course. Others felt that only those on the tenure track, such as assistant professors, should be evaluated. The TEC was asked to consider this issue and to make recommendations to resolve the questions. After discussion, they recommended that tenure-track faculty be evaluated annually, that tenured associate professors be evaluated at least every two to three years, that tenured full professors be evaluated at least every five years, and that the department head use discretion in evaluating all other faculty. The TEC further acknowledged that the department head would have final authority to decide which instructors would be evaluated.

Resisting a Focus on Negative Feedback

During implementation, one department head noted that the system emphasized what he perceived to be "negative" performance. He felt that the system was negative because it focused feedback on areas of teaching that needed improvement. We pointed out that the system indicated good or outstanding performance as well as performance that could improve. We also suggested that department heads could make notes indicating praiseworthy effort on the feedback form. We experimented with the possibility of adding computerized notes to the feedback report but dropped the idea because we felt that the feedback report already provided a balance of information for the department head and faculty member to discuss.

Improving Teaching

Another issue that arose during implementation had to do with using the information in the feedback reports. After faculty and their respective department heads reviewed several rounds of feedback, it became clear that improvements in teaching were needed in some cases. The way in which instructors were to go about making improvements was not clear, however.

We were asked how instructors would learn to improve their teaching. Some faculty and department heads noted that they needed some assistance to develop good teaching skills. They requested funds to cover sabbaticals, workshops, and consultations with teaching experts.

We confirmed that, according to the literature on teaching evaluation, instruction could improve through consultation with teaching experts. No such formal CVM program was developed, but we informed faculty and administrators about the services of a campus group that worked with faculty to improve teaching. This group had indicated a complete willingness to work with any faculty member to help improve teaching.

Updating the System

Once the system was operating, we recognized that we needed to devise some mechanism to allow for revision of objectives, indicators, or contingencies in case changes were needed over time. It was determined that the TEC would be the appropriate body to review and revise objectives, indicators, and collegewide teaching policy issues. Should changes in the contingencies be needed, the appropriate department contingency committee would be convened. It was also suggested that the TEC formally review the system on an annual basis.

Adopting the System

With the formal adoption of the student evaluation phase of the project, it became policy to include the evaluation results when making decisions about awards, merit raises, and promotion and tenure. The college was using data to make decisions and to guide improvement efforts. Although some problems with administration persisted, feedback reports were being provided on a regular basis, and faculty and administrators were accepting and using them. The first feedback reports were distributed in fall 1991, the formal policy decision to use the system was made in 1993, and as of this writing (spring 1996) the system has been in continuous use.

4

EVALUATING RESULTS AND ASKING TOUGH QUESTIONS

THIS CHAPTER WILL PRESENT the empirical results evaluating the ProMES student rating system. We will organize the discussion around the research questions listed in Chapter Three. We will restate each research question and provide the results relevant to that question. The data to be used in answering these questions come from observation, questionnaire data, and teaching evaluation data.

THE RESEARCH QUESTIONS

1. *Can the ProMES system be developed successfully in this environment?* Although the basic ProMES approach had been used successfully in a variety of organizational settings (Pritchard, 1995), as of the start of this project, it had not been implemented in a university setting. Thus, it was still unknown whether the system could be developed and implemented as a teaching evaluation system in an academic setting. In presenting our results, we will focus on whether the steps in the ProMES process were actually done successfully.

2. *Is the resulting system a valid measure of teaching effectiveness?* We must address several issues to answer the validity question. We will focus on the evidence regarding whether the steps in the process were done well, determining if the system produced variability in teaching effectiveness evaluations, answering a series of psychometric issues, ascertaining if the elements of the system produced the expected results, and establishing whether faculty and administrators perceived the system as valid.

3. *Will teaching effectiveness improve with feedback from the system?* Here we will focus on the effects of feedback on teaching effectiveness over time.

4. *Do faculty and administrators see the resulting system as valuable?* The focus here will be on whether the college continued to use the system and how different constituents judged the system's value.

5. *Is the new system better than traditional systems that provide measurement and feedback on teaching effectiveness?* Because traditional methods of student ratings are simpler to develop, it would not be appropriate to use the ProMES approach unless it produced better results. The question here is whether this new approach has proven superior to traditional methods.

RESEARCH QUESTION 1: CAN THE PROMES SYSTEM BE DEVELOPED SUCCESSFULLY IN THIS ENVIRONMENT?

To answer this question, we examined evidence pertaining to several issues. These issues are described below.

System Development

The first issue is whether the design committees were able to complete the steps in ProMES and do the other tasks needed to develop the system. The TEC was able to develop objectives with little difficulty. Developing indicators was somewhat more complicated (as is usually the case in ProMES projects) but was still accomplished with a reasonable amount of effort. All departmental contingency committees also succeeded in developing the contingencies.

The TEC and the contingency committees were able to present their work to their respective departments as well as to the administrators. Both of these groups had to approve the system before it could be used. These presentations were made with little difficulty. Committee members responded to questions and presented the logic behind their recommendations. All departments approved the components and the actual use of the system.

Another issue concerns whether the design committees achieved a true consensus regarding the system design. We answered this question by using a questionnaire developed for this project, called the Design Committee Questionnaire. A copy of this questionnaire is in Appendix B. The first questionnaire in Appendix B was used for the TEC, the sec-

ond for the department contingency committees. The two questionnaires assessed similar issues for the two different types of committees.
The responses to this questionnaire measured whether the different
design committees made agreements based on solid consensus or just to
move the process along.

Four of the five TEC members were present to complete the TEC
version of this questionnaire. All four either agreed or strongly agreed
that a true consensus was reached.

There were five contingency committees, one for each department,
with a total of twenty-seven members. Nineteen of the twenty-seven
committee members responded to a similar questionnaire that asked
them to describe their experiences as contingency committee members.
Of those nineteen, eighteen either agreed or strongly agreed that a true
consensus was reached within their committee; one individual indicated a response of "neither agree nor disagree." Thus, 95 percent
agreed that a true consensus was achieved. All design committee members completed this questionnaire after developing and approving the
objectives, indicators, and contingencies.

The Review and Revision Process

Another issue that we used to determine whether the system could be
successfully developed involved the approval process. Various groups
needed to approve the system at different points in the process. The
questions are whether this approval process was completed and how
the committees doing the system development reacted to this process.

The faculty, department heads, and the dean's office all needed to
approve of the system at various steps in the development process.
Departmental approval was obtained in all five departments either
through faculty responses to a questionnaire (the mechanism used to
obtain approval for the objectives and indicators) or through departmental faculty meetings (to obtain approval for the contingencies). The
results from the questionnaire in which faculty approved of the objectives and indicators were fairly positive. These results appeared in
Chapter Three. Faculty members approved all objectives and indicators. Although the meetings held to approve the contingencies were
very intense and lively, the faculty approved all the contingency sets
without exception.

The administration gave its approval of the system in two separate
steps. First, in a meeting held after the objectives and indicators were
completed, the dean, associate deans, and department heads approved

the objectives and indicators with only one minor modification. Second, the contingencies were presented to the associate dean for academic affairs (the administrative representative selected by the college administration to complete the approval process for contingencies). The associate dean approved all contingency sets without modification.

We also evaluated the approval process by having the aforementioned Design Committee Questionnaire include items measuring how committee members felt about the review and revision process. If they perceived that the process was completed fairly and reasonably, it would further demonstrate that the system could be completed in this environment.

A review of the TEC members' responses indicates that 100 percent agreed or strongly agreed that the review and revision process was fair and reasonable. For the contingency committee members, 88 percent either agreed or strongly agreed that the review and revision process was fair and reasonable. Those who did not agree with this question responded with "neither agree nor disagree." The individuals responding neutrally made written comments such as "Who knows? I wasn't there." Thus, these individuals seemed to be neutral out of a lack of information rather than a negative view of the process.

Summary of Results for Research Question 1

These findings indicate a clear affirmative answer to the research question of whether the ProMES system could be successfully developed in a university setting. We base this conclusion on the following evidence:

- Each of the ProMES steps was completed.
- Committee members perceived that a true consensus was reached.
- The appropriate approvals were obtained.
- The committee members felt the approval process was appropriate.
- The system was actually implemented.

RESEARCH QUESTION 2: IS THE RESULTING SYSTEM A VALID MEASURE OF TEACHING EFFECTIVENESS?

The validity question is difficult to answer. As the literature review indicated, no single criterion of teaching effectiveness can be used to validate the evaluation system. Rather, validity must be shown through a series of factors. This process of establishing overall validity by exploring multiple sources of information is generally known as *construct validity* (Brown, 1983; Cascio, 1987; Cohen, 1981; Cronbach & Meehl, 1955; Guion, 1965; Marsh, 1984, 1987). We will use this process and look at as many aspects of validity as possible to build a picture of the system's overall validity.

Quality of the Indicators

The system is founded on the seventeen items students use to rate the instructors. If these items are not of high quality, the overall system's validity suffers. The steps taken to develop these items, which were described in Chapter Three, included having the TEC reach consensus, pretesting the items with students, conducting a formal faculty review, and seeking approval from faculty and administrators. Thus, the process of generating the indicators was quite extensive in order to ensure their validity.

In addition, the research team reviewed the objectives and indicators to determine if they were consistent with what one would expect, based on the teaching evaluation literature. All seven objectives that the TEC selected were among the important teaching characteristics identified by the literature and summarized in Table 1.1. Further, the items on the student rating form, or indicators (see Figure 3.1), were also quite similar to those found on other measures of teaching effectiveness. The substance of all seventeen indicators can be found on commercially available student rating forms, although they sometimes have slight wording differences.

Variability

Another aspect of validity is variability in the ratings themselves and variability in the effectiveness and percentage of maximum scores developed by the ProMES system. These scores must vary to have validity. If little variability exists, students are making no discrimination between different instructors. This would certainly suggest a lack of validity, because all faculty and administrators involved in the design process strongly believed that such variability in teaching effectiveness existed in the CVM. Variability alone does not establish validity, but the system cannot be valid without it.

A frequency distribution of the mean student ratings for the first four semesters of system use (266 evaluations) appears in Figure 4.1. There were several ratings in the 2.5 to 2.75 range with evaluations up

Figure 4.1. Frequency Distribution of Mean Student Ratings.

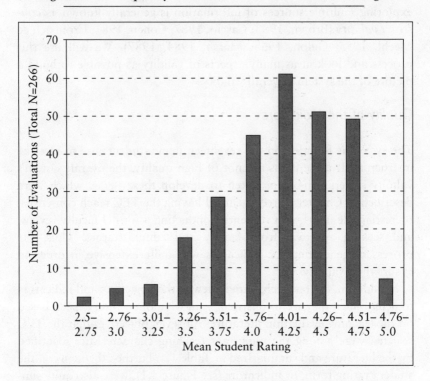

to the 4.76 to 5.0 range. As one would expect, the majority of the ratings were in the middle range, with fewer at the extremes.

Frequency distributions of overall average effectiveness scores and percentage of maximum scores show the same pattern (see Figure 4.2). Average overall effectiveness scores range from clearly below expectations to extremely high. Percentage of maximum scores show the same pattern, with some instructors receiving nearly perfect evaluations. These data indicate that the student ratings and the ProMES scores showed considerable variability.

Overall Effectiveness and Percentage of Maximum

The specifics of these two different overall teaching effectiveness scores—the average overall effectiveness score and the percentage of maximum score—are explained in Chapter Three. Recall that the average overall effectiveness score is the average of the effectiveness scores across the indicators. This calculation comes directly from the contingencies. The percentage of maximum score indicates in percentage

Figure 4.2.   Frequency Distribution of ProMES's Overall Effectiveness and Percentage of Maximum Scores.

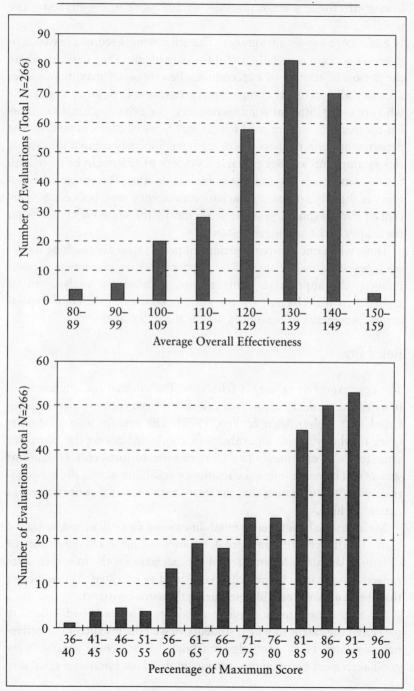

terms how close the effectiveness score is to the maximum possible effectiveness score. Both types of scores can range from 0 percent, the lowest effectiveness score possible, to 100 percent, the highest score possible.

Each score has its advantages. The effectiveness scores are easier to interpret and are especially useful for individuals. They indicate where the person is, relative to expectations. Percentage of maximum scores are especially useful for comparisons across people or groups of people who are using different contingency sets. For example, because different contingency sets are used for distinct types of courses and different departments, effectiveness scores are not completely comparable across these groups. An average effectiveness score of 125 might be quite high in one contingency set and not as high in another. Percentage of maximum is directly comparable across contingency sets, because 80 percent of the maximum possible score means the same no matter what the shapes of the contingencies are.

Thus, when one compares groups of people who are teaching different types of courses or are in different departments, percentage of maximum is the appropriate score to use. Because the analyses to be reported in this chapter are for various courses in different departments, percentage of maximum will be the index used.

Reliability

The next aspect of validity is reliability. The internal consistency reliability of the student ratings was calculated from each evaluation using Cronbach's alpha (Allen & Yen, 1979). The average internal consistency reliability across all evaluations conducted during the first three semesters was examined. The total number of instructor evaluations was 266. The mean internal consistency reliability across these evaluations was .90, suggesting that the instrument's internal consistency was extremely high.

Mean internal consistency reliabilities were also calculated by size of class. The upper half of Figure 4.3 shows the mean reliability for the different class sizes. Mean internal consistencies for the four class sizes ranged from .83 to .93, which is very good to excellent. This indicates that the items were reliably measuring the same construct.

We also considered interjudge reliability. This index of reliability measured the extent to which students viewed the instructor's effectiveness similarly. High interjudge reliability (.8 or above) suggests very good agreement between the students in the class. Interjudge reliability

Figure 4.3.   Reliability by Class Size.

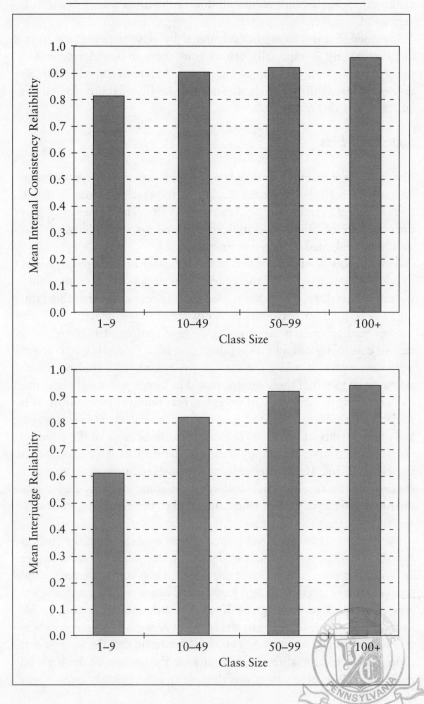

was calculated using intraclass correlations (Marsh, 1987). The average interjudge reliability across all 266 evaluations was .83, which is very good.

Interjudge means were also calculated by class size, because interjudge reliability is especially sensitive to the number of raters. The results appear in the bottom of Figure 4.3. Although the reliability for classes of less than ten students was low (.64), reliability for all the larger classes was quite good.

Sources of Bias

Bias in student ratings occurs when students rate the instructor based on some factor other than the quality of the teaching (Marsh, 1984, 1987; Stumpf, Freedman, & Aguanno, 1979). The presence of any major source of bias would indicate reduced system validity, so bias should be evaluated to help determine validity.

Two sources of bias identified in the literature review are quite easy to control. One is whether the instructor is present in the room when the ratings are done. The other is whether students know that these ratings will be used for personnel decisions about that instructor. Both situations lead to more positive ratings. These sources of bias are fairly easy to control by simply making them constant. To do this, instructors were never present when the ratings were done, and students in all classes were told that these ratings would influence personnel decisions.

Controlling another type of potential bias required more effort. It is possible that students might give an instructor very low ratings, regardless of the quality of teaching. This could occur because of the unpopularity of the course, the unpopularity of the instructor, or some other irrelevant factor. Understandably, this possible source of bias was a concern of the faculty. They believed that some students might rate instructors negatively for reasons unrelated to their teaching, thus spuriously reducing their ratings.

We evaluated this potential source of bias by examining the student ratings. The logic was that if a student were intentionally trying to give an instructor poor ratings, he or she would do so across all items. This would result in what we called *generalized negative ratings*. A student was considered to have given a generalized negative rating to an instructor if the mean rating by that student across all seventeen indicators was between 1.0 and 1.5. This would indicate that the student was rating the instructor at the bottom or near the bottom of the scale on all items. This level of rating was thought to reflect bias because it was not likely that any instructor was so ineffective that he or she would be rated this low on all seventeen indicators.

To assess whether this type of bias was present, we counted the number of students who gave such generalized negative ratings to each instructor. The data for the first four semesters appear in Figure 4.4. They indicate that in 258 of the 266 evaluations, there was not a single student who gave generalized negative ratings. In only seven evaluations, 2 percent of the students gave a generalized negative rating. In just one evaluation, 4 percent of the students gave generalized negative ratings. This indicated that generalized negative ratings were very rare.

The next question was how frequent generalized negative ratings needed to be in order to affect an instructor's mean student rating significantly. A meaningful decrease in an instructor's overall rating was defined as a .25 decrease in the average rating across all seventeen items. To produce such a decrease, approximately 18 percent of the students would have to give generalized negative ratings. Thus, not only were few generalized negative ratings given but the frequency was nowhere near enough to produce a meaningful decrease in an instructor's overall rating. Therefore, we concluded that generalized negative ratings were not a source of bias.

Evaluation of the Contingencies

Another way to determine the validity of the ProMES system is to evaluate the contingencies that were developed. Contingencies are what most clearly distinguish ProMES from other methods of teaching evaluation and feedback. Some of the advantages of ProMES contingencies are that they account for differential importance and nonlinearities and capture different purposes or missions for various courses and departments. These advantages have been discussed in detail in earlier chapters. The issue to be addressed here is whether these potential advantages were in fact realized.

NONLINEARITY. The majority of contingencies in previous ProMES applications have been nonlinear. The question is whether the same was true in this setting. This is determined by examining the contingencies that the department committees developed. If they were mostly linear, this potential advantage of ProMES was not realized.

Of the 136 contingencies that the five departments developed, only 10 were linear. These 10 linear contingencies were distributed across the five departments, and no department had more than 2 linear con-

Figure 4.4. Frequency of Generalized Negative Ratings.

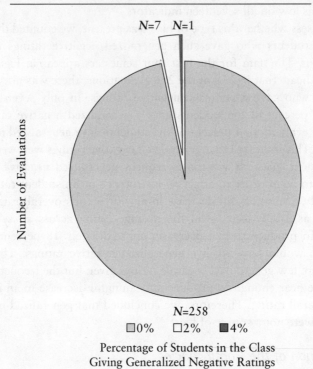

N=7 *N*=1

N=258

□0%   □2%   ■4%

Percentage of Students in the Class
Giving Generalized Negative Ratings

tingencies in each set of 17. This indicated that the vast majority of teaching behaviors were seen as having a nonlinear relationship with effectiveness in all five departments. Thus, ProMES contingencies were in fact nonlinear in this setting.

DIFFERENTIAL IMPORTANCE. We expected that the contingencies would capture differential importance, as demonstrated by each contingency's slope. A contingency with a steep slope reveals that the indicator is very important, because a small change in the indicator score will cause a large change in effectiveness. On the other hand, a contingency with a shallow slope means that the indicator is not very important, because even a large change in the indicator score will result in only a small change in effectiveness.

For example, the most important indicator in Figure 3.4 is in the upper left quadrant: "The instructor was well organized." Compared with the other contingencies, this has the steepest slope, with the effectiveness scores ranging from 20 to 170. The least important indicator is in the lower left quadrant: "The examination questions from this instructor were reasonable in difficulty." The range of effectiveness scores for this contingency go from 80 to 105.

We did a simple visual review of the contingencies, which demonstrated that they had differential slopes and therefore differential importance. To determine the differential importance more precisely, however, we compared the contingency with the steepest slope and the one with the most shallow slope for the seventeen contingencies in each set.

In the example we just mentioned with only four contingencies (Figure 3.4), the range for the steepest (most important) contingency is 170 – 20 = 150. For the least important of the four, the range is 105 – 80 = 25. The ratio of 150 to 25 indicates the degree of differential importance represented in the contingency set. In this example, the ratio would be 150 to 25, or 6 to 1, indicating that the most important contingency was six times more important than the least important. The larger this ratio, the larger the difference in importance between the contingencies in that set.

The ratios for the different sets in the five departments ranged from a low of 4 to 1 to a high of 10 to 1. Thus, all these contingency sets contained large variation in importance.

CAPTURE OF DIFFERENT TEACHING POLICIES. Another aspect of contingencies to evaluate is whether they captured different teaching policies. Contingencies with unique shapes reflect different policies, because they place varying importance on distinct aspects of teaching in different situations. Two situations are important here: different types of classes and different departments.

Different Courses

It was clear in this setting, as in most, that the teaching objectives and policies for undergraduate, graduate, and professional classes were different. For example, having examination questions that require the student to do more than recall factual information was more important in teaching graduate students than undergraduate students. Thus, when the same department committee created contingencies for different types of classes, they should have formed differently shaped contingencies for some of the items.

Two departments decided to take advantage of this feature of the system. One department developed three sets of contingencies, one for graduate, undergraduate, and professional (DVM) courses. Another developed two sets, one for the bulk of their courses and one for a type of laboratory course they held frequently. The other three departments developed only one set of contingencies.

There were two primary reasons that these three departments created only one contingency set. Some did not see the courses they taught as being very different, or they taught so few courses that were different that a second set of contingencies did not seem necessary. The other reason was that some contingency committees wanted to see how the first set worked out and decide later if they needed more.

In general, there was a clear pattern of differences in the contingencies that were expected to be different, and there was much similarity when the contingencies were expected to be alike. For example, in the department with three contingency sets, the contingencies were quite similar for undergraduates, graduates, and DVM courses on the items dealing with the instructor's being well organized, speaking clearly and being easily understood, creating an atmosphere facilitating learning, being courteous, and giving examinations that covered important concepts from the course and that were graded fairly.

The contingencies were also different for some items. For example, the top half of Figure 4.5 shows the three contingencies for the item "The instructor's examination questions required me to do more than recall factual information." The contingencies for undergraduate and professional DVM courses are the same, but the graduate contingency is quite different. This was a basic science department (physiology and pharmacology) in which both undergraduate and DVM courses were primarily designed to impart basic information. The graduate courses, however, led to advanced degrees in these disciplines and were designed to help students generate more knowledge.

These policy differences are reflected in the contingencies. Although the basic shapes of the three contingencies are similar, the graduate contingency has a higher expected value. An instructor in a graduate class should do this behavior very often (a value of 4 on the rating scale) just to meet expectations, whereas for undergraduate and DVM courses, performing the same task regularly (a value of 3 on the rating scale) meets expectations.

In addition, the graduate contingency ranges from 35 to 165 for a total of 130 effectiveness points. The corresponding ranges for undergraduate and DVM contingencies are both 87. Thus, as expected, this indicator was much more important for graduate classes. In addition, the negative consequences of not doing this teaching behavior are much greater in graduate classes. The drop in effectiveness from the expected level to the minimum in the graduate class is 100 minus 25, or 75 effectiveness points. The analogous drop for the DVM and undergraduate courses is only 30 effectiveness points.

A second example of differences in the three types of courses appears in the bottom half of Figure 4.5. These three contingencies are for the item "The instructor raised challenging questions or problems for consideration." The contingencies indicate that this teaching behavior is very important for the graduate classes (range: 198 − 35 = 163) and less important for DVM classes (range: 180 − 52 = 128) and for undergraduate classes (range: 165 − 52 = 113).

Different Departments

It is important to capture policy differences across departments, as well as across courses. That is, if two departments have different teaching policies, they should use uniquely shaped contingencies for different aspects of teaching. Because there were some clear differences in teaching policy, if the contingencies were all similar, the contingencies would not be capturing this difference. There were also some similarities, however, in the teaching policies of the different departments. Thus, there should have been some indicators for which the contingencies were similar. If all indicators showed large differences across departments for these contingencies that should have been similar, it could suggest that the contingencies were not valid reflections of policy.

The data generally matched these expected patterns. For example, consider the indicator "The instructor appeared to have a thorough knowledge of the subject." One would expect that the five departments would have a somewhat similar policy on this teaching behavior. No matter what the content, purpose of the course, or type of course, thorough subject knowledge should be important. Figure 4.6 shows the contingencies for the different departments on this indicator. For the two departments with more than one set of contingencies, we selected for comparison across departments the contingencies for the DVM courses, which constituted by far the majority of their courses.

These contingencies in the figure look similar. The overall importance for each department is very high, as reflected in the overall range. The lowest range was 145, the highest 176. They were nearly identical in the effectiveness score they gave to the minimum amount of the indicator. Four departments gave it 0 effectiveness points, one gave it 2. In all cases, not displaying a thorough subject knowledge hurt one's effectiveness more than having this knowledge helped one's effectiveness. This is apparent in the figure, because the drop in effectiveness from

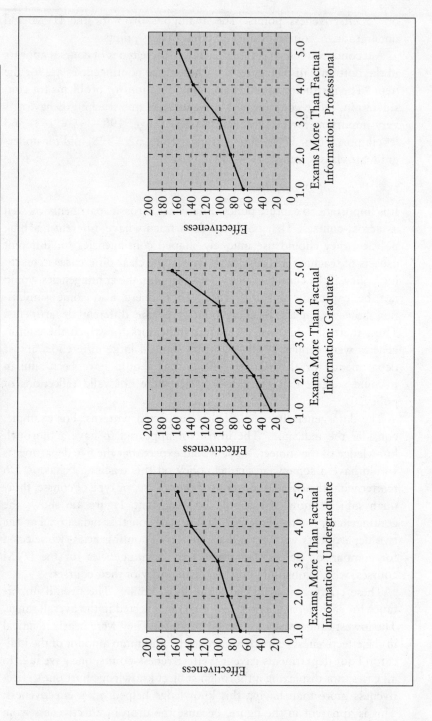

Figure 4.5.   Contingency Differences in Varied Course Types.

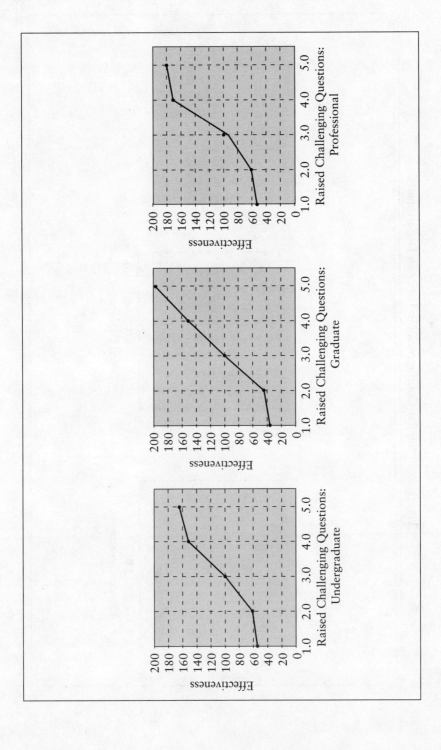

Figure 4.6. Similar Contingencies in Different Departments.

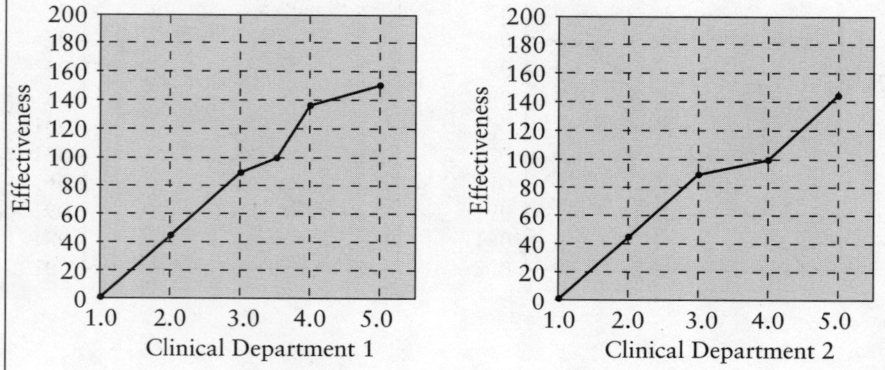

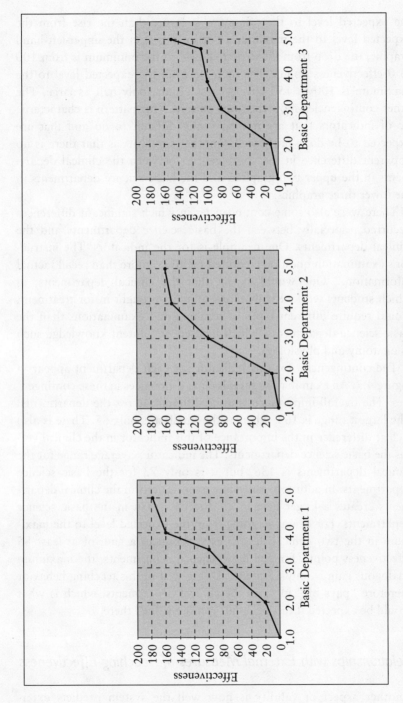

Indicator: The instructor appeared to have a thorough knowledge of the subject.

the expected level to the minimum is larger than the rise from the expected level to the maximum. For example, in the upper-left-hand graphic, the drop from the expected level to the minimum is from 100 to 0 effectiveness points. The increase from the expected level to the maximum is 100 to 150 effectiveness points, only half as large. The other contingencies show the same pattern. This pattern is characteristic of indicators that are not especially difficult to do and that are expected to be done fairly well. Another similarity is that there is no apparent difference in the contingencies between the clinical departments in the upper two graphics and the basic science departments in the lower three graphics.

There were also some contingencies in which significant differences occurred, especially between the basic science departments and the clinical departments. One example is for the indicator "The instructor's examination questions required me to do more than recall factual information." One would expect that the clinical departments, in which students worked with actual animals brought in for treatment, would require different types of teaching and examinations than the basic science departments, which focused on content knowledge such as anatomy and physiology.

The contingencies for this indicator for each department appear in Figure 4.7. An examination reveals clear differences in these contingencies. The overall importance is quite different across the departments. The largest range is 163, whereas the smallest is only 65. There is also a clear difference in the importance of this indicator in the clinical versus the basic science departments. The indicator's average range for the clinical departments is 136, but it is only 73 for the basic science departments. In addition, exceeding expectations in the clinical departments creates a larger gain in effectiveness than in the basic science departments. For example, going from the expected level to the maximum in the two clinical departments produces a gain of at least 85 effectiveness points. For the basic science departments, the maximum analogous gain is only 55 points. Doing well in this teaching behavior therefore "pays off" more in the clinical departments, which is what would be expected if this behavior is more valued there.

Relationships with External Measures of Teaching Effectiveness

Another aspect of validity is how well the system predicts external measures of teaching effectiveness. Even though there is no single criterion of effectiveness, some variables can serve as partial criteria.

We decided to use a type of peer rating as an external measure of teaching effectiveness.

To obtain peer ratings that would be as reliable and valid as possible, we asked department heads and faculty from the design committees for confidential nominations of all individuals whom they believed to be (1) highly effective classroom teachers, (2) teachers of average effectiveness, and (3) teachers of low effectiveness. We then examined these nominations.

Our intent was to have as pure a sample as possible of instructors who were high, medium, and low in teaching effectiveness. To do this, we included in the sample only those whom the different judges nominated for just one category and whom at least two people nominated for that category. For example, if two people nominated an instructor, but one nominated her for the most effective category whereas the other nominated her for the average category, we did not include her. If two or more people nominated someone for the most effective category and no one nominated him for any other category, then we included him. Twenty-nine instructors met these criteria: fifteen in the most effective group, eight in the average group, and six in the least effective group.

The next step was to compare the scores that the three groups received from the ProMES teaching evaluation system with their peer ratings. If the system is valid, it should clearly distinguish these three levels of instructors. The mean percentage of maximum scores for these three groups appear in Figure 4.8. A review of these means indicates that the faculty members judged to be the most effective had the highest percentage of maximum scores, those judged to be the least effective had the lowest percentage of maximum scores, and those judged to be of average effectiveness had a percentage of maximum scores in the middle. Therefore, there was some evidence to support the validity of the system.

To interpret such data better, one traditionally tests for statistical significance. Currently, however, a controversy surrounds the appropriateness of null hypothesis significance testing in the social sciences (for example, Cohen, 1994; Schmidt, 1992). Those in favor of abolishing significance testing argue that it gives distorted results that are not optimal, especially when one attempts to combine the information across studies. Instead of testing the significance of null hypotheses, they argue for using *effect sizes*—essentially the number of standard deviations of change from one group to another.

We find the arguments presented by those opposed to significance testing rather compelling. Much of the research community has not

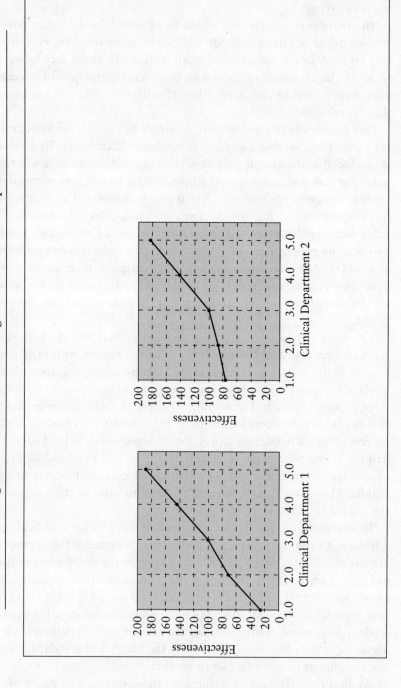

Figure 4.7. Dissimilar Contingencies in Different Departments.

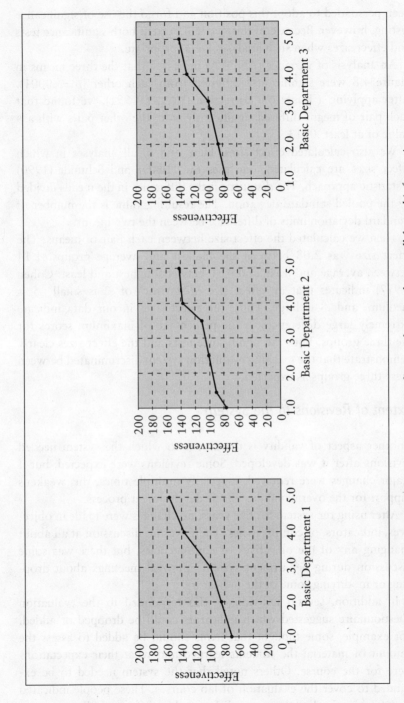

Indicator: The instructor's examination questions required me to do more than recall factual information.

been persuaded to adopt this position and forgo the use of significance testing, however. Because of this, we will present both significance tests and effect sizes when such analyses are appropriate.

An analysis of variance (ANOVA) indicated that the three means in Figure 4.8 were significantly different from each other ($p = .0001$). After applying a Bonferoni correction (Keppel, 1991), we found that each pair of means differed significantly from the other pairs with a p value of at least .0013.

We also calculated effect sizes. Here and in all analyses in which effect sizes are calculated, one uses the Hunter and Schmidt (1990) d-statistic approach. The d-statistic is the difference in the means divided by the pooled standard deviation. The resulting value is the number of standard deviation units of difference between the two means.

Then we calculated the effect size between each pair of means. The effect size was 2.08 between the highest and average groups, 1.14 between average and least, and 4.10 between highest and least. Cohen (1977) indicates that an effect size (d-statistic) of .2 is small, .5 is medium, and .8 is large. Thus, the effect sizes in our data indicate extremely large differences in the percentage of maximum scores for the three groups. Both the significance tests and the effect sizes clearly demonstrate that the teaching evaluation system discriminated between these three groups as expected.

Extent of Revisions to the System

Another aspect of validity is the extent to which the system needed revisions after it was developed. Some revisions were expected, but if major changes were required, especially multiple times, this weakens support for the overall validity of the development process.

After using the system for five years, no changes were made in objectives, indicators, or contingencies. There was no discussion at all about changing any of the objectives or contingencies, but there was some discussion during department system approval meetings about dropping or modifying some of the indicators.

In addition, several individuals who responded to the evaluation questionnaire suggested which indicators could be dropped or added. For example, some thought that items should be added to assess the amount of material the students learned and what their expectations were for the course. Others noted that the system needed to be expanded to cover the evaluation of lab courses. These people indicated that teaching in the lab was so different that different indicators were needed, not just the different contingencies that were already in use.

Figure 4.8.   Peer Evaluations Related to Teaching Effectiveness.

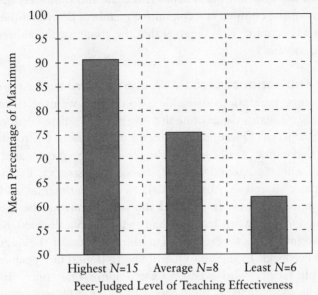

Because only a small minority of instructors made each of these sug-gestions, no changes were made. This suggests that the faculty and administrators saw the system as complete and accurate (that is, valid). To ensure that the system continued to reflect good teaching, the TEC decided to conduct an annual review to determine if there was a con-sensus to change any of the objectives or indicators. The department contingency committees were also encouraged to review the contingen-cies on an annual basis and to make any adjustments that the faculty deemed necessary.

The Perception of Validity

The final aspect of validity to be assessed is the perception of validity. Although the perception of validity does not necessarily mean that the system is valid, it is still an important issue. As with the other aspects of validity, this one factor is one piece in the entire construct validity picture.

DEVELOPMENT COMMITTEES. One source of validity perceptions comes from the committees designing the system. As shown in the De-sign Committee Questionnaire in Appendix B, TEC committee mem-bers were asked if they felt that the objectives and indicators were accu-rate and complete, and department contingency committee members were asked if the contingencies they had developed were accurate. All members of the TEC saw the system as accurate and complete, whereas 95 percent of the contingency committee members described the contingencies as accurate. This suggests that the committee members saw the system as valid.

FACULTY AND ADMINISTRATORS. We also measured the faculty's and administrators' perceptions of validity. To do this, we used three versions of an evaluation questionnaire. We sent the first version, the General Evaluation Questionnaire (found in Appendix C), to all faculty who had either (1) not been evaluated or (2) been evaluated only once. We sent the second version, the Administrative Evaluation Questionnaire (found in Appendix D), to all departmental and collegewide administrators. It included the same items as the General Evaluation Questionnaire but also had items specifically designed to measure administrators' reactions. The third version of the questionnaire, the Feedback Evaluation Questionnaire (found in Appendix E), went to all faculty who were evaluated more than once. It also included the same items as the General Evaluation Questionnaire, as well as additional items specifically designed to measure the reactions of faculty members who had the chance to improve their teaching performance based on system feedback.

The first two versions of this questionnaire (the General Evaluation Questionnaire and the Administrative Evaluation Questionnaire) were anonymous. The third version (the Feedback Evaluation Questionnaire) was not anonymous, because later analyses required the use of each individual's actual evaluation scores. Responses were in a five-point, agree or disagree format. Anchors were strongly agree (5), agree, neither agree nor disagree, disagree, and strongly disagree (1).

We pretested these questionnaires before administering them. This pilot test allowed us to ensure that the instruments and the instructions were clear and easy to understand, to conduct an item analysis, and to determine the instruments' internal consistency reliability. The details of this pretesting appear in Watson (1993).

QUESTIONNAIRE ADMINISTRATION. After the pretesting was completed, we distributed a total of 163 questionnaires to faculty and administrators. Of these people, 103 had been evaluated by the student evaluation system and 60 had not. They returned seventy-one questionnaires, for an overall return rate of 44 percent. Responses came from all five departments. The department with the largest representation comprised 25 percent of the sample, whereas the department with the smallest representation comprised 13 percent. Thus, all departments were represented.

Because only 44 percent of the questionnaires were returned, it was important to determine if those who responded to the questionnaire were representative of the faculty as a whole. Although one of the clinical departments was slightly underrepresented, the sample was fairly representative of the percentage of faculty affiliated with each department. The sample did not, however, accurately represent the number of faculty members evaluated. Of the faculty, 63 percent had been evaluated, whereas 85 percent of the sample had been evaluated. Thus, faculty who had been evaluated were overrepresented in the sample.

This was not surprising, because faculty who had not been evaluated were, for the most part, researchers who had very little classroom contact with students. Because they had few impressions of the student rating system and had not been meaningfully affected by it, it was not surprising that few of them chose to return the questionnaire. This also helps to explain why the general return rate was so low.

We also compared the teaching effectiveness scores of those who returned the questionnaires to the total. For all the data, 78 percent of the faculty received a percentage of maximum score of over 70 percent. Of those who returned the questionnaire, 78 percent had also received scores of over 70 percent. For all the data, 14 percent of the faculty received percentage of maximum scores between 60 percent and 69 percent, whereas for those who returned the questionnaire, only 13 percent received scores in that range. For all the data, 4 percent (11 people) received scores below 60 percent, whereas for those who returned the questionnaires, only 1.7 percent (1 person) scored this low. These results suggest that although the respondents' overall pattern of teaching effectiveness scores matched the pattern for the entire group, faculty who received the lowest teaching effectiveness ratings were underrepresented in the sample.

QUESTIONNAIRE RESULTS. Along with a series of other variables to be discussed later in this chapter, these questionnaires measured perceived validity. Each version of the evaluation questionnaire included four validity items, as Table 4.1 illustrates. The table shows the number of respondents *(N),* the mean, and the standard deviation. It also shows the percentage of respondents who either agreed or strongly agreed with the item (percent A + SA) and the percentage who disagreed or strongly

Table 4.1. Perceived Validity.

Item	N	Mean	SD	A + SA (percent)	D + SD (percent)
In general, I believe the student rating system is valid.	64	3.23	1.18	59	27
The student rating system includes all the important aspects of classroom teaching that students are able to observe.	66	3.26	1.13	58	24
Student ratings should be part of a comprehensive teacher evaluation system.	62	3.93	0.85	84	6
The students here are able to rate my classroom teaching performance accurately.	60	3.20	1.04	50	25

disagreed (percent D + SD). To simplify the presentation of these results, we will refer to these two values as the percentages agreeing and disagreeing. Note that these two percentages do not add up to 100 percent because the neutral response is not included.

The table indicates that the perceptions of validity were mixed. Most people do not want to be evaluated, though, so it is difficult for those being measured to endorse the validity of a system enthusiastically. This is especially true for instructors who received lower ratings than expected. Based on our experience, we would consider it positive if approximately two-thirds of the people being evaluated saw the system as valid. Overall, the values were close to this, but with a rating of 59 percent, the item most directly tapping validity was a bit below this.

In order to understand these mixed results more fully, we did additional analyses. One set of analyses separated out those faculty who had a fundamental disagreement with the idea that students should do faculty teaching evaluations. Such faculty would find any system that included student ratings invalid. Faculty in this category disagreed that students should be part of the evaluation system or that students could rate accurately.

There were fifteen individuals in this category. We removed them from the sample, leaving fifty-six respondents. We then recalculated the percentage of respondents. In this group, 71 percent of the respondents agreed that the system was valid, whereas only 12 percent disagreed.

Thus, removing those who felt students were not a valid source of data meaningfully increased the number of faculty who perceived the system to be valid.

Another issue to explore with the perceived validity data is to compare it by department. It was clear to us that three of the departments had a much more positive attitude toward the system than the other two. To determine whether this also held true for validity perceptions, we did this analysis by department. Of those who responded from the two clinical departments, 23 percent agreed that the system was valid; from the basic departments, 83 percent thought so. The percentage disagreeing that the system was valid was 49 percent for the clinics and 13 percent for the basic departments. Thus, there was a very large difference in the perceptions of the two types of departments. The basic departments perceived a high validity, whereas the clinics saw the system as having low validity.

Summary of Results for Research Question 2

Overall, the answer to this research question is positive. The developed system was valid. Many sources of information go into the validity issue. These results are summarized below.

- The indicators appeared to be of high quality. The development process was done well and was complete. The objectives and indicators that were developed were consistent with the literature.

- The student ratings showed good variability across instructors, as did the ProMES effectiveness scores and percentage of maximum scores.

- Internal consistency reliabilities were high. Interjudge reliability was high, except for very small classes. This lower reliability for small classes is not really a problem if one makes judgments of teaching effectiveness by using multiple classes.

- Potential bias from having the instructor present and having the students know that evaluations will be used for personnel decisions was controlled by never having the instructor present during evaluations and by always telling the students that the ratings would be used for personnel decisions.

- Generalized negative ratings, another source of potential bias, were not a problem.

- The potential advantages of the ProMES contingencies did occur. Nonlinearities were present in the vast majority of indicators. There were clear differences in the importance of the indicators in each contingency set. Those departments that developed contingency sets for different courses developed contingencies that were similar when indicators were expected to be similar and different when dissimilarities would be expected in indicators. The contingencies also appeared to capture various policies across different departments accurately.

- The evaluations produced by the system were clearly related to reliably developed independent peer evaluations.

- Major revisions did not have to be made to the system.

- Perceptions of validity by the development committees were high. Perceptions by faculty were adequate. A strong majority of the faculty in the basic science departments saw the system as valid, but many fewer faculty members in the clinics did. When faculty who philosophically opposed the idea of using students to rate faculty were removed from the sample, the large majority saw the system as valid.

RESEARCH QUESTION 3: WILL TEACHING EFFECTIVENESS IMPROVE WITH FEEDBACK FROM THE SYSTEM?

Because one of the key objectives of the project was to give feedback that would help instructors improve teaching effectiveness, a critical question is whether the system actually accomplished that objective.

Teaching Effectiveness After Feedback

To assess whether the feedback caused improvement, we examined teaching effectiveness over time. We considered the first feedback reports given to instructors as the baseline, because the instructor's first feedback report evaluated teaching done without benefit of feedback from the system. We then compared these scores with the scores of successive semesters.

Selecting individuals to be used in this analysis was complicated by the fact that students in different levels of courses (that is, undergraduates, graduates, and professional students) differ in the mean ratings they give instructors (Aleamoni, 1981; Braskamp, Brandenburg, & Ory, 1984). Although the ProMES contingencies can neutralize these differences, not all departments chose to use different contingency sets to do this.

To deal with this potential problem, we included in the analysis only instructors who taught the same level of class (undergraduate, graduate, or professional). For example, if an instructor taught an undergraduate course for three semesters, she would be included in the data as having taught for three semesters. If that same instructor then taught a graduate course for the first time in the fourth semester, she would not be counted as having taught a fourth semester, because this would be a different level of course.

As it turned out, including only instructors who taught courses at the same level over multiple semesters had very little effect on the overall results. The sample size for all the data when the matching was not done was only slightly larger than the sample size for matched data. Apparently, the vast majority of instructors teach the same pattern of courses over time. Thus, the conclusions from the unmatched data would be the same as the matched.

Of the available data, 86 individuals were evaluated at the same class level two different times. Of those 86 individuals, 54 were evaluated a third time, and of those 54, 24 were evaluated a fourth time. There were not enough instructors who were evaluated more than four times to provide reliable results, so these analyses were limited to four semesters of evaluation. Specifically, only 13 instructors were evaluated five times and only 8 of these were evaluated six times.

Figure 4.9 shows the initial analyses of these data. The upper left quadrant displays the data based on the largest sample, those evaluated twice. The figure indicates that the baseline mean for these instructors was approximately 78 percent of maximum. After feedback, the mean rose to approximately 81 percent of maximum. The upper right quadrant shows that for those evaluated three times, their teaching effectiveness continued to rise. The lower left quadrant shows that the increase seems to be maintained over four evaluations.

The lower right quadrant presents comparison group data. These data come from thirty-eight departments in four colleges (liberal arts, business, architecture, and agriculture) at the same university. The number of individual student evaluations making up the mean in each semester ranges from a low of 34,880 to a high of 53,689. The approximate number of classes making up each semester mean ranges from a low of 450 to a high of more than 700. These data come from the traditional teaching evaluation system used by these departments. The CVM had never used this traditional system. The comparison group

Figure 4.9.   Changes in Teaching Effectiveness over Time.

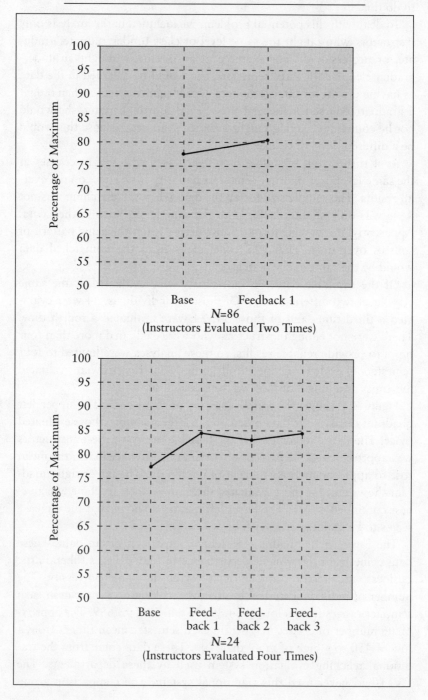

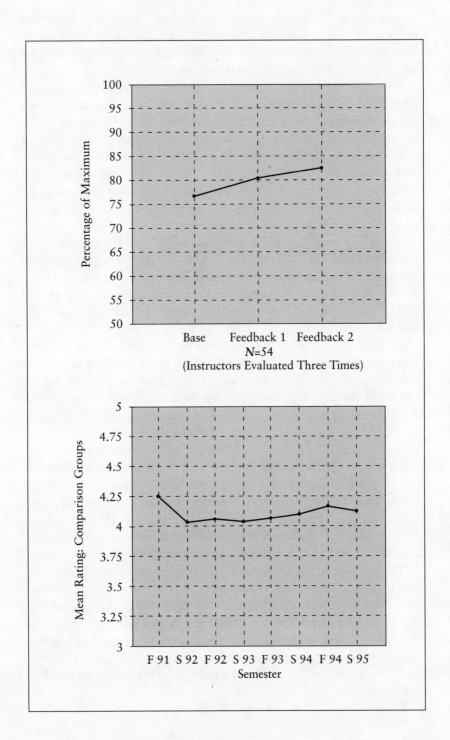

system is based on a questionnaire that students complete at the end of the semester. The means of these student ratings are provided to the instructor, the department, and the college administrators each semester. The evaluations are done on a five-point scale.

We attempted to express the results on a similar scale so that relative changes in the figures between the ProMES system and the comparison groups would be as comparable as possible. The three graphs of the ProMES effects range from a percentage of maximum of 50 percent up to 100 percent, the highest possible score. Of course, percentage of maximum in the ProMES sense was not available for the comparison group data. To match this range as closely as possible, we made the scale for the comparison groups go from the mean of that rating scale (3.0) to the maximum possible score (5.0).

We did significance tests on the means of the ProMES data in Figure 4.9 using an ANOVA *(F)* test. The *p* values for the overall *F*'s appear in Table 4.2 for the data from two periods (Baseline and Feedback 1) and for the data with three and four periods. In all cases, this overall *F* is highly significant, indicating that the means are different from one another.

In addition, we made a priori mean comparisons (Keppel, 1991), comparing the baseline mean with the mean of the feedback periods. In the case of the data with only two periods, these two analyses are the same. For the data with more than one feedback period, however, they are different. The table shows that in all cases, the mean percentage of maximum under feedback is significantly higher than baseline.

We also calculated effect sizes, comparing the baseline mean to the mean percentage of maximum under feedback. For example, the effect size shown for four periods compares the baseline mean with the mean of the three feedback semesters. We calculated this mean for three feedback semesters by taking each instructor's mean over these three feedback semesters. These effect sizes show a small improvement for the first semester, increasing to a moderate improvement after three semesters.

Taken together, the graphs in Figure 4.9 indicate a small but meaningful increase in teaching effectiveness after one semester of feedback and a moderate increase after that. The figure also indicates that over the same time period as the ProMES system, there was no overall increase in the level of teaching effectiveness throughout the university. Thus, the improvement in teaching effectiveness in the CVM could not be attributed to university-wide improvements in teaching effectiveness.

Table 4.2. Teaching Effectiveness over Time: Means, Effect Sizes, and p Values.

	MEANS				OVERALL F	COMPARISON OF BASELINE TO MEAN OF FEEDBACK PERIODS	
	Baseline	Feedback1	Feedback 2	Feedback 3	p Value	Effect Size	p Value
2 Periods	77.6	80.4			.022	.22	.022
3 Periods	76.4	80.3	82.4		.001	.44	<.001
4 Periods	77.8	84.5	83.1	84.3	.008	.57	<.01

Change in Teaching Effectiveness by Initial Effectiveness Level

To interpret the data further, we looked at the effects of the feedback as a function of initial level of teaching effectiveness. We believed that someone who taught well initially would have little room to improve. As indicated by their teaching scores, many of the instructors in the CVM were good instructors before we implemented ProMES. Thus, this large number of good instructors could be masking some of the system's effects.

To do this analysis, we classified the instructors as high, medium, and low initial performers. We did this by examining the frequency distribution of percentage of maximum scores in Figure 4.2. There seemed to be three distinct groups in this frequency distribution: high scorers with percentage of maximum scores above 80, a middle group with scores between 56 and 80, and a lower group with scores below 56. Using these intervals, we categorized all instructors as being in the high, medium, or low group based on their scores the first time they were evaluated by the system.

Once we formed these subgroups, we first analyzed those who had been evaluated twice. This analysis is shown graphically in the upper left quadrant of Figure 4.10. For each of the three subgroups, the baseline and feedback means are shown. The sample sizes for each group appear at the bottom of the graphics.

This graphic shows that those instructors who were initially high performers did not change significantly after their first feedback from the system. Those who were initially medium performers showed large changes, however, and those who were initially low performers showed dramatic increases in teaching effectiveness.

The appropriate test of significance for these differences is to measure the relation between the changes. We did an ANOVA for three groups by two time periods; the group by time interaction was significant at $p < .001$. This indicates that the change after feedback was significantly different for the three groups. The effect sizes for the three groups were as follows: $-.13$ for the high group, $.40$ for the medium group, and 2.06 for the low group. This indicates no appreciable change for the instructors who were initially very good, a moderate improvement for those who were initially medium, and a very large increase for those instructors initially low in effectiveness.

It was difficult to continue these analyses over a longer period, because the number of low performers with two or more semesters of feedback was too low to analyze separately. To compensate for this, we combined the low and medium groups to increase the sample size. The upper right graph shows the result of this combination for those evaluated twice, and the two lower graphs show the results for those evaluated three and four times. In all cases, the group by time period interaction was statistically significant with a p value of .004 or less.

These results confirm very clearly that the amount of improvement from the system depended on the initial level of teaching effectiveness. Those who were lower in performance showed very strong increases in teaching effectiveness, whereas those who were in the middle showed moderate improvements, and those who were initially effective instructors did not change as a result of the system.

Frequency of Low Performers

Another way to look at the effects on low performers is to examine the frequency of low-performing instructors before and after feedback from the system. To do this, we needed a definition of low performance that would include more instructors in the analysis. Low performers were defined as those whose first-semester evaluation (baseline) was at or below the mean percentage of maximum score of those instructors who had been identified by their peers as low performers. This mean is shown in Figure 4.8, which shows the comparison of the student evaluations with peer evaluations. The figure indicates that the mean score of low-performing instructors was 62. Thus, any evaluation with a percentage of maximum of 62 percent or less was treated as low.

In the first analysis, we calculated the percentage of low performers evaluated one time, the percentage evaluated two times, and so forth. The results of this analysis appear in the upper half of Figure 4.11. The data are shown for six semesters. There were 139 instructors evaluated once, as noted by the N for the first semester. Only eight instructors were evaluated for six semesters. The figure shows a dramatic drop in the number of low performers. Although more than 12 percent of those evaluated only once were low performers, for those who were evaluated more than four times, the percentage had dropped to zero. Thus, after feedback from the system, those who were initially low performers increased their teaching effectiveness.

We also examined the data by year. That is, we looked at what percentage of the evaluations were low the year the feedback started (1991) and how the percentage changed over time. Again, the effects are dramatic. When the feedback first started in 1991, almost 13

Figure 4.10.   Changes in Teaching Effectiveness by Initial Score.

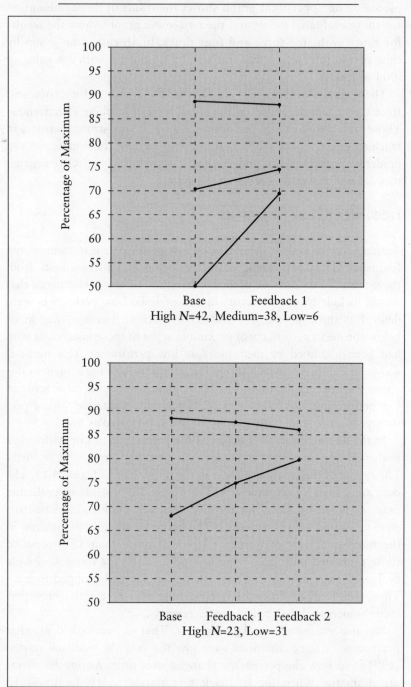

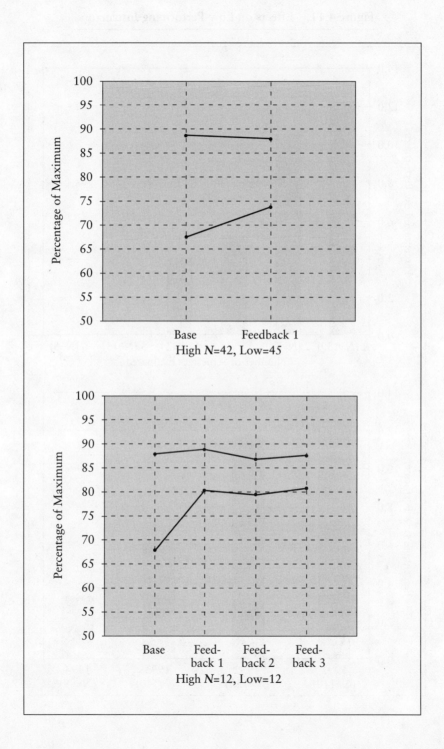

High N=42, Low=45

High N=12, Low=12

Figure 4.11.   Effects on Low-Performing Instructors.

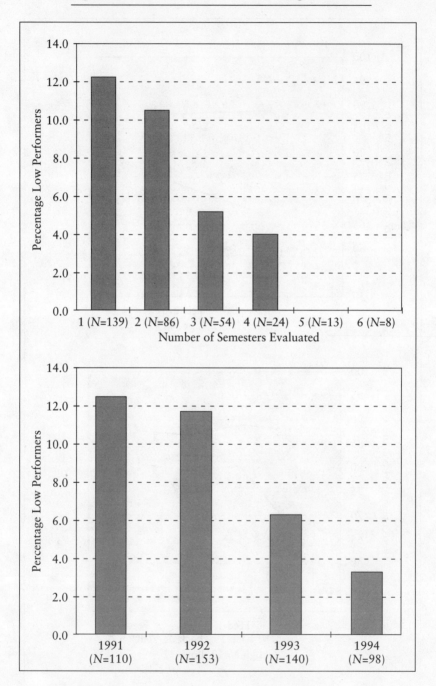

percent of the 110 instructors evaluated were low performers. By 1994, only about 3 percent were low. Thus, there were more than four times as many low evaluations in 1991 as in 1994.

One explanation for why the frequency of low performers decreases over time is that the low performers were no longer teaching. This explanation is unlikely, however, given the results in Figure 4.10. There, the *same* instructors are measured over time; in all the analyses, the low-performing instructors show the largest improvements. To evaluate attrition further as a possible explanation of the results, we looked at the instructors from 1991 to 1994. For the high-performing instructors (percentage of maximum scores above 80) who had evaluations in 1991, 43 percent also had evaluations in 1994. For the instructors who were low performers in 1991, 40 percent had evaluations in 1994. Thus, there was no meaningful differential loss of low-performing instructors. When we take these results together, it seems clear that the number of low-performing instructors decreased because their teaching performance increased.

Summary of Results for Research Question 3

Overall, the answer to Research Question 3 is that feedback from the system did have a positive effect on teaching effectiveness.

- There was a small to moderate improvement in teaching effectiveness when all instructors were combined.
- The improvement was maintained at least over three semesters.
- During this period, there were no corresponding improvements in teaching effectiveness in other units of the university.
- The teaching effectiveness of instructors who were initially highly effective did not change significantly as a result of feedback from the system. Those who were initially moderate in teaching effectiveness showed moderate improvements. Those instructors who were initially low in teaching effectiveness showed dramatic improvements and maintained these improvements for at least three semesters.
- The number of low-performing instructors decreased dramatically after teachers received feedback from the system.

RESEARCH QUESTION 4: DO FACULTY AND ADMINISTRATORS SEE THE RESULTING SYSTEM AS VALUABLE?

This teaching evaluation system is complex and costly to develop, especially in terms of faculty time. Therefore, it is important to determine whether college personnel saw ProMES as valuable.

Perceptions of Usefulness and Cost-Effectiveness: Faculty

One element of value is the system's perceived usefulness and cost-effectiveness. We included items to measure these perceptions in all three forms of the evaluation questionnaire in Appendixes C, D, and E. Three items assessed the way faculty perceived the system's usefulness and accepted it. The items asked if the system produced results that had been helpful for (1) self-improvement, (2) departmental evaluations, and (3) college administration's evaluations of faculty. An additional item directly assessed the faculty's perception of the system's cost-effectiveness by asking if faculty believed that the benefits of using the system outweighed its costs. Means, standard deviations, and response frequencies for these items appear in Table 4.3.

The table indicates that although most faculty felt that the system helped them improve, there was clearly a mixed reaction to the other items. Before we interpret these results, however, we need to consider differences across departments.

Further analysis of the data indicated great differences in the reactions of different departments. As in the case of the validity perceptions, the three basic science departments were much more positive than the two clinical departments. For example, on the cost-effectiveness question, the average percentage agreeing that the system was cost effective in the basic science departments was 67 percent, whereas only 11 percent disagreed. For the two clinical departments, the respective figures were 4 percent and 58 percent. The same pattern occurred with all the items. In sum, the basic departments were quite positive, whereas the clinical departments were quite negative.

Perceptions of Usefulness and Cost-Effectiveness: Administrators

Departmental and collegewide administrators (that is, department heads, associate deans, and the dean) were also asked about the system's usefulness and cost-effectiveness. The results appear in Table 4.4. The results indicate that the administrators generally viewed the system

Table 4.3. Perceptions of Usefulness and Cost-Effectiveness: Faculty.

Item	N	Mean	SD	A + SA (percent)	D + SD (percent)
The student rating system has produced results that have been useful in *helping me improve* my teaching performance.	62	3.35	1.01	58	16
The student rating system produces results that are useful in *helping the administrators in my department evaluate* the quality of teaching.	60	2.95	1.17	40	35
The student rating system produces results that are useful in *helping the College administrators evaluate* the quality of teaching at the CVM.	62	2.95	1.17	39	32
The student rating system provides benefits that outweigh the costs (e.g., time, energy, effort, etc.) of using it.	64	3.16	1.07	42	27

quite positively—more positively than the faculty did. The only item on which administrators were not highly positive related to cost-effectiveness. We believe that the lower percentage of agreement on this item may result from the department heads in the clinical departments.

Satisfaction with the System

In addition to perceptions of usefulness and cost-effectiveness, we looked at faculty satisfaction with the system. We used four items to assess the faculty's overall level of satisfaction and included the items in

Table 4.4.　Perceptions of Usefulness
and Cost-Effectiveness: Administration.

Item	N	Mean	SD	A + SA (percent)	D + SD (percent)
The student rating system has produced results that have been useful in *helping me improve* my teaching performance.	3	4.00	0	100	0
The student rating system produces results that are useful in *helping the administrators in my department evaluate* the quality of teaching.	4	3.75	.58	75	0
The student rating system produces results that are useful in *helping the College administrators evaluate* the quality of teaching at the CVM.	6	4.00	.40	83	0
The student rating system provides benefits that outweigh the costs (e.g., time, energy, effort, etc.) of using it.	7	3.57	1.07	57	14

the evaluation questionnaires in Appendixes C, D, and E. Those items had the same five-point, agree or disagree format described previously. The items assessed the level of satisfaction participants felt about the system's design, implementation, and use. Table 4.5 summarizes the results. They show that although satisfaction with the design of the system was moderately high, satisfaction with the implementation of the system and the use of the data was quite low.

As with the other attitude analyses, we broke down the satisfaction results by department. As before, the basic science departments were substantially more satisfied than the clinical departments. For example, for the item on satisfaction with the system's design, 74 percent of fac-

Table 4.5.   Faculty Satisfaction with the System.

Item	N	Mean	SD	A + SA (percent)	D + SD (percent)
In general, I am satisfied with the design of the student rating system (e.g., items on the student rating form, the contingencies, and the feedback reports).	65	3.88	0.98	55	22
In general, I am satisfied with the implementation of the student rating system (e.g., scheduling of the evaluations, decisions regarding who will be evaluated and how often, the speed with which feedback is received, etc.).	65	2.54	1.13	26	52
In general, I am satisfied with how the administration in my department uses the data from the student rating system.	50	3.02	1.06	36	26
In general, I expect I will be satisfied with how the College Administration (i.e., the Deans and Associate Deans) will use the data from the student rating system.	57	2.70	1.07	23	35

ulty in the basic science departments were satisfied, whereas only 8 percent were dissatisfied. In contrast, for the clinical departments, the analogous percentages were 34 percent and 37 percent. For the item on department administrators' use of the data, 45 percent of faculty across the basic science departments were satisfied and 15 percent were dissatisfied. For the clinical departments, however, the analogous percentages were 25 percent and 48 percent.

In addition to measuring faculty's satisfaction with the system, we also explored the following factors to see if they were related to satisfaction: (1) the level of participation in the system's design, (2) the level of ratings received, (3) the evaluation's consistency with the instructor's expectations, and (4) the extent to which the teacher believed that evaluations would be used for tenure and other rewards. Items in the questionnaires in Appendixes C and E assessed all of these measures.

Although these analyses are discussed more fully in Watson (1993), we can summarize the overall results here. Two factors showed significant correlations with satisfaction with the system: perceived validity ($r = .59$, $p < .0001$) and degree of participation in the system's design ($r = .36$, $p < .004$). The correlations with self-reported evaluations, match with expectations, and perceived consequences were all insignificant, ranging between $-.01$ and $.07$, with all p values being greater than .62.

Continued Use of the System

Although perceptions of usefulness, cost-effectiveness, and satisfaction are important, the ultimate criterion of value is whether the system continues to be used after its development. Our involvement in the use of this student rating system ended after the first semester, with the exception of occasional questions that arose. Since that time, the CVM has completely administered the system. At the time of this writing, the system has been in continuous use for six years since its development. Therefore, in the overall judgment of the college, the system was indeed worthwhile.

In addition, the dean, associate deans, and department heads declared during the fourth semester that the student rating system was to be used throughout the college for administrative reviews of teaching, as well as for developmental feedback (prior to this decision, the system had been used only for developmental feedback). This statement of policy indicated the administrators' clear support of the system and was further evidence that the system would continue to be used.

Summary of Results for Research Question 4

As a whole, the perceptions of the system's value when measured by questionnaires were generally positive. The questionnaire results also revealed, however, that some CVM personnel had doubts about the system's value. For example, administrators and those in the basic science departments were very positive, whereas faculty members in the clinical departments were negative. Yet the system has been in continuous use since it was implemented in 1991.

- The faculty's perception of usefulness and cost-effectiveness was mixed.
- Faculty members in the basic science departments had a much more positive reaction to the system's usefulness and cost-effectiveness than faculty in the clinical departments.
- Overall, administrators were quite positive about the system's usefulness and cost-effectiveness.
- Satisfaction with the system's design was fairly high; satisfaction with the system's implementation was low.
- Satisfaction with the system's design and implementation was higher in the basic science departments than in the clinical departments.
- Satisfaction with the system was significantly correlated with perceived validity of the system and degree of participation in the system's design. Satisfaction was not significantly related to self-reported evaluations, match between evaluations and expected evaluations, or perceived consequences of the evaluations.
- Most important, the system is still in use.

RESEARCH QUESTION 5: IS THE NEW SYSTEM BETTER THAN TRADITIONAL SYSTEMS?

The ProMES approach to measuring and improving teaching effectiveness is more involved and more difficult to use than traditional teaching evaluation systems. Because of this, it was important to determine

whether the system produced results that were better than more traditional systems. In posing this question, we assume that *traditional systems* are questionnaires that ask students to rate instructors on a
quantitative scale. Afterward, the means and frequency distributions of
these ratings are reported to faculty and administrators.

Impact on Teaching Effectiveness

One way to compare traditional systems to the ProMES system is to
refer back to the ProMES system's effects on teaching evaluations and
to measure those results against the comparison group data. Because
the comparison group used a traditional student evaluation system,
this comparison is relevant. These results appear in the lower right
quadrant of Figure 4.9.

The results clearly indicate that teaching effectiveness with the
ProMES system improved more than with the traditional system.
Although these results support the conclusion that the ProMES system
was superior, however, they do not demonstrate this conclusively.
There are two problems in making this comparison. First, we cannot
directly compare the two types of scores, percentage of maximum versus mean student ratings, because they are different metrics. We cannot
even compare the underlying mean student ratings of the ProMES system with that of the comparison groups, because they are different
items. Thus, any comparison of the absolute level of teaching effectiveness under the two systems is not possible. We are left with comparing
the amount of change produced by the two approaches.

This leads us to the second problem. Specifically, these data do not
compare the introduction of a student-based quantitative evaluation
system for both groups. The comparison group data were based on
departments that had used that system for some time. Because it was
not newly introduced, as was the ProMES system in the CVM, it is not
appropriate to conclude that the ProMES system produced improvements and the traditional system did not or that the ProMES system is
therefore superior.

The CVM did have another type of teaching evaluation system in
place before we introduced the ProMES system, however. The original
system was a qualitative evaluation in which students answered several
questions about the course, instructor, and curriculum. The faculty and
the administration received copies of these written answers. Consequently, we can at least say that meaningful improvement occurred

when the ProMES system replaced this qualitative type of teaching evaluation system.

Another way of answering the question of whether the ProMES system was superior comes from comparing the gain in teaching effectiveness under the ProMES system with the gain reported in the literature from using traditional systems.

This literature indicates that feedback from teaching evaluations using student ratings can cause higher ratings of teaching effectiveness (for example, Aleamoni, 1974; Centra, 1972, 1973a; Doyle, 1975; Miller, 1972; Pambookian, 1973, 1974; Root, 1931). Two meta-analyses have been done on this literature (Cohen, 1980; L'Hommedieu, Menges, & Brinko, 1990). In the most recent review, L'Hommedieu, Menges, and Brinko looked at twenty-eight studies. Most of these studies used a pretest and posttest design with a control group that received no feedback. The experimental groups received feedback (that is, student ratings) at midsemester and at the end of the semester. Control groups only received ratings at the end of the semester. Researchers examined the change in ratings from midsemester to the end of the semester. The second set of ratings showed an increase over the first, with an average effect size of 0.34. The earlier meta-analysis by Cohen (1980) found an average effect size of 0.38.

The effect sizes of the improvements that ProMES produced were 0.22 after one semester, 0.44 after two, and 0.57 after three. These results are difficult to compare. The meta-analysis data come from studies in which students gave feedback during the semester and then did a second rating at the end of that semester. One could argue that this design maximizes the chances for improvement, because the teaching behaviors with which that particular group of students are concerned are very salient and the instructor has the opportunity to change those specific behaviors before the next evaluation. With an approach that spans semesters, the instructor loses the ability to tailor any changes in teaching behavior to the concerns of that particular group of students. Therefore, one might expect smaller effect sizes with ProMES. On the other hand, having data over several semesters to make changes and to see their results could in time produce larger effects.

One needs to keep these problems of interpretation in mind. We can say, however, that if one compares data only from one semester, the traditional systems are slightly better at improving teaching effectiveness. If we look at data over time, the ProMES system shows larger improvements than those reported in the literature.

Effects of ProMES on Extreme Evaluations and on Improvement Priorities

Another way to evaluate the comparative value of the ProMES teaching evaluation system is to see whether using it leads people to make different decisions than they would make with more traditional methods. We will examine two types of decisions—those related to the composition of extreme groups and priorities for making improvements in teaching. In other settings, ProMES has been shown to cause quite different decisions than other methods of obtaining overall scores (Pritchard and Roth, 1991). The question, however, is whether ProMES and traditional methods would find similar results in this setting.

COMPOSITION OF EXTREME GROUPS. The first issue is whether ProMES contingencies change the composition of extreme groups of instructors, meaning those who are extremely good or extremely poor. Many of the uses of teaching evaluations have consequences for instructors in these extreme groups. For example, various types of teaching awards, raises for teaching, tenure decisions, and other forms of special recognition go to the best teachers. The poorest teachers have special counseling, remedial training, and problems obtaining tenure. Thus, it is very important to determine the membership in these extreme groups of best and worst instructors.

One way to assess the impact of the contingencies is to see if using ProMES changes the membership in these extreme groups. For example, if the best and worst teachers are the same people when measured by ProMES as when measured by more traditional methods, ProMES has less unique value as an evaluation method. Put another way, if there is no difference in the composition of these extreme groups when ProMES is used, then both methods lead to exactly the same decisions.

To make this comparison, we will examine the overall teaching effectiveness score produced by ProMES and compare it with overall scores generated by more traditional methods. We will examine three of these more traditional methods.

In the first method, the overall teaching effectiveness score is based on the mean student rating. The average rating on each item across the students in the class is first calculated. Then the mean of all the items is calculated. This produces a single number for the mean overall teaching effectiveness for the instructor for that course.

As part of the next method of evaluation, the students are asked to make an overall judgment of the instructor's effectiveness. This is typically done with a single item. The overall index is the mean student rating on this one overall item. This method allows the students to combine the various aspects of teaching in any way they choose.

In the third method, an attempt is made to weight the student evaluation items by how important they are. For example, if Item 3 is twice as important as Item 6, Item 3 is multiplied by 2 before the two items are averaged. Students can determine the importance weights, but the faculty more typically assigns them. To calculate the overall score, one multiplies students' mean rating on an item by the weighting factor. One then averages these products to arrive at a single number, which is the overall teaching effectiveness score.

In comparing ProMES with these more traditional methods, we will look at four overall measures of teaching effectiveness. To generate the four measures, we did the following calculations:

1. We found the mean rating of the seventeen items for all the students in the class.

2. We determined the mean for all students in the class on a single item assessing overall teaching effectiveness. This item was not part of the normal student rating form; we added it to a sample of ratings to do this analysis. Thus, for these classes, there was an eighteenth item: "Overall, this instructor demonstrated effective teaching." The response format for this item was the same frequency format used for all the other items.

3. We multiplied the mean rating provided by the students on each of the seventeen items by an importance rating, which the faculty provided. We determined this importance rating by first asking the contingency committee in each department to rate the importance of each of the seventeen items on scale from 1 to 9. We then averaged these ratings across the committee members. This resulted in seventeen importance weights for each department. We determined the overall score by multiplying the importance weight for that department by the mean student rating on that item and averaging the products.

4. We found the ProMES overall score simply by using the average overall effectiveness score that came from the instructor reports.

The data used for these analyses were collected in fall 1992 when seventy-two instructors were evaluated. An average of 130 students were in each class and the total number of student evaluations was 8,840. For each of the seventy-two evaluations, we calculated the four different overall indexes of teaching effectiveness.

The first way of comparing the overall performance scores produced by the four methods is simply to correlate them. These correlations appear in Table 4.6. The correlations are very high between the four methods. ProMES correlates with the other methods in the high 80s and low 90s. This could be interpreted as indicating that ProMES does not add much to any of the other three methods. This conclusion is not warranted from these correlations, however.

Mathematically, no matter how they are weighted, composites formed from the same variables (items) will correlate very highly with each other when there are more than ten items and there are even moderate correlations between the variables (Wilks, 1938; Ree, Carretta, & Earles, 1997). Because there were seventeen items and some correlation is expected between different aspects of teaching, extremely high correlations are expected simply on a mathematical basis. Furthermore, as Pritchard and Roth (1991) have shown, even with highly nonlinear contingencies, correlation coefficients are poor indexes of whether the composites lead to different decisions.

A more appropriate method is actually to examine the composition of extreme groups. To do this, we used each set of overall teaching effectiveness scores to identify high- and low-scoring instructors. If the individuals that ProMES identifies as being the top instructors (for example, the top 5 percent) are the same as those identified by the other methods, then ProMES is not adding anything unique to the decisions made about these instructors. If, however, the individuals identi-

Table 4.6.   Correlations Between the Four Methods.

	Mean Rating	*Overall Rating*	*Mean Multiplied by Importance*	*ProMES*
Mean	1.00			
Overall	.96	1.00		
Mean multiplied by importance	.97	.91	1.00	
ProMES	.92	.93	.87	1.00

fied by ProMES are different from those that other methods identify, then ProMES is adding unique information.

To make this comparison, we identified instructors in the top and bottom 2 percent, 5 percent, 10 percent, and 20 percent by using the overall score from each of the four methods. Next, we compared the percentage of instructors who were *different* in the ProMES method with those from the other three methods. For example, in the analysis involving the top 10 percent of instructors, the top 10 percent based on the ProMES overall score was compared to the top 10 percent as determined by the average student rating method. If the exact same set of instructors were in both groups, there would be 0 percent difference. If none of the top 10 percent based on ProMES were in the top 10 percent group based on mean student ratings, there would be 100 percent difference. We made similar comparisons for the overall student rating method and the mean student rating weighted by importance method.

Results of these analyses appear in Table 4.7. Pairs of rows show the different types of extreme group examined (bottom and top 2 percent, 5 percent, 10 percent, and 20 percent). The middle three columns show results for the three methods being compared to ProMES, and the last column presents the mean of each of these three methods. The cell

Table 4.7. Changes in Group Composition Between ProMES and the Other Methods.

		METHOD			
Percentage (Overall N = 72)		Mean Rating (percent)	Overall Rating (percent)	Mean Multiplied by Importance (percent)	Mean of Three Methods (percent)
2	Bottom	50	100	50	67
	Top	33	67	33	44
5	Bottom	25	0	75	33
	Top	25	50	25	33
10	Bottom	14	14	43	24
	Top	25	75	75	58
20	Bottom	14	14	21	16
	Top	25	50	33	36
Overall	Bottom	41	46	58	48
	Top	22	48	33	34
Combined					41

entries represent the percentage of instructors identified by ProMES who are not in the analogous group for the other methods.

For example, in the bottom 2 percent group, 50 percent of the instructors ProMES put into this group differ from the instructors that the mean student rating technique assigned to this group. Of the instructors ProMES put into this group, 100 percent differ from the instructors that the overall student rating method put into this group.

The results are very clear. ProMES puts very different instructors into the top and bottom groups, compared with the other three methods. If we combine top and bottom and all percentages, we see that 41 percent of the instructors selected by ProMES differ from those that the other methods selected. If teaching awards, raises, and decisions about tenure and termination were made on the basis of these teaching evaluations, very different people would be receiving these positive and negative consequences under ProMES than under the other methods. Thus, when it comes to the composition of extreme groups, ProMES leads to very different decisions.

CHANGES IN IMPROVEMENT PRIORITIES. The previous discussion focused on the evaluation aspects of the ProMES approach. A second way to evaluate ProMES's unique contribution is to focus on its feedback aspects, which are designed to cause improvements in teaching. Specifically, we can compare the ways that the different methods suggest for instructors to improve.

Based on the contingencies, ProMES makes very specific recommendations about what teaching factors (items) to focus on to improve teaching effectiveness maximally. By indicating in the feedback report how much gain can be made in overall effectiveness by improving in each of the items, ProMES suggests priorities for enhancing performance. Chapter Three further discusses this aspect of the feedback reports, and Table 3.3 provides an example.

Two of the methods examined here do not give any information on priorities for making improvements. Both the average student rating and the overall student rating offer no such information. The method in which student ratings are weighted by importance, however, does give this information. Because that method includes the importance of each teaching factor (item), it imparts some priority information. Specifically, to maximize the overall score, this method implies that an instructor should make improvements on the items with the highest importance ratings. If these items are already at their maximum, instructors should direct efforts at those items with the next highest importance. Any individual instructor can derive priority information for making improvements by using these rules.

For ProMES, the nonlinear nature of the contingencies indicates that gains in effectiveness can differ significantly, depending on where the instructor is performing in relation to the contingency. The critical characteristic of contingencies is that an indicator's importance depends in part on how well it is already being done. The question here is whether the ProMES priorities give information that differs from simple importance weighting. If the priorities suggested by ProMES are the same as those for importance weighting, ProMES does not offer unique information.

We compared ProMES and the importance-weighted method. For each of seventy-two faculty members, we used both methods to determine the item that, according to the measurement system, should receive the highest priority in making improvements. We made a calculation of the percentage of times ProMES suggested a *different* top improvement priority than the weighted method.

If for every instructor the two methods identified the *same* teaching factor (item) as deserving the highest priority, the percentage of cases in which ProMES offered unique information would be 0 percent. On the other hand, if in every case ProMES suggested a *different* item, the score would be 100 percent, indicating that ProMES offered unique improvement information.

We also did this analysis for the top five items with the highest improvement priorities by identifying and comparing them. For a match to occur between the two methods, it was only necessary that the same five items be in the set. The sequence of the five items was not important.

The results indicated that for the single top improvement priority, ProMES identified a different item in 96 percent of the cases. For the top five priorities, ProMES identified different items in 99 percent of the cases. These findings indicate that ProMES very definitely suggests different improvement priorities from the importance-weighted approach.

Taken together, the conclusions from the analyses in this section very clearly suggest that ProMES offers substantially unique information compared with the other techniques studied. This does not necessarily mean that the unique ProMES information is better, only that it is different. This information is only better if the ProMES system is in fact valid. Because the large amount of data presented in the validity section indicates that this is indeed the case, however, it is likely that this unique information is valid as well.

Comparison with Traditional Systems: Perceptions

In addition to generating and examining more objective data, we also found it useful to assess perceptions of ProMES's superiority. To do this, we solicited administrators' views. We decided to ask administrators because they had more experience with different evaluation systems. Many of the faculty had not used any other systems and thus could not make a judgment. We collected the data for this comparison from responses to items on the Administrative Evaluation Questionnaire (in Appendix D).

We gave this version of the questionnaire to department heads, the dean, and the associate deans (a total of eleven individuals). Of those eleven, eight returned their questionnaires, for a return rate of 73 percent. Four of these individuals were department heads, whereas the remaining four were at the level of dean or associate dean.

We asked respondents to compare the new system to a more traditional system, in which only the means and frequency distributions of student ratings were reported to faculty and administrators. The overall item said, "Is the system an overall superior measure of teaching effectiveness?" The mean across the seven respondents was 3.57 with a standard deviation of .88. Whereas 57 percent agreed, only 14 percent disagreed; many more therefore agreed than disagreed.

Summary of Results for Research Question 5

The overall picture of the results indicates that ProMES is superior to traditional systems. There is some ambiguity in the data, however. Some data suggest a definite superiority, whereas other data are simply not clear.

- Use of the ProMES system over time produced improvements in teaching effectiveness, whereas the traditional system used in the comparison groups did not. This is not conclusive, though, because the traditional system had been in place for some time in the comparison groups and was not newly introduced as the ProMES system was.
- The ProMES system produced meaningful improvements in teaching effectiveness when it was substituted for the existing qualitative student evaluation system.

- Comparing the ProMES improvements with those found in the literature was inconclusive because of differences in the nature of the available data. If one compares data only from one semester, the traditional systems are slightly better at improving teaching effectiveness. If we look at the situation over time, however, the ProMES system shows larger improvements than those reported in the literature.

- The instructors making up extreme groups (those considered to be excellent or poor teachers) are a very different group of people under ProMES than under traditional systems.

- The improvement priorities that ProMES identified are very different from the improvement priorities that traditional systems identified.

- Because there is strong evidence that the ProMES system is valid, it is quite likely that these differences in the composition of extreme groups and the improvement priorities are valid as well. This suggests the superiority of ProMES over traditional systems.

- Many more administrators agreed than disagreed that the ProMES system was superior to traditional systems.

5

PHASE TWO

Adding Peer Evaluation to the System

THIS CHAPTER WILL DESCRIBE the process used to develop the second phase of the teaching evaluation system. Whereas Phase 1 involves student evaluation, Phase 2 is about peer evaluation. This chapter will also describe faculty reactions and concerns that arose during development and how we addressed them.

In addition, this chapter presents the empirical data available for this phase of the project. Because Phase 2 was not implemented, we will present it in much less detail than the student evaluation component.

BACKGROUND OF PHASE 2

From the very beginning of the project, our intention had been to combine student evaluations with peer evaluations. We decided to develop and implement the student evaluation component (Phase 1) and then add the peer evaluation (Phase 2). In addition, we intended that Phase 2 would examine all aspects of teaching, not just classroom teaching. For example, working with graduate students, advising, and performing other nonclassroom teaching activities were to be incorporated into the final system.

Faculty and administrators had very different reactions and expectations during Phase 2 from those they expressed in Phase 1. For example, whereas some faculty questioned students' ability to evaluate teaching behaviors during Phase 1, there was very high agreement that peers could provide useful evaluations of teaching. Another difference was that many concerns about Phase 1 related to people's uncertainty about the project. We had answered most of these questions about the system by the time we initiated Phase 2. Therefore, instead of questioning the processes to be used and the goals to be accomplished, people had concerns as we developed Phase 2 about the nature of the tasks to be accomplished.

Most important, people at the college had never used peer ratings and were confused about the specifics of that procedure. In addition, the current provost wanted to use teaching portfolios as a foundation for evaluating both tenured and nontenured faculty. This was also a new procedure, and the faculty and administration were unsure about how it was to be implemented.

While Phase 1 was developed and implemented, several workshops had been held on campus to teach faculty how to compile their own portfolio to document teaching efforts. The Center for Teaching Excellence sponsored these workshops. At the same time, the dean of faculties had worked with a group of faculty to develop recommendations about what should be included in a teaching portfolio. It was understood that in time, individuals being considered for promotion and tenure would be required to submit such a portfolio. This gave further impetus to Phase 2 because peer evaluations as well as student evaluations of all aspects of teaching could be the basis of a teaching portfolio. Another way to look at it is that the teaching portfolio, if constructed properly, could provide the necessary information for peer evaluations.

PRELIMINARY ISSUES

Before we actually began to develop Phase 2, we held a meeting in which we discussed this phase with the dean and the dean's executive committee. During this meeting, people identified the following issues concerning Phase 2:

1. What should be the focus of Phase 2?
2. Should objectives and indicators be the same for the entire college?
3. If a teaching portfolio is used, what should be included, and should the contents be consistent across departments?
4. What factors should be included under "teaching" in the system?
5. How often should the peer evaluation be done?

6. Which peers will evaluate the portfolios?

7. How do we express the amount of teaching done by an instructor?

8. How will the evaluations from the two phases be combined?

The recommendation of the dean and the executive committee was that the TEC should deal with these issues and make recommendations to the executive committee on the matters concerning college policy. A memorandum outlining these issues went to members of the TEC, and a meeting was scheduled.

The TEC reviewed these issues and recommended that the major thrust of Phase 2 be to incorporate peer evaluation into the system developed during Phase 1 and to evaluate all aspects of instruction, not just classroom teaching. Furthermore, the evaluation process should be in the form of a teaching portfolio that the faculty prepares and a committee evaluates. These evaluations would then be the basis of a feedback report that would be integrated with the student rating system in Phase 1. The development process should be analogous to that in Phase 1; that is, objectives and indicators should be developed to cover the relevant factors, and then contingencies should be developed for the indicators.

The TEC also recommended that objectives and indicators should be consistent across all departments. To develop the system at the college level, the TEC should therefore determine the factors to be included under "teaching" and should develop objectives and indicators, whereas departments should choose contingencies, as in Phase 1.

The portfolio contents should also be consistent across departments, with the specific portfolio content to be decided after objectives and indicators were determined. The selection of individuals to review the portfolios, however, should occur at the department level.

The TEC further recommended that the frequency of evaluation, weighting of the two phases, and determination of how to express the amount of teaching done by an instructor be resolved at a later time. The committee also felt that members of our research team should continue to act as facilitators at design meetings.

To implement these recommendations, the TEC decided that they should (1) define "teaching" (that is, determine what factors the system would include); (2) identify objectives; (3) develop indicators; (4) determine the specific content of portfolios; and (5) establish contingencies at the department level. We discuss each of these steps below, along with other design issues that arose during the process.

DESIGN ISSUES

As the steps listed previously make clear, Phase 2 used a similar process as Phase 1 but included some significant differences. This section clarifies the issues and tasks completed by the TEC and the faculty during the development of Phase 2.

Defining Teaching

During the first few meetings, the TEC attempted to reach a consensus about which aspects of teaching to include in the system. At the first meeting, to facilitate this process, we provided the design committee with possible factors based on a review of the literature. The factors included planning and preparing for the course, teaching in the classroom, evaluating student learning and providing feedback, advising students, developing curriculum, working with graduate students, and keeping up with the professional field in areas related to teaching performance.

The TEC achieved final consensus on the list of teaching functions to be included in the system after five meetings of approximately one and a half hours each. The committee agreed on the following list of teaching functions:

Teaching in the classroom

Staying current with the field

Developing and using procedures and methods for teaching

Publishing or otherwise disseminating materials (for example, articles on teaching, computer programs)

Showing team cooperation, leadership, and collegiality (both inside and outside the classroom)

Planning and preparing the course and curriculum

Advising students

Participating on the TEC Committee

After the design team met only a few times, it became apparent that not all members would be able to attend meetings regularly. In fact, two out of six representatives were absent more often than present. These two members represented the two clinical departments, and were absent because of their clinic duty schedules. The facilitators were concerned that the representatives' absences might lead to a lack of input and might affect their acceptance of the system in the long run.

In an effort to overcome this problem, we spoke with the absent representatives to impress upon them the importance of their input. We also sent them copies of decisions made in the meetings. In this way, they were informed and could provide feedback or ask for the meeting to be scheduled at a time when they could more likely attend. When they were able to attend, these two members were active, asking questions, giving input, and participating as part of the team. Handling their absences by using the meeting reports was an effective way to keep them informed.

To obtain more input from faculty, we asked all members of the design team to report regularly on the status of the peer evaluation portion of the system to their respective departments. This strategy seemed successful in widening faculty involvement, in that there was more consistent faculty participation during Phase 2 than in Phase 1.

Identifying Objectives

Once the committee reached consensus on the list of teaching functions to be included, they began to identify the corresponding objectives. Because Phase 2 was to include all aspects of teaching and not just classroom teaching, the objectives were expected to be broader in scope than the objectives for Phase 1. The discussions about objectives took longer and were more laborious than the discussions in the first phase. For example, there were times when the design team seemed to make no progress with their discussions. The broad focus of Phase 2, plus the group's unfamiliarity with teaching portfolios, made the task of developing objectives and indicators more challenging than it had been for Phase 1.

This lack of progress was very frustrating for the design team. As we saw it, part of the problem was that they were having trouble translating the components of the known ProMES student evaluation system into the unknown peer evaluation system. To help the design team, we gave them a comparison between Phase 1 and Phase 2. More specifically, we outlined for them the components of Phase 1 (that is, objectives, indicators, contingencies, evaluations, the way evaluations were combined into feedback, and the process in which feedback reports were produced and distributed). In addition, we indicated what group did each step in

Phase 1. Then we showed them an analogous set of steps for Phase 2. This seemed to help clarify the design team's task. As another aid, we gave them a hypothetical list of objectives and indicators that we developed from the literature on peer evaluation and portfolios.

This information seemed to help considerably and the design team was then able to move forward and make decisions about objectives. They included five objectives in the system:

1. The instructor was an effective teacher in the classroom or laboratory.
2. The instructor demonstrated efforts to improve teaching.
3. The instructor showed evidence of influential scholarship in teaching.
4. The instructor demonstrated effective interpersonal skills related to teaching activities.
5. The instructor was an effective student adviser.

In creating these five objectives, the team aimed to cover all of the teaching functions identified above. Objective 1 related to the previously identified teaching function of classroom teaching. Objective 2 included staying current with the field and planning courses. The team dropped curriculum development from the list of teaching functions, because that was primarily the responsibility of the curriculum committee and, as such, seemed more appropriately a service function. The team split the function of developing and utilizing procedures for teaching into two different functions: developing new methods and being willing to learn about or use alternative teaching techniques that others developed. The latter function, using others' techniques, fell under Objective 2. Developing new methods, along with publishing teaching units, comprised Objective 3. Objective 4 included the function of showing team cooperation, leadership, and collegiality, and Objective 5 involved advising students.

Unlike Phase 1, in which the TEC finalized objectives before developing indicators, during Phase 2 objectives and indicators were developed somewhat simultaneously. More specifically, during the third meeting to identify objectives, the design team began to develop indicators as a way to help them determine and define the final list of objectives. As such, it is impossible to calculate separately the amount of time required to develop objectives and indicators. It took the design team six meetings of approximately one and a half hours each to reach a consensus on the list of objectives and indicators.

Developing Indicators

The design team experienced difficulty in identifying indicators, because they expected them to be somewhat uniform. In Phase 1, each of the indicators had been an item on a questionnaire. In Phase 2, however, uniformity among indicators was not appropriate. We explained that some indicators would be reported in simple descriptive amounts, such as the number of graduate students advised, whereas the other indicators would be reported through the use of qualitative information, such as copies of course syllabi. The indicator scores for qualitative information would have to be assigned by the portfolio reviewers. This helped the design team know what was appropriate. They could then identify indicators.

One of the questions that arose as they developed indicators had to do with the rating process itself. Design committee members wondered how the peer rater would use the objectives and indicators that had been developed. We suggested that faculty members receive checklist items to guide them as they evaluated the portfolio. Checklist items are examples of how the rater can make judgments about the indicator in question. In a way, they are indicators of the indicator.

For example, under the indicator "The instructor employed effective methods of evaluating students," checklist items included "exams were reasonable in difficulty," "exams were reasonable in length," and "exams were clear and well stated." Some checklist items indicated quality, whereas others indicated quantity. These items defined the indicators further. The design team developed each checklist item for the system and decided to allow departments to add or subtract checklist items as appropriate for their discipline or situation.

The final list of objectives, indicators, and checklist items appears in Figure 5.1, along with suggested sources for finding information about the items.

Determining Portfolio Content

In developing indicators, the design team questioned exactly how a portfolio would be constructed to match the objectives and indicators that they had developed. As none of the design team members had ever constructed a portfolio of their own, they could not clearly see how the

Figure 5.1. Objectives, Indicators, and Checklist Items.

The following list includes the objectives and indicators to be used in Phase 2 of the Teaching Evaluation System. The peer review committee will make ratings on each of the twelve indicators.

Under each indicator is a list of checklist items. These items define each indicator, identifying what the indicator is designed to include. Also shown for each indicator is the location of the information that will be used to evaluate that indicator.

Please note that the checklist items do not represent an exhaustive list of possible ways to demonstrate the behavior described in the indicator. In addition, please note that an individual instructor is not required to have done every item on the checklist to receive a high indicator rating. These checklist items are provided merely as guidelines to be considered in assigning indicator ratings.

Objective 1: The instructor was an effective teacher in the classroom or laboratory.

Indicator A. The instructor's course materials and methods of presentation were effective.

Checklist Items:

_____ Content was appropriate for the course and the curriculum.

_____ Course content was at a level appropriate to the class.

_____ The instructor used effective supporting materials, such as handouts, outlines, and so forth.

_____ Course information was current.

_____ The instructor used appropriate methods of presentation (such as lecture, demonstration, discussion, and so forth).

Information regarding this indicator could be found in some of the following items: instructor's statement about how the class was taught and why; and copies of class notes, slides, drawings, schematics, handouts, and course outlines.

Indicator B. The instructor employed effective methods of evaluating students.

Checklist Items:

_____ Exams were reasonable in difficulty.

_____ Exams were reasonable in length.

_____ Exams emphasized important concepts.

_____ Exam questions were clear and well stated.

_____ Exam questions elicited relevant information and facts.

_____ When appropriate, exam questions required students to integrate facts in order to arrive at solutions and to develop conclusions.

_____ Other methods for evaluating students (attendance, term papers, outside assignments, presentations, and so forth) were reasonable and appropriate.

Information regarding this indicator could be found in some of the following items: samples of assignments, papers, and exams.

Indicator C. The instructor provided constructive feedback to students.

Checklist Items:

_____ The instructor provided a review for students of exams or assignments.

_____ The instructor posted explanatory keys for exams or assignments.

_____ The instructor provided constructive comments on exams or assignments.

Information regarding this indicator could be found in some of the following items: samples of graded assignments, papers, and exams; samples of explanatory keys; and statement from instructor regarding whether or not exams were reviewed with students.

Objective 2: The instructor demonstrated efforts to improve teaching.

Indicator A. The instructor demonstrated a willingness to learn about or incorporate new information regarding the discipline.

Checklist Items:

_____ The instructor attended formal courses.

_____ The instructor attended professional workshops, scientific meetings, and so forth.

_____ The instructor participated in developmental leaves or visiting professorships.

_____ The instructor undertook independent study.

_____ The instructor included new material in course content.

Information regarding this indicator could be found in some of the following items: statement from instructor regarding participation in courses, workshops, meetings, and so forth; certificates of course or workshop completion; and updated course notes.

Indicator B. The instructor demonstrated a willingness to learn about or implement alternative teaching techniques.

Checklist Items:

_____ The instructor attended formal courses.

_____ The instructor attended professional workshops, scientific meetings, and so forth.

_____ The instructor visited other schools.

_____ The instructor participated in developmental leaves or visiting professorships.

_____ The instructor undertook independent study.

_____ The instructor implemented alternate teaching methods.

Information regarding this indicator could be found in some of the following items: statement from instructor regarding participation in courses, workshops, meetings, and so forth; and certificates of course or workshop completion.

Indicator C. The instructor effectively participated in course development.

Checklist Items:

_____ The instructor developed at least one new course.

_____ The instructor reconstructed or revised at least one course.

Information regarding this indicator could be found in some of the following items: syllabi of newly developed courses or reconstructed or revised courses; documentation of effective participation from team members, such as a statement or letter; documentation from previous courses to compare with the revised course; and documentation of honors courses.

Objective 3: The instructor showed evidence of influential scholarship in teaching.

Indicator A. The instructor developed new methods of teaching.

Checklist Items:

_____ The instructor created new approaches to teaching.

_____ The instructor developed techniques for evaluating teaching methods.

_____ The instructor obtained funding for research on teaching.

Information regarding this indicator could be found in some of the following items: the instructor's description of the new teaching method, including a written description, handouts, personal notes, and so forth; and documentation of teaching grants.

Indicator B. The instructor published materials related to teaching.

Checklist Items:

_____ The instructor participated in teaching research.

_____ The instructor published work related to teaching.

_____ The instructor had work cited by others.

_____ The instructor was invited to present work on teaching.

Information regarding this indicator could be found in some of the following items: samples of publications, such as journal reprints, textbooks, book chapters, videotapes, autotutorial materials, and so forth; other people's citations of the instructor's work in the literature; lists of the author's work; and invitations to present material on teaching.

Objective 4: The instructor demonstrated effective interpersonal skills related to teaching activities.

Indicator A. The instructor demonstrated cooperation and collegiality.

Checklist Items:

_____ The instructor cooperated with colleagues in teaching-related activities.

_____ The instructor worked harmoniously with other faculty.

_____ The instructor participated constructively on teaching-related committees (TEC, Curriculum Development, and so forth).

Information regarding this indicator could be found in statements or letters from other faculty members or administrators.

Indicator B. The instructor demonstrated leadership ability.

Checklist Items:

_____ The instructor served as course coordinator.

_____ The instructor chaired teaching-related committee (TEC, promotion, and so forth).

Information regarding this indicator could be found in statements or letters from other faculty members or administrators.

Objective 5: The instructor was an effective student adviser.

Indicator A. The instructor facilitated graduate students' progress toward their educational goals.

Checklist Items:

_____ The instructor assisted students in completing their M.S. and Ph.D. programs.

_____ The instructor assisted graduate students in publishing work.

_____ The instructor involved students in ongoing projects.

_____ The instructor effectively addressed students' career development needs.

_____ The instructor counseled students effectively.

Information regarding this indicator could be found in some of the following items: listing of students supervised and current status of degree program; letters from students regarding the effectiveness of graduate-level instructors; and questionnaires given to current and former students.

Indicator B. The instructor demonstrated willingness to counsel undergraduate and professional students.

Checklist Items:

_____ The instructor was readily available to undergraduate and professional students.

_____ The instructor participated in the TAMU Mentor program.

_____ The instructor served on Student-Faculty Relations Committee.

_____ The instructor participated as faculty adviser for student clubs and organizations.

_____ The instructor received or was nominated to receive Distinguished Achievement Award in Student Relations.

Information regarding this indicator could be found in some of the following items: log of students counseled, including frequency and number of students; questionnaires administered to former students; and letters or testimonials from former students.

---

peer review process would work. To assist the design team and to create a guide for the instructors who would have to prepare portfolios, we made a list of recommendations regarding which items to include in a portfolio for each indicator.

We derived our list somewhat from a set of items that the dean of faculties recommended for inclusion in the portfolio. Some of the items on our list of proposed portfolio contents included copies of class notes and handouts, course syllabi, samples of class assignments, certificates of completion from workshops to improve subject matter knowledge or teaching skills, and documentation of leadership activities related to teaching. Again, the design team decided that departments could add or delete items from the suggested list as appropriate for an instructor's discipline or situation.

One important concern of the design team was the use of direct observation of teaching in the peer review. The primary reason for considering direct observation was that it had significant support among faculty and administration. We discussed with the design team the many problems associated with direct observation. The most important issues were its lack of validity (as discussed in Chapter One) and the amount of faculty time such observations would take.

The design team considered having the instructor videotape one or two lectures and submit these recordings with the portfolio. Peers would then evaluate the tapes. To overcome problems with validity, however, the team realized that they would have to use multiple peers, create another structured evaluation or rating system, and train raters on its use. When the committee members understood the time and effort needed to do all this, especially the actual viewing and rating of the videotapes, they reluctantly decided not to use direct or videotaped observations.

Structuring the Peer Rating System

Another question regarding implementation had to do with identifying the people who would be responsible for actually providing the ratings. After some discussion, the design team agreed that department heads should appoint the raters. Promotion and tenure committees within departments could rate teaching portfolios as part of their duties, but department heads should have the prerogative to select a separate group and give them the responsibility of evaluating the portfolios. The team of evaluators could also include individuals from outside the department or college if they possessed the expertise to provide the ratings. The guideline would be to include raters who could be considered peers of the instructor being evaluated.

The final step in developing objectives and indicators for Phase 2 was for the design committee to choose anchors to be used for the contingencies. Although five anchors had been used for Phase 1, several design team members thought that Phase 2 should have more anchors, because faculty could make finer discriminations about teaching behavior than students could. The group came to a consensus on recommending that seven anchor statements be used to rate the portfolio. The anchors selected were never, almost never, rather seldom, sometimes, fairly often, very frequently, and always.

As the design team members completed Phase 2, they wondered whether or not the Phase 2 results should be combined with Phase 1 results. The teaching literature suggests that all teaching effectiveness data be combined into a single index of effectiveness to assist with making personnel decisions, such as promotion, tenure, and salary increases (Doyle, 1983; Seldin, 1990). This single index is necessary because decisions are not made on the basis of a variety of numbers; instead, they derive from an overall assessment. Each administrator makes this overall assessment by using either subjective, individual judgments or some formally agreed-upon method. The literature also prefers formal, objective methods of combining data to more subjective, clinical judgments (Sawyer, 1966). Based on this logic, the team decided to combine the results of the student rating system (Phase 1) and the peer evaluation system (Phase 2).

This decision led the team to question how they should weight the scores from the two systems in making this combination. There would be an overall ProMES score from the student evaluation system and one from the peer evaluation system. The design committee felt that they should weight the two scores according to the relative importance of the teaching functions contained in the two systems.

A confounding issue was that both phases included assessments of the effectiveness of classroom teaching. If each of these elements received separate weighting, classroom teaching might be weighted too heavily, despite its obvious importance. There was a great deal of discussion about the optimum weight for components of the two phases. The final decision was to give one weight to the function of classroom teaching; this weight would include data or ratings from both phases.

The team obtained weightings by asking each member of the design team to recommend certain weights privately for each component. When we compared the individual recommendations, we discovered a great deal of agreement in the weightings. The design team finalized the following set of recommended weightings. The weightings for each function can be interpreted as percentages of the total teaching function. In other words, a weighting of 58 percent indicates that this component accounts for 58 percent of the overall teaching function.

COMPONENTS OF THE TEACHING FUNCTION	WEIGHTING OF EACH FUNCTION
Effectiveness of classroom teaching	58 percent
Effective interpersonal skills related to teaching	13 percent
Efforts to improve teaching	12 percent
Influential scholarship	10 percent
Student advising	7 percent

Because both phases covered classroom teaching, it was necessary to determine how much of the total 58 percent for classroom teaching each evaluation system was to cover. Only when this was determined could the weighting of the peer and student evaluation systems be determined.

To make this judgment, the team first identified the components of classroom teaching. For students, evaluating classroom teaching meant assessing the instructor's communication skills, organization, subject mastery, rapport with students, fairness in evaluating students, encouragement of critical thinking, and ability to motivate students to learn. Classroom teaching as evaluated by peers included the instructor's course materials and presentation methods, methods of evaluating students, and provision of constructive feedback to students.

The design team felt that the peer evaluation components of classroom teaching represented approximately 10 percent of the total 58 percent associated with classroom teaching. Thus, the student ratings would cover 48 percent (58 percent – 10 percent) of the factors in classroom teaching. The peer evaluation would include the 10 percent that peer reviews contributed to evaluating classroom teaching plus the 42 percent of teaching outside the classroom (12 percent + 10 percent + 13 percent + 7 percent, from the percentages in the list above) for a total of 52 percent. Because the two were nearly equal (48 percent versus 52 percent), the team decided to weight the peer evaluation overall score and the student evaluation overall score equally in determining the final teaching effectiveness score.

Presenting Objectives and Indicators to the Faculty

After the TEC selected objectives and indicators, each department held meetings to discuss the TEC's recommendations about the design and implementation of Phase 2. The TEC then compiled and discussed a list of issues expressed in those meetings.

A vocal minority in several departments had concerns about having peers observe classrooms and about videotaping. During the meetings, we explained to the faculty the logistical problems associated with coordinating observations and ensuring reliability. Even after we pointed out these drawbacks, some departments expressed strong support for having classes observed or videotaped. Because we felt that gaining faculty acceptance was critical for the project's long-term success, we decided that either classroom observation or videotaping could be incorporated into Phase 2 if the department felt strongly that it should be included. We developed guidelines for the use of peer observation and shared them with faculty to ensure that ratings would be reliable and valid.

Several questions about objectives, indicators, and checklist items also arose during department meetings. One concern was that it would take a good deal of time to prepare a portfolio. In response to this, we pointed out that the dean of faculties would be requiring instructors to submit a portfolio for promotion and tenure review; therefore, some type of portfolio would have to be prepared no matter what form the evaluation took. Design team members also explained that the system belonged to the faculty and could be modified to suit their needs. If the faculty members felt that the suggested portfolio had too many requirements and would take too much time to develop, they could change it to contain only the most essential items.

Another concern raised in the faculty meetings related to faculty who taught only a limited amount. The evaluations of the teaching that those faculty did should have less impact on their overall assessment than the evaluations of faculty who did extensive teaching. We explained during the meetings that the department head could take this into consideration when evaluating faculty. The departments would also have the option of evaluating only those individuals who spent a specific minimum percentage of their time teaching, so that faculty whose primary responsibilities did not include teaching were not evaluated with this system.

As faculty reviewed the objectives and indicators, some of them pointed out that their department did not provide them with resources to perform some of the tasks and behaviors suggested by the checklist items, such as attending conferences on teaching. We reminded faculty that checklist items were provided to give examples of tasks or behaviors that could be rated; checklist items were not required. An instructor would have the option of including information in the portfolio indicating that a request for travel funds had been made but not honored. As a result of these discussions, the recommendation was made that the CVM take the lead in sponsoring conferences to allow for broad participation among its faculty.

In many cases, the design team decided to follow their initial decision when reviewing the list of concerns collected during the department approval meetings. In the case of videotaping, as mentioned earlier, the team made allowances to include videotaping in the portfolio. In order to foster support for the system, the team kept a list of faculty concerns and recorded how and why they resolved each concern.

They circulated this document to the faculty so that it was clear that the concerns they expressed in department meetings had been reviewed and taken seriously. The team felt that this approach was worthwhile and helped acceptance.

Developing Contingencies

As in Phase 1, Phase 2 contingencies were developed at the department level to reflect individual departments' policies better. One of the clinical departments asked not to create Phase 2 contingencies at that time. After considerable discussion between the department head and the dean, this request was approved. Design committees for the remaining departments included three to five department representatives. The majority of these representatives had also been members of Phase 1 contingency design teams and thus were quite familiar with the process. The development of Phase 2 contingencies mirrored that of Phase 1.

One issue that arose at the beginning of contingency development was that within each of the departments, some instructors were primarily researchers and some were primarily teachers. Part of the faculty felt that there would be different priorities for the two types of instructors. For example, faculty members who were primarily researchers would not be expected to publish works about teaching, whereas faculty who were primarily teachers would be more likely to do so. Such differences would affect the contingencies.

It was decided that each department would consider developing a separate set of contingencies for the two types of faculty if they felt that the differences were great enough to warrant a separate set. All departments approached this task first by developing the complete contingency set for faculty who were primarily researchers (which represented the majority of faculty) and then by reviewing each contingency individually. They tried to determine whether it should be changed to reflect more accurately the priorities of faculty members who were primarily teachers. Only one of the four departments decided to create a different set. In this particular department, seven of the twelve contingencies were not changed for faculty who were primarily teachers.

The process of developing contingencies went very smoothly in Phase 2. Discussions in all of the design meetings continued to be lively, but committee members were able to reach a consensus much more quickly than they had during Phase 1. This seemed to be due to the experience they gained during Phase 1. Departments were able to develop contingency sets in approximately two to eight hours.

After contingencies were created, they were reviewed in department meetings. During these meetings, members of the contingency committee presented the contingencies to their fellow faculty and department head and answered their questions. Representatives from the research team were also present at these meetings to help answer questions. Although there were some disagreements with contingency committee decisions, after some discussion the contingencies remained relatively unchanged.

A complete set of contingencies for one department appears in Figure 5.2. As in Phase 1, the contingencies show considerable variability and nonlinearity.

RESULTS

The amount of available empirical results for Phase 2 is limited because Phase 2 was not implemented. We shall discuss this implementation issue in Chapter Six. We can report some empirical results, however. The overriding project objective was to determine whether the ProMES approach could be successfully implemented in this setting. These were the specific research questions for Phase 2:

1. Could Phase 2 be developed in this environment?
2. Was the resulting system valid?

We had planned other research questions for Phase 2, such as whether the resulting system was useful and cost effective. Unfortunately, because it was never actually implemented, it was not possible to answer these additional questions.

Research Question 1: Could Phase 2 Be Developed in This Setting?

As in Phase 1, we answered this question by examining evidence from several different sources. We describe these sources of evidence below.

SYSTEM DEVELOPMENT. As noted earlier in this chapter, the TEC was able to develop objectives and indicators, and department contingency committees were successful in designing contingencies. Once again, administrators and department personnel approved the system components (objectives, indicators, and contingencies) with little difficulty.

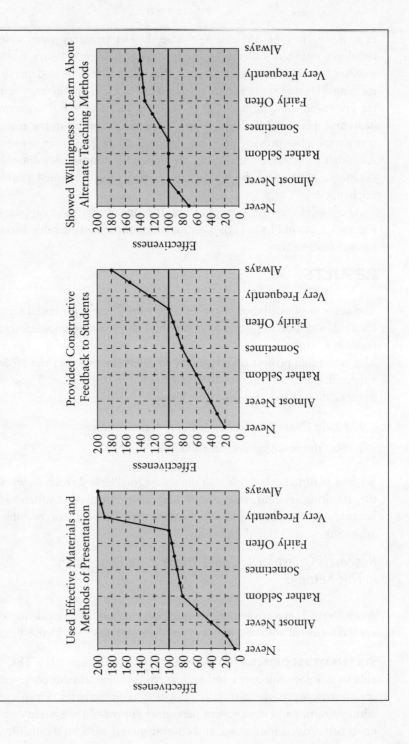

Figure 5.2. Sample Contingency Set.

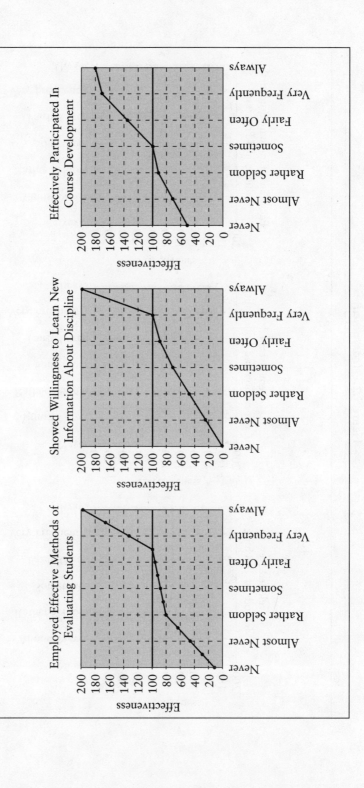

Figure 5.2. (continued)

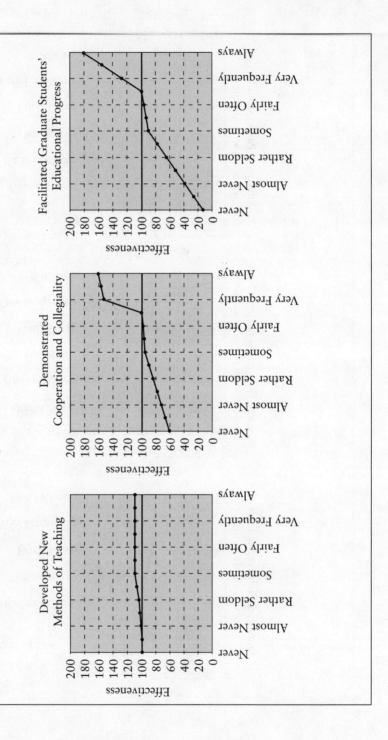

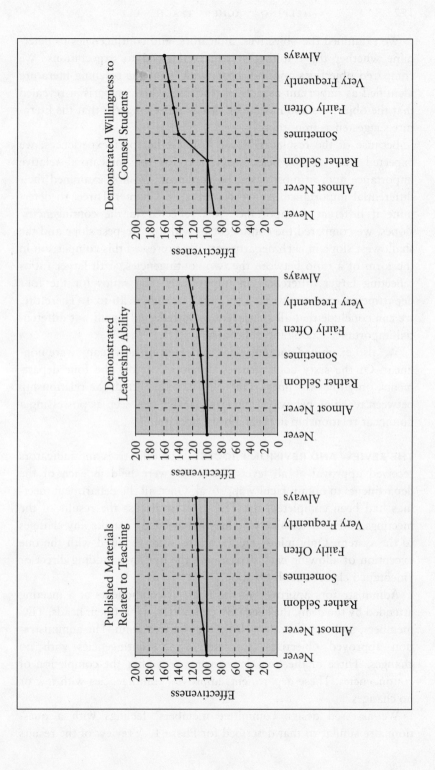

We examined the objectives, indicators, and contingencies to determine whether the resulting system conformed to expectations. We compared objectives and indicators with what the teaching literature identified as important aspects of teaching. This comparison revealed that the objectives and indicators closely reflected areas that the literature suggested as important.

Because of the results of Phase 1 and other past experiences, we expected that contingencies would express the indicators' relative importance and, in most cases, be nonlinear. We first examined their differential importance. As we described in Chapter Three, to determine if differential importance was reflected in the contingencies' slopes, we compared the contingencies with the steepest slope and the shallowest slope in each department. We expressed this comparison in the form of a ratio between the two contingencies, with larger ratios reflecting larger differences in importance. The ratios for the four departments were as low as 3 to 1 and as high as 20 to 1. Therefore, we can conclude that all contingency sets reflected significant differential importance among the indicators.

We also examined contingencies to determine how many were nonlinear. Of the sixty contingencies developed across the four departments, only one was linear. Once again, as expected, the relationship between teaching behaviors and effectiveness was seen as possessing a nonlinear relationship in the majority of cases.

THE REVIEW AND REVISION PROCESS. The objectives and indicators received approval at all levels. Meetings were held in each of the departments to obtain faculty approval. Once all the department meetings had been completed, the TEC met to discuss the results of the meetings and to determine whether they needed to make any changes to the system. Only minor modifications were required with the one exception of allowing each department the option of adding direct or videotaped classroom observation.

Administrators approved of the Phase 2 components at a meeting attended by the dean, the executive committee, department heads, TEC members, and representatives from the research team. The administration approved objectives, indicators, and contingencies with no changes. Three of the four departments met after the completion of contingencies. These departments approved contingencies with few or no changes.

We assessed design committee members' feelings with a questionnaire similar to that described for Phase 1. A review of the results indicated that 67 percent of TEC members and 70 percent of contingency committee members felt that the review and revision process was fair and reasonable.

In summary, the answer to the first research question is a clear yes; Phase 2 could be developed in this environment.

Research Question 2: Was the Resulting System Valid?

Because the system was not actually implemented, much of the information needed to assess validity is simply not available. Some preliminary indications of the faculty's perceptions of the system do appear, however, in design team members' responses to two items on the questionnaire that they received. This questionnaire was similar to that given under Phase 1 and described in Chapter Three.

Design committee members were asked to indicate the level of consensus achieved within their committee. A high level of consensus could be one indication that committee members perceived the system as a valid measure of teaching effectiveness. Responses indicated that 100 percent of TEC members and 92 percent of department contingency committee members felt that a true consensus had been reached.

A second item on this questionnaire asked committee members to indicate how accurate and complete the system was. Responses indicated that 100 percent of TEC members and 92 percent of contingency committee members perceived the contingencies as accurate.

Consequently, although these results are not conclusive, they do provide some evidence that the system was perceived as valid.

Summary of Results: Phase 2

There are clearly fewer results to report on the Phase 2 attempt to include peer evaluations and all aspects of teaching. In general, the design of this part of the system went quite well once the initial problems were overcome. Committees were able to do the work and it went much more smoothly than in Phase 1, undoubtedly because the committees, faculty, and administration had gained experience during Phase 1. Faculty and administrators seemed to perceive the Phase 2 system as accurate and complete and generally regarded it highly.

Thus, it is clear that it was indeed possible to use the ProMES approach here, as well as for the student ratings. The most interesting result, however, was that the system was never implemented. We shall discuss this issue in detail in the next chapter on conclusions.

6

DRAWING CONCLUSIONS AND MAKING RECOMMENDATIONS

THIS CHAPTER FOCUSES ON the conclusions that we can draw from this project. We will frame the discussion around the research questions identified in Chapter Three and discussed in Chapter Four, as well as the list of characteristics of an ideal teaching evaluation system provided in Chapter One.

THE RESEARCH QUESTIONS

In previous chapters we described the research questions that guided this project and reported our conclusions as they related to each phase. Here we review the questions one final time, focusing on what we learned across the entire project.

Can the ProMES System Be Developed Successfully in This Environment?

The results indicated that the components of the system for both Phase 1 and Phase 2 could indeed be successfully developed in this setting. All the components were developed and approved in both phases.

Is the Resulting System a Valid Measure of Teaching Effectiveness?

There are considerable data in Phase 1 to support the conclusion that the resulting system was valid. There were considerably less data in

Phase 2, because it was not implemented, but what was available supported that system's validity.

Will Teaching Effectiveness Improve with Feedback from the System?

The data showed clear improvements in teaching effectiveness with feedback from the ProMES system. Instructors made improvements over the existing qualitative system. As instructors in the college did so, teachers at other colleges in the university showed no improvement. The system was especially effective at improving the teaching effectiveness of instructors who were initially less effective.

Do Faculty and Administrators See the Resulting System as Valuable?

Overall, the results were basically positive but quite variable. There are a few issues to be considered here.

DIFFERENCES BETWEEN BASIC AND CLINICAL DEPARTMENTS. One major source of variability was the difference between the faculty in the basic science departments and the faculty in the clinical departments. If we just look at the results from the college administration and the basic science faculty, we would conclude that the system was seen as very valuable. If we just consider the results from the faculty from the clinical departments, our conclusion would be nearly the opposite.

This difference was rather pervasive. It surfaced in the validity perceptions, many aspects of the perceptions of system value, and the reactions to Phase 2. The differences were quite large. For example, in terms of satisfaction with the system's design, 74 percent of faculty in the basic science departments were satisfied, whereas only 34 percent of faculty in the clinical departments were satisfied.

There seem to be several reasons for this difference. One was that the clinical departments did much less classroom teaching than the basic departments. The clinical departments focused more on small-group, laboratory-type courses in which instructors worked with students to diagnose and treat specific cases. Thus, the time and effort that clinical faculty required in developing and using the system were not as beneficial, because the ProMES system did not cover much of their teaching.

The clinical departments also seemed to experience more problems with actually implementing the system. We will discuss this issue in more detail below. Briefly, the clinical faculty had more problems than the basic faculty with making schedules and keeping people informed. These problems occurred for many faculty members when the system was first implemented, but they persisted for the clinical faculty.

Finally, at least some people in the clinical departments seemed more skeptical of the motives of the college administration in using the system. Essentially, they trusted the administration less than the faculty in the basic departments did.

Although it is not clear how much of the dissatisfaction derived from these three factors, it is clear that these negative experiences did indeed contribute to the clinical faculty's unhappiness with ProMES.

DISSATISFACTION WITH IMPLEMENTATION. Another source of variability in people's perceptions of ProMES's value was the difference between the system's design and its implementation. In general, perceptions of system design were more positive than perceptions of system implementation. The explanation for this difference is rather straightforward. There were a number of significant problems in the initial administration of the student evaluation system.

The worst problem was that some faculty members were not informed that they were to be evaluated. Without prior scheduling, a person simply showed up one day in class expecting to administer the student evaluations. Naturally, this was not well received.

There were other problems with the system's administration, such as lack of clarity about who was responsible for implementing it. Specifically, who decided which faculty were to be evaluated, who was actually to visit the classrooms, and who had responsibility for managing the data once collected? Although all these issues had been addressed, it was apparently not clear to all concerned what final decisions had been made.

To make matters worse, it took several semesters to resolve these problems, which added to the faculty's frustration. These issues still had not been worked out when we administered the questionnaire about the faculty members' perceptions of ProMES. Their low levels of satisfaction seem to reflect this frustration.

In fact, although the most critical problems of administration were eventually solved, the process is still not running to the satisfaction of the dean and many faculty members. The primary problem is the logistical complexities involved in collecting the data and putting it into feedback reports. It still takes the college two to three months after a course ends to give faculty feedback reports. We will have more to say about this issue later in the chapter.

Even with all these issues, however, the most important indication of the system's perceived value is that it is still in use.

LACK OF PHASE 2 IMPLEMENTATION. Another important aspect of system value is that Phase 2 was not implemented. It is instructive to look at the reasons for this. If Phase 2 was seen as valid and it was important to a significant minority of faculty to include peer evaluations, why was this phase not implemented?

We spent considerable time attempting to answer this question and decided that a number of factors are involved. One factor was that the associate dean responsible for implementing Phase 2 died unexpectedly in the middle of the year, and there was no one to take his place immediately. Because he had the responsibility of overseeing the implementation of Phase 2, his absence slowed down the effort considerably.

Another administrative issue was significant turnover in key administration positions. In particular, the person who was provost and acting president moved to another position. He had been the primary force behind the use of teaching portfolios. There was some resistance to the idea of faculty members' developing teaching portfolios because of the effort involved. Phase 2 had become somewhat tied to the portfolio idea, as it seemed that peer ratings could best be done if a portfolio were developed. Without this pressure for portfolios and with the faculty's resistance to them, there was less enthusiasm for Phase 2.

A third administrative reason concerned the reduction in discretionary CVM funds. The CVM, similar to other parts of the university, was experiencing a decrease in resources due to the university's general economic conditions. This caused people to focus the limited financial and time resources on essential functions. Phase 2 was seen as a desirable but not essential function and thus received a lower priority.

We believe, however, that faculty members were the primary reason that Phase 2 was not implemented. When we introduced Phase 2, the problems of administering Phase 1 had still not been resolved. The faculty members were very frustrated with this and were concerned about implementing an even more complex system. Their trust in the administration was at somewhat of a low point because of this, which diminished their support for Phase 2. This was certainly true for the clinical departments but was also true for the more basic departments, to some extent. Finally, both faculty members and administrators began to see how much effort it would actually take to implement Phase 2 the way they had designed it and started to question whether it would add sufficiently to what Phase 1 provided.

Some of these issues were fixable but some were not. Clearly, we could not have predicted the decreasing discretionary resources, the unexpected death of the associate dean, and the growing resistance to creating teaching portfolios. One lesson we learned here, however, is the importance of having one part of a teaching evaluation system run smoothly before adding other components. Another lesson is that it is very important to keep the system as manageable as possible. In the design phase, it is easy to add complexity in the interest of making it a better system. If the system becomes too complex, however, it will not be easy to implement. A less-than-perfect system that is used is better than a nearly perfect one that is not.

Is the New System Better Than Traditional Systems?

Because it takes more effort to do a ProMES teaching evaluation system than a traditional student evaluation system, it is important that the potential gains outweigh the additional costs. We addressed this issue in Chapter Four and concluded that there were indeed areas in which the ProMES approach was superior. Except for the added work of developing and administering the ProMES system, there were no areas in which the traditional approach was superior.

Another way to look at this issue is to compare ProMES and traditional systems on the set of criteria outlined in Chapter One for an ideal teaching evaluation system. These criteria fall into the categories of overall structure, measures to use, measurement characteristics, and feedback characteristics. The specific factors appear in Tables 6.1 through 6.4. The tables indicate whether each factor was present in Phase 1, Phase 2, and a typical traditional system. As in Chapter Four, we define a traditional system as one in which students rate faculty and in which faculty and administration receive means and frequency distributions. Students can also write qualitative comments, which are also returned to the faculty.

The first row of Table 6.1 shows the factor "The objectives of the teaching evaluation system must be clear and publicly stated." The three columns to the right of the factor indicate that it is or can be present in all three approaches. The judgments shown in some of the cells are difficult to make but still serve as a general comparison.

Table 6.1. Comparisons with Ideal Characteristics: Overall Structure.

Factors	Phase 1	Phase 2	Typical System
1. The objectives of the teaching evaluation system must be clear and publicly stated.	Yes	Yes	Yes
2. The evaluation system should be based on quantitative information.	Yes	Yes	Yes
3. The evaluation system must give an overall index of teaching effectiveness, as well as information on more specific aspects of teaching.	Yes	Yes	No
4. The evaluation system must capture teaching policy accurately.	Yes	Yes	No
5. Both instructors and the administration must understand the system and accept it as accurate and useful.	Mixed	?	Mixed
6. The system must be cost effective to develop and maintain.	Yes	?	Yes
7. The system should be developed with significant and meaningful instructor participation.	Yes	Yes	No
8. If it is important to evaluate how well instructors teach, it is also important to assess how well the evaluation system is working.	Yes	?	?

As Table 6.1 shows, the primary structural differences are that ProMES provides an overall score, captures policy more accurately because of the contingencies, and has more faculty participation in its design. Acceptance was mixed in Phase 1, as is usual in the typical student rating system. There are question marks in a number of the Phase 2 factors, because without implementation, these were not possible to assess.

Table 6.2 indicates that the ProMES system compares more favorably because it can assess all teaching activities, uses multiple measures, and adds peer ratings.

Table 6.3 shows that ProMES accounts for differential importance and nonlinearities, allows for comparisons across class types, and captures different teaching missions.

Table 6.2.   Comparisons with Ideal Characteristics: Measures to Use.

Factors	Phase 1	Phase 2	Typical System
1. Teaching is multidimensional. Thus, the system must measure a variety of teaching behaviors.	Yes	Yes	Yes
2. Critical teaching behaviors must be identified before the measurement system is developed.	Yes	Yes	Yes
3. To give a complete assessment of teaching contribution, the evaluation must include all aspects of teaching, not just classroom instruction.	No	Yes	No
4. Because there is no one perfect measure of teaching effectiveness, multiple measures should be used to complement each other.	No	Yes	No
5. Student ratings are a practical and valid source of instructor evaluation and should be part of the system.	Yes	Yes	Yes
6. To improve the validity of the overall measurement system and promote acceptance by those skeptical of student ratings, the system needs to supplement these ratings with other measures. The best supplement is peer evaluations made after a review of teaching materials but not based on classroom observation.	No	Yes	No
7. To avoid bias in student ratings, the instructor should be absent from the classroom when the ratings are done, the ratings should be anonymous, and all students should be told that their ratings can have effects on personnel decisions.	Yes	—	Yes
8. Instructors should only be measured on factors over which they have control.	Yes	Yes	Yes

Table 6.3. Comparisons with Ideal Characteristics:
Measurement Characteristics.

Factors	Phase 1	Phase 2	Typical System
1. The measurement system must show three types of reliability: internal consistency, interjudge, and test-retest reliability.	Yes	?	Yes
2. The system must be valid.	Yes	Yes	Yes
3. The system should be able to account for differential importance of teaching factors.	Yes	Yes	No
4. The system should be able to account for nonlinearities.	Yes	Yes	No
5. The system should allow for direct comparisons across different types of classes.	Yes	Yes	No
6. The system must be flexible enough to allow for different teaching missions.	Yes	Yes	No
7. The system should be sensitive to the importance of teaching in the instructor's overall work.	Yes	Yes	?

In Table 6.4, of the two systems, ProMES does a better job of meeting the requirements of the first factor. Although a traditional system may provide faculty with information on the aspects and manner of measurement and the use of the information, it may not specify how the measures will be combined. In a ProMES system, however, the manner in which the measures are combined is formally identified through the contingencies and the feedback reports. Other areas of superiority include indicating how good the student rating is and identifying improvement priorities.

Thus, there are a number of areas in which ProMES is superior and none in which the traditional approach is superior, except for ease of use. If these areas of potential superiority are important, then ProMES should be considered as a foundation for a teaching evaluation system.

WHERE THE SYSTEM COULD BE IMPROVED

Overall, the evaluation of the system is positive. There are several areas, however, in which it could have been improved substantially. These areas should receive special attention in future attempts to use the system.

One major problem was the logistics of administering the system. The process of collecting student ratings in class, having machines score the student questionnaires, putting this output through the computer program that generated feedback reports, and distributing these reports proved to be more complex than expected. Even with a good faith effort on the part of the dean's office, it still took far too long to give the feedback reports to the faculty. To improve this, two options seem worth consideration. One is to devote more administrative resources to the project. It would help if someone in the dean's office has responsibility for this effort and if it is made a priority. In times of tight resources, however, this is difficult. Even with more resources, the process is complex and could break down in one step or another.

A second alternative is to increase the efficiency of the process when designing the system. Our recommendation is that students be required to enter their evaluations each semester on a computer terminal. The college would keep information on whether each student did, in fact, do the evaluations. A single computer program would then collect and process the ratings and the feedback report would be printed. This should greatly reduce the logistical steps involved in generating reports and should speed the process considerably. Such a system would also allow for more sophisticated feedback reports, including graphic representations of the results.

Another improvement would be to involve department heads more. We did as many things as we could think of to involved faculty in the process but spent less time with department heads. We should have spent more time here, involving heads with planning, designing, and implementing the system.

Another major improvement would have been to use the teaching evaluation feedback more effectively. In its normal application, ProMES includes meetings with those receiving the feedback to discuss its meaning and to plan improvements. This is considered to be a very important part of the system. We did not include this step in the project, although there was much discussion about doing so. For future applications, we suggest that this be an essential part of the system.

Table 6.4.   Comparisons with Ideal Characteristics:
Feedback Characteristics.

Factors	Phase 1	Phase 2	Typical System
1. Faculty should know what is going to be measured, how it is going to be measured, how the measures are to be combined, and how the information is to be used.	Yes	?	Mixed
2. Measurement and the resulting feedback should occur on a regular, predictable basis.	Yes	Yes	Yes
3. The feedback should be given in a timely manner—as soon after the evaluation as is practical.	Yes	?	Yes
4. The feedback should include not only how the instructor scored on each factor but also how good that level of performance is.	Yes	Yes	No
5. The feedback should help improve teaching performance. It should communicate the differential importance of the various aspects of teaching, communicate the existing nonlinearities, and allow for the identification of priorities for improving teaching.	Yes	Yes	No

After each semester, interested faculty should meet and discuss their evaluations. This meeting would have several functions. First, it would educate faculty members who are new to the system about the meaning of the feedback reports. Second, it would allow faculty to share ideas about how to improve teaching. Third, it would allow for a continuous evaluation of the system itself so that any needed changes could be made. Finally, it would make the evaluation process salient to faculty and administrators.

7

DOING TEACHING
EVALUATION
IN OTHER SETTINGS

IN THIS CHAPTER we turn to some practical suggestions for designing and implementing teaching evaluation systems. We have learned much from doing this particular project, as well as measurement and feedback projects in other contexts (for example, Pritchard, 1995). At the end of Chapter Six, we discussed several of the issues that were especially important for improving the CVM project. In this chapter we want to share the more general lessons we have learned with others who are thinking of starting their own systems.

The chapter is divided into two sections. The first deals with general issues that should be addressed in designing any type of teaching evaluation system. The second section addresses issues that arise in implementing a ProMES teaching evaluation system. In each of these sections we list issues and offer suggestions on that subject.

GENERAL ISSUES IN DESIGNING AND IMPLEMENTING A TEACHING EVALUATION SYSTEM

Before you even start to design a teaching evaluation system, you should address a series of issues. Some of these are quite complex and difficult to handle. They will definitely have an impact on the project at some point, though, and should therefore be considered early.

Organizational Trust

One key factor is the issue of trust, which is especially important between the administration and the faculty. The collaborative nature of a teaching evaluation system makes it imperative that an atmosphere of mutual respect and trust exists between administrators and instructors.

If the instructors do not possess at least a minimal amount of trust in the administration, it may impair the system's success in at least two ways. First, the instructors are unlikely to be willing to develop a system that the administration may use against their interests. Second, if a system is imposed on instructors who distrust the administration, they will find a way to sabotage or interfere with the system.

It is also important for the administration to trust the instructors. We strongly encourage a bottom-up approach in which the faculty initially develop the system and then submit it to the administration for approval. In order for administrators to be comfortable with this method, they must respect and trust the faculty to some extent.

If a reasonable level of trust does not exist, it is probably not going to be possible to develop a good teaching evaluation system. Our advice would be to first work on improving trust directly. Only when trust has been improved to a reasonable level should one start to develop the system.

Importance of Administrative Support

It is critical that the project has the administration's support. The administration must view the project as important, commit resources to it, be interested in the effort's results, and defend the project if it is challenged. Without this commitment, the project will in all likelihood fail, regardless of the system's quality. It is especially crucial that the most senior administrator support the project. For example, if the project includes all the departments in a college, it will be important for the college dean to be committed.

This support must not only be present, but others must also perceive that it is present. In other words, the administration's support for the project must be visible to everyone in the college. This can be achieved through formal announcements of support from the administration, administrators' appearances at collegewide information meetings about the project, requests for information about the program, and completion of administrative tasks associated with the system.

Early in the planning of the project, it is important to remind the administration of the role they play in developing and operating a successful effort to improve teaching. The administration should also be given a realistic picture of (1) the cost of designing and implementing the system, (2) the system's potential benefits, (3) a methodology to assess these benefits, (4) a realistic timetable for acquiring these benefits, and (5) the importance of providing visible and long-range support. To guarantee the administration's continued support, it is crucial to keep administrators abreast of the project's progress and to give them tangible evidence of its success.

Teaching Evaluation Climate

The feelings about teaching evaluation varied considerably across individuals in our project. The administration was very supportive of the idea. Faculty members ranged from liking the idea to verging on paranoia. In general, though, most of the people favored the idea.

It is very important to assess this climate before proceeding with the project. Most people resist change, especially change that involves how they are to be evaluated. As such, it is important for people to be convinced that this evaluation system is in their best interests. One argument that helps reduce people's concerns is to point out to them that their teaching is already being evaluated. Peers, department heads, and the dean all do evaluations for raises, promotions, tenure, and so forth. If there is no formal teaching evaluation system, they base this evaluation on factors that they do not know about and a process into which they had no input. A formal system, on the other hand, allows them to design the method used in their evaluation so that they have more control over the assessment process.

In spite of these arguments, it is unlikely that everyone will be in favor of the project. By acknowledging the faculty's concerns, however, you will likely get the faculty to cooperate enough at least to try the system. Then, once they are familiar with it, they may resist the system less.

Participation

A frequent concern throughout the project was the faculty's participation in designing and implementing the system. From our previous work (Pritchard, 1995) and that of others (for example, Weiss, 1984), we realized the importance of faculty participation. When instructors help design and implement the system, it makes them more confident in the system, increases their perceptions of its validity, and ultimately leads to their greater acceptance of the system. Because of this, we tried hard to invite faculty participation. Actual participation was low, however. For example, when we asked for reactions to Phase 1, only 27 percent of the faculty returned the questionnaire.

Participation is a complex issue in academic settings. On the one hand, there seems to be a heightened need for participation, compared with other types of organizations. Academics, by their very nature, seem to feel that participation is important and have significant concerns when their sense of appropriate participation is violated. On the other hand, there is little reward for participation. Most faculty members are very busy and it is difficult for them to become heavily involved in a project such as this because of the time required and the competing demands on that time.

These two competing forces of time and participation created another problem. A small but vocal minority voiced strong concerns about participation but did not have the time to participate when invited. When others completed the system design, these faculty members again complained that they had not had input into the system.

There are several important conclusions to be drawn here. It is very difficult to obtain broad-based participation for such a project. Because of this, every effort should be made to offer such participation on a regular basis. Even if this is done, however, system designers should not expect everyone to be comfortable with their level of input. It is important that system designers accept this limitation.

You should work out how you will encourage participation before you start the project. Early on, you should give a presentation to all faculty members. It should outline the reasons for the project, its goals, and how you will accomplish these goals. This presentation should be attended by the highest-level administrator involved with the project, who should introduce and formally support the effort.

Once system development begins, instructors should receive periodic progress reports at faculty meetings. In addition, you should conduct formal meetings after every major step to keep them apprised of new developments and to obtain their feedback. If it is impossible to convene meetings after any of these steps, you should give memos to faculty outlining the project's progress and requesting their input.

After you solicit feedback, it is important to inform the faculty of any resulting changes in the system. This information should include the rationale behind the changes—that is, which specific faculty concerns led to changes in the system. You should also give an explanation for any faculty concerns that did not result in changes. This step is important because it demonstrates that the design team is taking faculty feedback and concerns seriously, even if no change was made. It is important to recognize, however, that human nature being what it is, no matter what you do, some people are unlikely to pay attention to the project until it starts to affect them personally.

Finally, as we discussed in Chapter Six, it is important to include department heads in all phases of design and implementation.

Trade-Offs Between Accuracy and Complexity

During system development, the design team must repeatedly make decisions about the level of completeness or accuracy in the system. You can design a system that measures in great detail and gives correspondingly detailed feedback. A system can also assess components in multiple ways in order to reduce measurement error. In general, however, the more complete, detailed, and accurate the system is, the more complex it is to develop, implement, and use.

Thus, there is a trade-off between the level of completeness and accuracy on the one hand and the time and effort required to develop and use the system on the other. This is a delicate balance to find. Most design teams will tend toward complex, accurate systems that become too cumbersome to use effectively. Such systems eventually collapse under their own weight. The amount of time and effort required to use the system outweighs the gains obtained from using the system. The design team and its facilitator need to guard against this tendency to overcomplicate.

You can take a couple of steps to avoid this problem. First, it is important to make faculty understand the trade-off between accuracy and cost. Second, it is helpful to estimate the amount of time and effort required to incorporate ideas proposed for the system. You can disseminate this information to the faculty, and then they can decide if the cost is worth the benefit. Finally, if people are uncertain or cannot agree about the "cost" of a particular aspect of the system, they can initially include this measure and then reevaluate it later.

Instructors' Resistance to Being Measured

Personnel often resist new measurement systems that will affect them (see, for example, Pritchard, 1995). One of the facilitators' responsibilities is to determine the source of this resistance. In most cases, some of the opposition can be attributed to the general resistance to change that most organizations experience when they attempt to implement something new. People, in general, do not like to change established routines.

There are other possible reasons for resistance, however. In some instances, people may be concerned about the amount of work required to develop the system or the additional paperwork that the system may create. Many times, you can handle such issues by explaining the system's potential benefits and by assuring personnel that you will carefully monitor the administrative work related to developing and using the system. In other words, you should explain to the personnel that the system will be cost effective or that you will revise the system until it is.

A more difficult problem is that most people simply do not like to be evaluated. Although many like to receive feedback about their work, they usually prefer to be the only ones with access to this feedback, especially if it is not positive. This is a very natural and common feeling. People are accountable for their work, though. As such, information about their performance, both positive and negative, must be accessible to others.

Faculty may resist the system's development and implementation primarily because they do not want to be evaluated. They will rarely cite this as their reason for opposing the system, however. In many cases, they will propose other reasons for their lack of support. This produces a problem for the facilitators and design team, because these people will continue to resist the idea regardless of the facts or assurances they hear.

One way to deal with resistance to measurement is to recognize their concerns formally, discussing them openly and fully. It is also worthwhile to note that any anxiety faculty are experiencing is perfectly natural. Furthermore, you should make it clear that these concerns should not prevent the college from developing a system that could improve teaching effectiveness. It may also be helpful to point out that their performance has been evaluated in the past for promotions, tenure, and pay raises and will continue to be assessed in the future with or without this system. Therefore, faculty members need to decide whether they want to continue being evaluated in the present manner or whether they would like some control over the assessment method.

People often express resistance by saying, "You can't measure teaching effectiveness!" Because there may have been no method of measurement in the past, instructors assume that none is possible. One way to address this is to ask instructors if they have any idea how well they or their colleagues teach or if they can judge when their or others' teaching is becoming better or worse. If they say yes to any of these questions, point out that what they are doing is measuring teaching effectiveness. The question is how to convert that measurement system to one that is more public and less subjective.

Although this line of reasoning will have some effect, it may not entirely put their fears to rest. One approach that has proven successful is to have instructors agree to try the system and see how it goes. Once they go through the process, their doubts usually decrease.

Importance of Being Responsive to Faculty Concerns

It was fairly common for faculty to express specific concerns about aspects of the system as it was being developed and implemented. For example, instructors were concerned about students' giving generalized negative ratings if they did not like the material or the instructor; faculty worried that these negative ratings would bias the evaluation. This concern was especially salient for faculty who did not think students should be doing teaching evaluations.

To respond to this, we did a series of analyses (described in Chapter Four), which indicated that (1) it would take a considerable percentage of such negative evaluations to have any significant impact and that (2) the actual frequency of such ratings was far below what it would take to have such an impact. We then presented these results to the faculty.

It is very important that the system designers be responsive to such concerns. Listening to faculty's objections can enhance the system's content. More important, such responsiveness communicates to the faculty that their concerns are important and will be taken seriously. This helps considerably with the overall acceptance of the system.

Importance of Planning the System's Initial Administration

One of the mistakes that we made in Phase 1 was not doing enough planning for the initial and later administrations of the student ratings. A series of important decisions must be made, such as how to choose the faculty who will be evaluated, how to notify them, how to schedule the classroom visits, who will explain the new system to the students, what to say during this explanation, who will do the classroom visits and collect the student ratings, how to process the ratings and turn them into feedback reports, how to distribute the feedback reports, who will receive copies, and what sort of discussions, if any, will occur between the instructor and, for example, the department head. It needs to be clear how all these steps will be done and who will do them.

Lack of proper planning and the subsequent problems in administering the system are very damaging to the credibility and acceptance of the entire project. Even when great effort has been made to include faculty in planning the system's design and implementation, much of the support for the project can be lost without careful implementation.

We strongly urge you to think carefully about all the implementation issues listed above and to develop a workable plan that makes everyone comfortable. It is especially important to clarify who has responsibility for what steps. We also recommend doing a small pilot project for the first administering of the system using faculty volunteers. Such a pilot will help uncover problems in the system's administration and give the system designers a chance to work them out before beginning full-scale implementation.

Students' Evaluation of Teaching

Some faculty members believe that students should not evaluate instructors. Instructors will usually cite students' lack of knowledge of teaching and the subject matter, as well as concerns about students' giving biased ratings based on instructor or course popularity.

There are indeed some dimensions of teaching effectiveness that students are not well qualified to rate. For example, in general students are poorly qualified to rate an instructor's subject matter knowledge, because they typically lack background in a particular field. Peers are much better qualified to rate this dimension.

Students do form impressions, however, that can provide useful information about teaching effectiveness. They have the greatest amount of contact with the instructor, which means that they base their ratings on multiple observations of behavior. No one can judge better than the student whether the subject matter was presented clearly. In some cases, therefore, students provide the best source of information about teaching effectiveness.

The literature concerning teaching evaluation shows that students can provide reliable, valid ratings of teaching. As such, the literature recommends that student ratings be included as one source of information about teaching effectiveness.

Our recommendations for dealing with such faculty, who are typically in the minority, are first to summarize the literature on the validity of teaching effectiveness. This information appears in Chapter One.

That will probably have a small effect but not much more. Next, start student evaluations on a pilot basis. In doing so, collect and report reliability and validity data similar to that in Chapter Four. Most important, have students rate skeptical faculty members and report the data back to the faculty confidentially. That is, do it so that the instructor can see the results but so that no one else can associate the instructor's name with the results. In most cases, skeptical instructors who see that their evaluations are reasonable will be much more supportive of student ratings. These steps will help, but even with them, one should not expect total agreement about the appropriateness of students' doing ratings.

Beliefs That Student Learning Is the Ultimate Criterion of Teaching Effectiveness

Many faculty members will posit that student learning is the ultimate criterion of teaching effectiveness and should be used as the measure of instructor effectiveness. At the very least, they will say, it should serve as a validation of other measures of teaching effectiveness.

In theory, it seems ideal to use student learning as the ultimate criterion of teaching effectiveness. If a student has not learned, it suggests that something may be wrong with the teaching. As we discussed in Chapter One, however, measuring student learning presents some significant difficulties. Potential contaminants include the student's motivation to learn, prior knowledge of the subject, differing abilities among students, and the student's interest in the subject. To interpret student learning meaningfully, one must account for these factors.

This is typically accomplished by developing pretests and posttests to measure these factors and then remove their influence. Even if one could do this, however, one would have to make test materials comparable. Not only must pretests and posttests be similar in content and difficulty across all instructors but if new material is added to a course, tests must also be changed to make them comparable with those given before the material was added. Therefore, the difficulty involved in executing this type of study makes it virtually impossible to use as a measure of individual faculty performance.

The only situation in which such efforts are justified is when the entire teaching effort of a large unit is being evaluated. National board examinations given in some professions as well as knowledge tests given to all children in the country are examples of such a situation.

Even with such efforts, it is generally not clear how much the students versus the teachers are accountable for the resulting scores.

Design Team's Frustration at Lack of Progress

There will be times during system development when members of the design team will become frustrated at what appears to be a lack of progress. The most likely time for this to occur is during the development of indicators. It can also happen if other members of the department or college, such as department heads or deans, put pressure on the design team members to complete the system.

To prevent this frustration, it helps to explain carefully to the design team at the beginning of the project how long the process is likely to take. If you explained this initially, you can later remind the people involved with the project of this. A second way to reduce frustration is to inform the design team that other schools that have tried to introduce teaching evaluation have also taken considerable time; the designers' experience is not unique. It can also be useful to point out to the group where they are in the developmental process and how much they have already accomplished. Finally, it is important to stress to the group that it takes time to develop a truly good system. The time invested in system development will be rewarded many times over when the system is used.

Disagreement on a Measure

There may be times when administrators and instructors on the design team disagree about how something should be measured. Actually, this situation occurs much less frequently than one might expect. If the design team is working together successfully, they reach compromises easily, because it usually becomes clear that both sides have valid points. There may be times, however, when a compromise is not easily achieved.

For example, in one manufacturing plant, the design team was composed of incumbents and a supervisor. There was a difference in opinion as to whether the measurement system should include the amount of unscheduled maintenance due to equipment breakdowns. The supervisor felt that the system should include that amount because the frequency of breakdowns was related to the manner in which the unit used the equipment. The incumbents, on the other hand, contended they should not be held responsible for unscheduled maintenance because the management did not give them time to perform all the scheduled maintenance set forth in the equipment manuals. Consequently, they felt that the breakdowns resulted from a lack of proper maintenance rather than worker misuse.

If the instructors and the administrators cannot agree, the first strategy is to try to compromise. The facilitator should encourage compromise and suggest possible options if it becomes necessary. In the manufacturing example, the agreed-upon compromise was that the unit would be held accountable for the amount of unscheduled maintenance only if they were allowed to do all the scheduled maintenance.

Another possible strategy, if a compromise is not apparent, is simply to let some time pass. In most situations, it is better to postpone the discussion of the debated indicator until the next meeting than to let the level of conflict in the group become too severe. Many times, group members will come up with a solution before the next meeting. Sometimes bringing in an outside expert can help resolve the issue. This is especially true if the point of contention is an issue of fact or information. If a compromise cannot be reached, one solution may be to have the group try it one way for a while, with the understanding that they will reexamine the issue later.

The most important thing in these situations is for the facilitator not to allow people to become so firmly entrenched in their positions that it becomes nearly impossible for one side to "give in" to the other. If this occurs, it becomes much more difficult to reach a compromise.

Dependence of Measures

Frequently, the measures being considered are dependent or correlated. In other words, if one goes up, the other will tend to improve also. For example, if the instructor raises more challenging questions in class, the learning environment will also probably improve. This is typically the case, but it usually is not a problem. The factors causing the indicators to vary are still different from one another. For example, the factors that determine how well challenging questions are raised are related but are not the same as those that control the type of learning environment. Consequently, it is appropriate to measure both indicators so that people are encouraged to improve both things. Correlated indicators only become a problem if they are actually measuring the same factor. In these situations, only one of the two indicators should be used.

Need for Classroom Observations or Videotaping

Some faculty members feel very strongly about the importance of classroom observation in peer evaluations. More recently, there has been an interest in videotaping class lectures for evaluation purposes.

The problem, which we have addressed several times in earlier chapters, is that the literature shows that classroom observation by peers is not reliable. It is a snapshot of teaching performance. In other words, the observation team may come on the best or worst day of the semester. Both of these procedures are invasive, and can disrupt teaching. They may alter the environment, rendering the evaluation invalid. Although these difficulties can be overcome by having multiple classroom observations, multiple raters, and carefully developed evaluation schemes accompanied by careful training, these solutions are very time consuming and logistically difficult for regular teaching evaluation.

The only exception to this is that observation can be an effective tool for mentoring. Trained observers can obtain very useful information to help individual instructors improve. This intervention is not practical on a regular basis for all instructors.

Observation is a good example of the issue we raised previously regarding the quality of the data and the cost of collecting it. There is little doubt that, properly done, observation would add to the accuracy of the evaluation and the usefulness of the feedback to the instructor. To do it well, however, would make the cost extremely high.

In dealing with this issue with faculty, our suggestion is first to point out the problems with collecting data from observations. We summarized these pitfalls earlier and discussed them in more detail in Chapter One. Then, you could indicate what would have to be done to overcome these measurement problems (for example, multiple observations, multiple raters, special observer training). The final argument is to have the faculty estimate the amount of time that would be required of the peer evaluation committee to include observations.

For example, say there is a department of thirty people in which half the instructors were evaluated each year. Each instructor would prepare one videotape from each of four classes taught over the past year or two. Only two committee members would watch these four tapes and would then complete a rating form evaluating the tapes. This is the absolute minimum structure we would suggest for reliable evaluations. It would be better to increase the number of tapes and evaluators, but in the interest of estimating the time required, we will proceed with the minimum scenario. Assume further that each tape was forty-five minutes long and that it took thirty minutes for the pair of raters to discuss the tapes and make the ratings. Finally, suppose there is a six-person committee to do ratings in the thirty-person department.

Under this scenario, each faculty member would evaluate five instructors and spend 6.5 hours on each one, for a total of 32.5 hours. With time to coordinate committee efforts and compare evaluations, they would need most of a week each year just to do the observations. Added to that would be the time to do the rest of the peer evaluation and combine it with the student evaluations. Thus, it could easily take six to seven days a year for each committee member to do the teaching evaluations. When faculty members hear scenarios such as these, their interest in peer observations tends to decrease.

Frequency of Evaluations

There are no clear criteria that can be used to determine how often faculty should be evaluated. Common sense indicates, however, that individuals who are not yet tenured but who are on a tenure track should be evaluated regularly. A reasonable recommendation would be that nontenured faculty of this type be evaluated annually. It is probably not necessary for tenured faculty to be evaluated annually. Also, faculty with a clear record of good teaching would not need to be evaluated as often. Faculty preferences should also be a factor, though. Many faculty members wish to be evaluated on a regular basis for the feedback.

Addition of Names to Feedback Reports

When a teaching evaluation system is finally put into regular use, it is obviously necessary to have instructor names associated with the evaluations. When a new teaching evaluation system is being developed, however, the faculty's acceptance is critical. To build acceptance, we recommend that there first be a trial period in which the system is not used for decision-making purposes. During the trial period, instructors and possibly their respective department heads would receive feedback reports that identified individuals by name. Reports sent to higher administrators should exclude names, however. Such a trial period allows faculty to develop some acceptance of the system, while allowing top-level administrators to see that the system operates smoothly. When the system has been evaluated and is running smoothly, names can be added to all feedback reports. At this time, participants should have enough experience with the system to feel comfortable with it.

Assignment of System Overseer

A number of steps are associated with the feedback reports. Instructors to be evaluated must be identified and informed of the upcoming evaluation. The logistics of collecting the data must be coordinated with faculty. Once the data are gathered, the feedback reports must be prepared and distributed. It is easy for a well-designed system to fail at this point, and for that reason, it is critical that this process be done well.

Someone should be formally assigned to oversee the process. In addition, people also need to be formally appointed to carry out each of the steps required to complete the process. The administrator assigned to oversee the process should communicate to those responsible for preparing the feedback reports that these duties are a regular and permanent part of their job. Preparation of the feedback reports can be significantly delayed if nobody is formally responsible for each step. This is important, because a delay in the distribution of the reports can diminish the feedback's usefulness.

One issue that occurs with outside facilitators is that the department becomes dependent on them to produce feedback reports. Because the facilitators have the most experience with the system, it is tempting to have them do the work involved with generating the reports. This may be appropriate at the start of the process, but the facilitators should very quickly turn the responsibility over to organizational personnel. A firm commitment to do the work associated with producing the feedback reports should be viewed as part of the commitment to the project.

Inclusion of Extraneous Information in Feedback Reports

At times, it is useful to include information in the reports that is not formally part of the system. Typically, this situation arises when some information will aid in the interpretation of the data. For example, suppose renovations were being made near an instructor's classroom. The distracting noise from the renovation may have affected some or all of the indicators. Another example might be if an instructor tried an innovative teaching method for the first time. In both these cases, it may be appropriate to mention this information somewhere on the feedback report.

Including additional information can also be a useful way to achieve compromises in developing measures. For example, if instructors feel that factors beyond their control may adversely affect their performance, putting a measure in the feedback report that will help make correct attributions can at times help resolve conflicts about whether to use the measure. For example, if teaching of a course involves equipment that has a history of breaking down, it may be a good idea to include the number of times that the equipment was unavailable due to malfunctions.

Importance of a Mechanism for Improving Teaching

As we discussed at the end of Chapter Six, a formal part of the usual ProMES process is that people receiving the feedback reports take the time to review them and discuss with other faculty some strategies to improve performance. We did not include that part in this project. We discussed this issue with some faculty beforehand, indicating that they might need guidance in making improvements. Although everyone supported this idea, no resources were actually committed for this purpose. We told faculty that the Center for Teaching Excellence had offered to help any faculty member requesting assistance. Few faculty took advantage of this option, however.

In planning a system, you should give considerable thought to the availability of such a mechanism. Faculty members have a legitimate point when they argue that the college evaluates them but does not give them any means to learn how to improve. Most universities have something like the Center for Teaching Excellence, which will coach faculty members; you should make this option clear to faculty. At least in this project, however, faculty preferred working with people in their own departments or college. One suggestion that most evaluated positively but that was not implemented was to have a panel of master teachers who would work with faculty. For example, a panel of excellent teachers could be formed who would meet on a regular basis with groups of faculty who wished to discuss teaching improvements.

ISSUES ARISING DURING PROMES SYSTEM DEVELOPMENT

The previous section addressed general issues to consider in starting any teaching evaluation system. In this section, we focus on issues specific to starting a teaching evaluation system with the ProMES approach.

Replacing Existing Evaluation Systems with ProMES

Some departments may already possess a system that collects data and gives feedback to instructors regularly. In these situations, it is worth considering whether ProMES is worth the effort.

In order to answer this question, it must be determined whether the current measurement system adequately meets the department's needs, thereby motivating and aiding the instructors to be effective teachers. The system must be examined to determine if the measures validly reflect what the instructors should be doing, if they are under the instructors' control, and if they are complete. In other words, does the system meet the criteria required for a good measurement system that we outlined at the end of Chapter One?

The best source of information is usually the instructors in the department. In some situations, however, the instructors may be hesitant to criticize the existing system, because people in the current administration may have put it in place. The instructors are more likely to be reluctant when the exact role of the person asking for their opinions is unclear. Consequently, it is often important to establish a good rapport with the instructors to determine their real views on the existing system.

If it is determined that the existing system does not meet the department's needs, ProMES can be used to modify, replace, or supplement it. If people in the organization hold the existing system in high regard, however, any changes must be handled with some delicacy.

It may also be useful to implement some aspects of ProMES when the existing system does contain good measures. By developing contingencies for the existing measures, you could add new features to the system. Some of these could include (1) creating a single index of effectiveness, (2) allowing instructors to judge how well they are doing relative to expectations, (3) aggregating effectiveness across departments, and (4) comparing effectiveness between departments. If adding these features to the existing system would make it more useful to the department, then it would be worthwhile to develop ProMES contingencies even in a department that possesses a system of high quality.

Composing ProMES Design Teams

ProMES design teams formed to develop measures for a department typically include a facilitator and three to five instructors. It may also be beneficial to include the department head or assistant. That person's role would be to (1) supply information to the team on relevant matters, such as the meaning of different measures; (2) provide guidance to the group so that they do not omit important issues or policies; and (3) act as an intermediary between the instructors and facilitator. This function is important, because the instructors and the facilitator will most likely have different perspectives on the work and the project. Other administrators could be added as needed, but care must be taken that the administrators do not dominate the meetings.

If a department is small (six faculty members or fewer), it may be possible for the entire department to be on the design team. This would be impractical with larger departments, though. If choices have to be made, it is usually best for the administrators or facilitator to approach key opinion leaders or instructors in key departmental positions. Another acceptable method of selection may be for the instructors to select some or all of the design team members.

If the design team is developing measures for more than one department, there should be at least one representative from each department. Whether the design team is developing measures for one department or several, however, the design team should have between five and eight people. Design teams larger than these tend to be slowed down by the size of the group. Consequently, care must be taken in forming design teams in large departments, because it is difficult to have small design teams be representative of the larger unit.

Using Outside Facilitators

Someone who is acquainted with ProMES and is skilled in group processes (conducting meetings, listening, reaching consensus, and so forth) is the ideal choice for an outside facilitator. If it is not possible to obtain such a person, however, someone within the organization can function in this role. It is not required that this person be an expert at teaching, because the administrators and instructors will provide the expertise required to design the system. The facilitator should, however, possess a thorough understanding of ProMES and be skilled at working with groups. It is also ideal for the facilitator to be someone whom the other design team members respect.

In most situations, it is better to use two facilitators so that they can assist each other and review the design team's progress together. This is especially true when the facilitators do not possess much experience with ProMES. This allows them to give each other feedback about how they are handling the process.

It is possible to gain considerable knowledge about how to do ProMES from studying this book and a book by Pritchard (1990). Direct training is better, but these sources contain considerable information that will help a person who is experienced in facilitating groups.

Consulting in Addition to Facilitating

One temptation that may arise during system development is for facilitators to become organizational consultants. In other words, they may be tempted to take a more direct role in attempting to solve organizational problems. The most common instance of this is when facilitators perceive that they can clear up a problem that arose in system development meetings by going directly to someone in the administration to work out a solution. Many times in these situations, the facilitator can actually solve the problem. Consequently, there is often pressure for the facilitators to meet with personnel outside the design team to try to create solutions.

Although it may be tempting for the facilitator to solve problems for the unit, that course of action is usually a mistake for several reasons. The first is that meeting with someone external to the design team to work out solutions can become very complicated and time consuming. Second, it is often difficult for facilitators to extract themselves once this process has started. Finally, facilitators may be perceived as advocating one position or another if they take on the role of consultant. This in turn can influence personnel, both inside and outside the department, to perceive the facilitators as less than fully objective.

The predicament for many facilitators is that there are certain situations when the facilitators *should* meet with personnel external to the design team to exchange information or to resolve problems that arise during system development. Consequently, it becomes a matter of judgment about when facilitators should go beyond simply helping to develop the system. One general guideline is that facilitators should only take that step when it is directly related to system development.

Having Doubts About ProMES's Subjectivity

ProMES is based on the combined judgments of the design team and administration. Subjectivity is present in determining the objectives and indicators and especially in developing contingencies. Traditionally, subjectivity is associated with lack of accuracy, unverifiability, and measures that are of lesser quality than those based on "objective" data. In dealing with teaching effectiveness, however, subjectivity is not only acceptable but it is both desirable and essential. This is true because determining what represents good or poor teaching is a matter of policy.

The components of ProMES are statements of this policy. Objectives, indicators, and contingencies denote which activities are important to the group (and, by omission, which ones are not), the relative importance of various activities, the expected level of each activity, and how effective different levels of each activity are. This is policy, which is by nature a matter of judgment; thus, it is inherently subjective.

ProMES offers a technique for determining and communicating policy formally. By discussing, quantifying, and presenting policy for the administration's formal approval, one can reduce existing ambiguity in policy. This process also offers a way of developing an explicit policy where none existed before.

It is important to recognize that all measurement systems are subjective in the sense that determining what measures to include is subjective. The important thing, therefore, is not whether there is subjectivity in the system but whether the measurement system accurately reflects department policy. In order to achieve this, two conditions must be met. First, the list of objectives and indicators must be complete, so that important aspects of teaching effectiveness are not omitted. Second, the system must identify what teachers should be doing. In other words, the objectives, indicators, and contingencies must be consistent with policy and be correctly scaled on effectiveness.

In developing a ProMES system, design teams meet these necessary conditions for identifying policy by including a clear process of system approval by the administration. During system development, members of the design team discuss objectives and indicators at length. Once they have reached a consensus, they take the objectives and indicators to the department heads and deans for modification and approval. They then repeat the process for the contingencies. Consequently, all levels of the department or college directly involved with teaching have two separate opportunities to review and formally concur with the policy that will guide the department. This developmental procedure maximizes the chances that the measurement system will correctly reflect policy.

Having Doubts About Reducing Teaching to a Number

Some faculty and administrators will take the position that something as complex as teaching effectiveness cannot be simplified into a single number. They believe that to do so means you have lost the essence of the phenomenon. Although it is true that some information is lost whenever a single number summarizes a complex set of information, it is important to realize that this is already being done whenever decisions are made about promotions, pay raises, and so forth. For example, all the complex information in a tenure decision must come down to a yes or a no. That is, administrators decide whether a professor has performed above a certain level of performance or not. This is equivalent to combining all the tenure information into a single index and deciding whether or not the resulting value is above a critical threshold.

Consequently, instructors need to ask themselves two questions. First, is it better to have each administrator use their own personal, subjective strategy to identify and combine the information they deem important about teaching, or is it better to determine explicitly the relevant factors, their relative importance to teaching effectiveness, and the method used to combine them? According to the literature (Sawyer, 1966), mechanical methods of combining multiple indicators are superior to clinical strategies. The second question is whether instructors want to help develop the measurement system used to evaluate their performance, or whether they would rather that the administration do it without their input. In most cases, people prefer to have the opportunity to provide their input into the measurement system.

Meeting with Only Part of the Design Team

At times, it is appropriate to meet with only a part of the design team. One of these times is when some of the team members do not possess the necessary expertise to make reasonable judgments. This situation will most likely occur during contingency development. For example, some design team members may simply have no knowledge about what is a reasonable maximum, what the shape of the contingencies should be, and so forth. In these situations, it is appropriate to meet with only those members who have reasonable expertise.

Another time it may be appropriate to meet with only part of the design team is when scheduling conflicts make it impossible for the entire team to meet. In an ideal world these situations never occur, but in the real world conferences, illness, and so forth may make it impossible for everyone to attend every meeting. Every attempt should be made to schedule meetings so that all members can attend, even if this means postponing meetings for a week or two. If the only way to achieve perfect attendance is to postpone meetings for an extended period, however, it may be better to meet with only part of the team.

Several conditions should be met in these situations. First, the absent members must be completely comfortable with the arrangement. Second, absent members should be kept apprised of the work done at the meetings they could not attend. Finally, meetings should not be convened if only a small percentage of the design team can attend. For example, in the CVM project, the design team that developed objectives and indicators consisted of six faculty members. Meetings would not be convened if fewer than three team members were able to attend.

Developing Only Linear Contingencies

Past experiences with ProMES indicates that completely linear contingencies are possible but rare. Thus, it is almost impossible to develop a system in which the majority of the contingencies are linear. If the design team is developing linear contingencies, there is probably something wrong with their development process. They may not fully understand the contingencies and what they represent. If this is the case, it may be advantageous to review what contingencies are and to show them examples of contingencies from other departments or the project described in this book.

Many times, the cause of this problem stems from the contingency template itself (see Figure 3.2). Once the minimums, maximums, and expected levels have been placed on the template, there may be a tendency for the design team simply to draw a straight line from the expected level to the maximum and from the expected level to the minimum. If this happens, it is useful to ask whether there are any points between the expected level and the maximum at which things change for any reason. In most cases, such points occur when the effectiveness increases or decreases at a different rate. This consideration will help the design team identify inflection points that will, in turn, reduce the contingencies' linearity.

Including Effectiveness on a Contingency's Vertical Axis

Technically, *effectiveness* is defined as the relationship between measures of output and the organization's expectations or goals. When a contingency such as collegiality is developed for an indicator, the amount of collegiality that the instructor exhibits is compared with expectations and is expressed in an effectiveness score. A value above the expected level means that it exceeds expectations. The larger the value, the more it exceeds expectations. Conversely, a value below the expected level means that it falls below expectations.

Thus, the scores that the ProMES process generates are technically effectiveness measures. This is true even when the indicator is a measure of efficiency. For example, one measure of a faculty member's efficiency might be his or her success at publishing academic articles. This could be measured by comparing the number of articles actually published per year to the number of articles written per year. For this indicator, the contingency would demonstrate how the instructor's level of efficiency compares to expectations, or how effective that level of efficiency is. There is nothing magical about the term *effectiveness,* however, and if system users prefer another term, they can work with that one.

Giving Two Contingencies Equal Rankings

It is not unusual for the design team to have trouble deciding which one of two indicator maximums is most important. If this occurs, it is perfectly acceptable to give them the same rank. If the design committee cannot decide between the maximums that are ranked fourth and fifth, for example, both should receive a rank of 4. The next most important indicator would have a rank of 5. When the effectiveness value for indicator maximums is calculated, the equal indicators should receive the same maximum effectiveness value.

Determining Improvement Priorities

When designers determine improvement priorities in the feedback report (see Table 3.3), they must select the size of the increase to use in calculations. Remember that priorities depend on the change in effectiveness that would result with an increase in each indicator. This issue requires some thought, because the size of the increase used to determine the change in effectiveness will be important. If the increase in one indicator is less than in another, the one with the smaller increase will seem less important to improve, even when the two contingencies are exactly alike.

Contingencies are set up with the values on the horizontal axis ranging from the minimum to maximum possible. Between these two extremes, there could be many different values or very few.

The solution to this problem is to use approximately the same number of intervals for all of the contingencies. If minimums and maximums are interpreted as having the same degree of negative or the same degree of positive for each indicator, the range of possible values between the two extremes represents a standard sort of range. Consequently, it is appropriate to divide each of them into the same number of intervals. In this project, with ratings on a five-point scale, we selected an interval of .25 because we thought it represented a meaningful difference.

There are other situations in which one cannot easily break the measures used into intervals. This is true of the number of works an instructor publishes on teaching. In such a case, a good rule of thumb is to use five to seven intervals. It may not always be possible to have exactly the same number of intervals for each contingency. In that case, make the number of intervals as close as possible.

Having Different Indicators in Departments

Whether or not separate departments have different indicators is a matter of policy. If the policies within the different departments are similar, then there would probably be no need to develop different indicators for each department. If policy varies significantly across departments, however, then the system's added accuracy might make it worthwhile to develop and use different indicators. Bear in mind, however, that using different indicators adds a significant amount of additional work when the system is used. Also remember that many dissimilarities in policy can be incorporated by using different contingencies in the various departments, as was done in the project described here.

Interpreting Percentage of Maximum Based on Different Standards

The most effective way of comparing teaching effectiveness across departments is to use the percentage of maximum index. Remember that it is calculated by expressing an instructor's actual overall score as a percentage of the maximum possible. The departmental percentage of maximum is then determined by calculating the average percentage of maximum for the instructors evaluated within the department. If the overall percentage of maximum for one department is 73 percent and another is 82 percent, the second department is more effective.

This is an appropriate way of comparing departments, as long as the standards used for determining maximums are the same for all the departments. In other words, the effectiveness scores for the maximum possible indicator values must be defined in the same way for all departments. If one department uses maximums that are easier to achieve than a second department, it will be easier for the first department to have a high percentage of maximum. Consequently, the comparison between the two departments would be distorted.

Obviously, then, the maximums must be defined in the same way if there are to be comparisons across departments. The best way to ensure this is to have the effectiveness scores associated with the maximums reviewed by a group of administrators or, at the very least, one administrator who is responsible for all the departments to be compared. The idea is to have people who are completely familiar with the departments' functioning judge whether the effectiveness maximums are equally high. A group of knowledgeable administrators, such as department heads, can be used if no one is totally familiar with all the departments. In this case, the issue should be explained to the group. They should then review the maximums of the departments together and make their best judgment.

Avoiding a Negative Tone in Feedback Meetings

Ideally, administrators (usually department heads) should meet with faculty to discuss their teaching evaluation. This is especially true for untenured faculty. If the administrator conducts the feedback meetings improperly, both parties may have a negative experience. For example, the administrator may spend only a few moments noting areas in which the instructor has high scores and then spend the majority of the time focusing on areas in which the instructor has lower scores. This usually makes the meeting into a negative experience. The experience is even more negative if the administrator assumes a blaming attitude with the instructor. Instructors whose overall effectiveness has improved significantly but who receive predominantly negative feedback in the meetings feel quite frustrated.

The best way to deal with this situation is to have facilitators train administrators in how to conduct feedback meetings. Administrators need to know about the negative consequences that result from blaming and focusing only on the low scores or decreases in effectiveness. If, once the feedback meetings have begun, facilitators become aware that the meetings are becoming negative experiences for people, they should tactfully point it out to administrators, usually in private, and help them to improve.

Preventing Instructors from "Gaming" the System

All feedback systems can be "gamed." In other words, there is always a way for people to distort the information so that they look good. An example here would be if instructors knowingly used a less effective teaching approach simply to obtain better ratings from the students. Although it is desirable to develop a system that is minimally susceptible to such distortion, it is impossible to design one that is completely immune to it. The way to control gaming is to design a system that instructors do not want to distort.

ProMES attempts to achieve this by making sure that instructors are involved in all aspects of system development. If instructors see the system as their own, they will be less inclined to attempt to distort it. It is equally important that the system be valid. If the instructors perceive it as valid, they will be much less likely to attempt to distort it.

A CONCLUDING COMMENT

In this chapter and throughout the book, we have raised a whole host of issues that are important to the design of a teaching evaluation system. All these issues may seem overwhelming, but we urge you not to quit. If all parties are sincerely trying to develop a good measurement and feedback system, they will indeed complete the job. We mention all these issues to help you avoid some pitfalls, many of which we have encountered ourselves in this and other feedback projects.

APPENDIX A: FACULTY EVALUATION QUESTIONNAIRE FOR OBJECTIVES AND INDICATORS

Directions included a brief summary of the project and stated objectives and items similar to those in Figure 3.1.

1. Do the questions cover all important aspects of classroom teaching?

_____ Yes _____ No

Comments:

2. Are the questions clear and understandable?

_____ Yes _____ No

Comments:

3. Would results from this form be likely to aid teachers in improving classroom performance?

_____ Yes _____ No

Comments:

4. Would responses from students to these questions be useful to administrators in determining students' perceptions of teachers' performance?

_____ Yes   _____ No

Comments:

APPENDIX B: DESIGN COMMITTEE QUESTIONNAIRES (TEC AND CONTINGENCY COMMITTEES)

TEACHING EXCELLENCE COMMITTEE QUESTIONNAIRE

Please indicate your feelings about each of the following statements by circling the number that corresponds to how strongly you agree or disagree with the statement.

1. The objectives our committee developed are accurate.

1	2	3	4	5
Strongly Disagree	Disagree	Neither Agree nor Disagree	Agree	Strongly Agree

Comments:

2. The indicators our committee developed are accurate.

1	2	3	4	5
Strongly Disagree	Disagree	Neither Agree nor Disagree	Agree	Strongly Agree

Comments:

3. True consensus was reached on the various decisions the group made about objectives and indicators.

1	2	3	4	5
Strongly Disagree	Disagree	Neither Agree nor Disagree	Agree	Strongly Agree

Comments:

4. The final list of objectives (after review by administration) is accurate.

1	2	3	4	5
Strongly Disagree	Disagree	Neither Agree nor Disagree	Agree	Strongly Agree

Comments:

5. The final list of indicators (after review by administration) is accurate.

1	2	3	4	5
Strongly Disagree	Disagree	Neither Agree nor Disagree	Agree	Strongly Agree

Comments:

6. The process of administrative approval of the objectives and indicators was fair and reasonable.

1	2	3	4	5
Strongly Disagree	Disagree	Neither Agree nor Disagree	Agree	Strongly Agree

Comments:

7. The administration valued our input when making their decisions concerning the final list of objectives and indicators.

1	2	3	4	5
Strongly Disagree	Disagree	Neither Agree nor Disagree	Agree	Strongly Agree

Comments:

CONTINGENCY COMMITTEE QUESTIONNAIRE

Please indicate your feelings about each of the following statements by circling the number that corresponds to how strongly you agree or disagree with the statement.

1. The contingencies our committee developed are accurate.

1	2	3	4	5
Strongly Disagree	Disagree	Neither Agree nor Disagree	Agree	Strongly Agree

Comments:

2. True consensus was reached on the various decisions the group made about contingencies.

1	2	3	4	5
Strongly Disagree	Disagree	Neither Agree nor Disagree	Agree	Strongly Agree

Comments:

3. The process of administrative approval of the contingencies was
   fair and reasonable.

1	2	3	4	5
Strongly	Disagree	Neither Agree	Agree	Strongly
Disagree		nor Disagree		Agree

   Comments:

4. The administration valued our input when making their decisions
   concerning the final list of contingencies.

1	2	3	4	5
Strongly	Disagree	Neither Agree	Agree	Strongly
Disagree		nor Disagree		Agree

   Comments:

APPENDIX C: GENERAL EVALUATION QUESTIONNAIRE

This questionnaire was sent to all faculty who had either (1) not been evaluated or (2) been evaluated only once.

This questionnaire is designed to evaluate Phase 1 of the CVM teaching evaluation system, i.e., the student rating system. Please note that we are referring to the student rating system, not the newly proposed peer evaluation system.

PART I. BACKGROUND INFORMATION

1. Which of the following statements best describes your level of participation in the development of the student rating system? Please check all statements that apply to you.

    _____ I was a member of the Teaching Excellence Committee during the development of this rating system.

    _____ I was on the committee that developed the contingencies in my department.

    _____ I provided input at departmental meetings when modifications of the system were discussed.

    _____ I attended at least one departmental meeting when the system was reviewed.

    _____ I attended at least one of the collegewide presentations regarding the system.

    _____ I was aware that a system was being developed, but I was not involved in any way in its development or approval.

    _____ I was unaware that this system was being developed.

    _____ I was not at the University when the system was being developed.

2. Have you been evaluated by the student rating system?

    _____ Yes, at least once.

    _____ No, I have not been evaluated by the student rating system.

3. On average, what has your Percentage of Maximum score from the student rating system been?

    _____ Below 50 percent.

    _____ Between 50 percent and 59 percent

    _____ Between 60 percent and 69 percent.

    _____ Between 70 percent and 79 percent.

    _____ Between 80 percent and 89 percent.

    _____ 90 percent or above.

    _____ I have not been evaluated.

4. Which of the following statements best reflects how consistent your student ratings were with your expectations?

    _____ On average, my ratings were lower than I expected.

    _____ On average, my ratings were at the level I expected.

    _____ On average, my ratings were higher than I expected.

5. In which department is your primary appointment?

PART II.   GENERAL SYSTEM EVALUATION

This section of the questionnaire is designed to evaluate your reactions to the *student rating system*. The "Does Not Apply" response is to be used with any question for which you have no opinion or have had no experience.

Satisfaction with the System

The next four questions ask about your satisfaction with the student rating system. Some of the questions ask about your satisfaction with the *design* of the system (e.g., the items on the student rating form, the contingencies, and the feedback reports); some ask about your satisfaction with the *implementation* of the student rating system (e.g., the scheduling of the evaluations, decisions regarding who will be evaluated and how often, the speed with which feedback is received, etc.); finally, some ask about your satisfaction with *how the data from the system have been (or will be) used* by either departmental or college administrators. Please think carefully about your level of satisfaction with each of these different components and then answer the following questions.

6. In general, I am satisfied with the design of the student rating system (e.g., items on the student rating form, the contingencies, and the feedback reports).

Strongly Agree	Agree	Neither Agree nor Disagree	Disagree	Disagree Strongly	Does Not Apply

7. In general, I am satisfied with the implementation of the student rating system (e.g., scheduling of the evaluations, decisions regarding who will be evaluated and how often, the speed with which feedback is received, etc.).

Strongly Agree	Agree	Neither Agree nor Disagree	Disagree	Disagree Strongly	Does Not Apply

8. In general, I am satisfied with how the administration in my department uses the data from the student rating system.

Strongly Agree	Agree	Neither Agree nor Disagree	Disagree	Disagree Strongly	Does Not Apply

9. In general, I expect I will be satisfied with how the College Administration (i.e., the Deans and Associate Deans) will use the data from the student rating system.

Strongly Agree	Agree	Neither Agree nor Disagree	Disagree	Disagree Strongly	Does Not Apply

Satisfaction with the Overall Teacher Evaluation System

10. If peer evaluations (with the option of direct or videotaped classroom observation) are added to the student evaluation system, I will be satisfied with the combined overall teaching evaluation system.

Strongly Agree	Agree	Neither Agree nor Disagree	Disagree	Disagree Strongly	Does Not Apply

System Validity

11. In general, I believe the student rating system is valid.

    Strongly   Agree   Neither Agree   Disagree   Disagree   Does Not
    Agree   nor Disagree   Strongly   Apply

12. The student rating system includes all the important aspects of classroom teaching that students are able to observe.

    Strongly   Agree   Neither Agree   Disagree   Disagree   Does Not
    Agree   nor Disagree   Strongly   Apply

13. Student ratings should be part of a comprehensive teacher evaluation system.

    Strongly   Agree   Neither Agree   Disagree   Disagree   Does Not
    Agree   nor Disagree   Strongly   Apply

14. The students here are able to rate accurately my classroom teaching performance.

    Strongly   Agree   Neither Agree   Disagree   Disagree   Does Not
    Agree   nor Disagree   Strongly   Apply

Cost-Effectiveness and Usefulness of the System

15. The student rating system has produced results that have been useful in *helping me improve* my teaching performance.

    Strongly   Agree   Neither Agree   Disagree   Disagree   Does Not
    Agree   nor Disagree   Strongly   Apply

16. The student rating system produces results that are useful in *helping the administrators in my department* evaluate the quality of teaching.

    Strongly   Agree   Neither Agree   Disagree   Disagree   Does Not
    Agree   nor Disagree   Strongly   Apply

17. The student rating system produces results that are useful in *helping the College administrators evaluate* the quality of teaching at the CVM.

    Strongly   Agree   Neither Agree   Disagree   Disagree   Does Not
    Agree   nor Disagree   Strongly   Apply

18. The student rating system provides benefits that outweigh the costs (e.g., time, energy, effort, etc.) of using it.

Strongly Agree   Agree   Neither Agree nor Disagree   Disagree   Disagree Strongly   Does Not Apply

Participation in System Development

19. I was given as much opportunity as I wanted to participate in the development of the student rating system.

Strongly Agree   Agree   Neither Agree nor Disagree   Disagree   Disagree Strongly   Does Not Apply

Underlying Factors That Contribute to System Effectiveness

20. The student rating system has helped faculty understand what is perceived in their departments as good teaching.

Strongly Agree   Agree   Neither Agree nor Disagree   Disagree   Disagree Strongly   Does Not Apply

21. The student rating system has motivated faculty to make changes in the way they teach their classes.

Strongly Agree   Agree   Neither Agree nor Disagree   Disagree   Disagree Strongly   Does Not Apply

22. The feedback from the student rating system shows faculty what they need to change to improve their teaching.

Strongly Agree   Agree   Neither Agree nor Disagree   Disagree   Disagree Strongly   Does Not Apply

Organizational Support for the System

23. My Department Head appears to support the student rating system.

Strongly Agree   Agree   Neither Agree nor Disagree   Disagree   Disagree Strongly   Does Not Apply

24. College Administration appears to support the student rating system.

Strongly Agree   Agree   Neither Agree nor Disagree   Disagree   Disagree Strongly   Does Not Apply

25. I expect that the results of the student rating system will be used in making promotion and tenure decisions.

Strongly Agree	Agree	Neither Agree nor Disagree	Disagree	Disagree Strongly	Does Not Apply

26. I expect that instructors who are rated highly by the student rating system are more likely to be rewarded (e.g., receive teaching awards, promotion, tenure, merit increases, etc.) for their teaching.

Strongly Agree	Agree	Neither Agree nor Disagree	Disagree	Disagree Strongly	Does Not Apply

Utilization of the Feedback Provided

27. Faculty are offered assistance in improving any teaching deficiencies they may have.

Strongly Agree	Agree	Neither Agree nor Disagree	Disagree	Disagree Strongly	Does Not Apply

28. Resources are available to faculty to help them improve their teaching.

Strongly Agree	Agree	Neither Agree nor Disagree	Disagree	Disagree Strongly	Does Not Apply

APPENDIX D: ADMINISTRATIVE EVALUATION QUESTIONNAIRE

This version of the Administrative Evaluation Questionnaire was sent to all departmental and collegewide administrators. It included the same items as the General Evaluation Questionnaire in Appendix C but also included items that were specifically designed to measure administrators' reactions.

This questionnaire is designed to evaluate Phase 1 of the CVM teaching evaluation system, i.e., the student rating system. Please note that we are referring to the student rating system, not the newly proposed peer evaluation system. It has two purposes: (1) to assess your overall responses to the student rating system, and (2) to assess whether you feel the student rating system is superior to a more traditional system. It is an anonymous questionnaire.

PART I.   BACKGROUND INFORMATION

1. Please indicate what administrative position you hold:

   _____ Dean or Associate Dean

   _____ Department Head

   _____ Collegewide Promotion and Tenure Committee

2. Which of the following statements best describes your level of participation in the development of the student rating system? Please check all statements that apply to you.

   _____ I was a member of the Teaching Excellence Committee during the development of this rating system.

   _____ I was on the committee that developed the contingencies in my department.

_____ I provided input at departmental meetings when modifications of the system were discussed.

_____ I attended at least one departmental meeting when the system was reviewed.

_____ I attended at least one of the collegewide presentations regarding the system.

_____ I was aware that a system was being developed, but I was not involved in any way in its development or approval.

_____ I was unaware that this system was being developed.

_____ I was not at the University when the system was being developed.

3. Have you been evaluated by the student rating system?

_____ Yes, at least once.

_____ No, I have not been evaluated by the student rating system.

4. On average, what has your Percentage of Maximum score from the student rating system been?

_____ Below 50 percent.

_____ Between 50 percent and 59 percent.

_____ Between 60 percent and 69 percent.

_____ Between 70 percent and 79 percent.

_____ Between 80 percent and 89 percent.

_____ 90 percent or above.

_____ I have not been evaluated.

5. Which of the following statements best reflects how consistent your student ratings were with your expectations?

_____ On average, my ratings were lower than I expected.

_____ On average, my ratings were at the level I expected.

_____ On average, my ratings were higher than I expected.

6. In which department is your primary appointment?

PART II.   GENERAL SYSTEM EVALUATION

This section of the questionnaire is designed to evaluate your reactions to the student rating system. The "Does Not Apply" response is to be used with any question for which you have no opinion or have had no experience.

Satisfaction with the System

The next four questions ask about your satisfaction with the student rating system. Some of the questions ask about your satisfaction with the design of the system (e.g., the items on the student rating form, the contingencies, and the feedback reports); some ask about your satisfaction with the implementation of the student rating system (e.g., the scheduling of the evaluations, decisions regarding who will be evaluated and how often, the speed with which feedback is received, etc.); finally, some ask about your satisfaction with how the data from the system have been (or will be) used by either departmental or college administrators. Please think carefully about your level of satisfaction with each of these different components and then answer the following questions.

7. In general, I am satisfied with the design of the student rating system (e.g., items on the student rating form, the contingencies, and the feedback reports).

Strongly Agree	Agree	Neither Agree nor Disagree	Disagree	Disagree Strongly	Does Not Apply

8. In general, I am satisfied with the implementation of the student rating system (e.g., scheduling of the evaluations, decisions regarding who will be evaluated and how often, the speed with which feedback is received, etc.).

Strongly Agree	Agree	Neither Agree nor Disagree	Disagree	Disagree Strongly	Does Not Apply

9. In general, I am satisfied with how the administration in my department uses the data from the student rating system.

Strongly Agree	Agree	Neither Agree nor Disagree	Disagree	Disagree Strongly	Does Not Apply

10. In general, I expect I will be satisfied with how the College Administration (i.e., the Deans and Associate Deans) will use the data from the student rating system.

Strongly Agree	Agree	Neither Agree nor Disagree	Disagree	Disagree Strongly	Does Not Apply

Satisfaction with the Overall Teacher Evaluation System

11. If peer evaluations (with the option of direct or videotaped classroom observation) are added to the student evaluation system, I will be satisfied with the combined overall teaching evaluation system.

Strongly Agree	Agree	Neither Agree nor Disagree	Disagree	Disagree Strongly	Does Not Apply

System Validity

12. In general, I believe the student rating system is valid.

Strongly Agree	Agree	Neither Agree nor Disagree	Disagree	Disagree Strongly	Does Not Apply

13. The student rating system includes all the important aspects of classroom teaching that students are able to observe.

Strongly Agree	Agree	Neither Agree nor Disagree	Disagree	Disagree Strongly	Does Not Apply

Cost-Effectiveness and Usefulness of the System

14. The student rating system has produced results that have been useful in *helping me improve* my teaching performance.

Strongly Agree	Agree	Neither Agree nor Disagree	Disagree	Disagree Strongly	Does Not Apply

15. The student rating system produces results that are useful in *helping the administrators in my department evaluate* the quality of teaching.

Strongly Agree	Agree	Neither Agree nor Disagree	Disagree	Disagree Strongly	Does Not Apply

16. The student rating system produces results that are useful in *helping the College administrators evaluate* the quality of teaching at the CVM.

Strongly Agree	Agree	Neither Agree nor Disagree	Disagree	Disagree Strongly	Does Not Apply

17. The student rating system provides benefits that outweigh the costs (e.g., time, energy, effort, etc.) of using it.

Strongly Agree	Agree	Neither Agree nor Disagree	Disagree	Disagree Strongly	Does Not Apply

Participation in System Development

18. I was given as much opportunity as I wanted to participate in the development of the student rating system.

Strongly Agree	Agree	Neither Agree nor Disagree	Disagree	Disagree Strongly	Does Not Apply

Underlying Factors That Contribute to System Effectiveness

19. The student rating system has helped faculty understand what is perceived in their departments as good teaching.

Strongly Agree	Agree	Neither Agree nor Disagree	Disagree	Disagree Strongly	Does Not Apply

20. The student rating system has motivated faculty to make changes in the way they teach their classes.

Strongly Agree	Agree	Neither Agree nor Disagree	Disagree	Disagree Strongly	Does Not Apply

21. The feedback from the student rating system shows faculty what they need to change to improve their teaching.

Strongly Agree	Agree	Neither Agree nor Disagree	Disagree	Disagree Strongly	Does Not Apply

PART III.   COMPARISON OF THE NEW SYSTEM TO A TRADITIONAL SYSTEM

This last section is designed to determine if you feel that the Phase 1 student rating system is superior to a more traditional system for administrative purposes. An example of a traditional system is the student rating system used by the remainder of the colleges at your university. *In a traditional system students complete a student rating form, and only the item averages and frequencies are reported back to the faculty and administration.*

In contrast to this traditional system, *the student rating system used by the CVM provides the average student ratings, the average overall effectiveness and percentage of maximum scores that correspond to those student ratings, and priorities for improvement.*

The questions below ask you to compare making administrative decisions using these two systems. The "Does Not Apply" response is to be used with any question for which you have no opinion or have had no experience.

22. The student rating system provides better data than a traditional system for evaluating the teaching skills of individual instructors.

Strongly Agree	Agree	Neither Agree nor Disagree	Disagree	Disagree Strongly	Does Not Apply

23. Compared to a traditional system, the data from the student rating system allows me to make better comparisons regarding the effectiveness of different individuals within a specific department, even when they taught different types or levels of class (e.g., undergraduate lectures, graduate seminars, professional labs, etc.).

Strongly Agree	Agree	Neither Agree nor Disagree	Disagree	Disagree Strongly	Does Not Apply

24. The data from the student rating system allow me to compare the effectiveness of individuals across different departments better than a traditional system would.

Strongly Agree	Agree	Neither Agree nor Disagree	Disagree	Disagree Strongly	Does Not Apply

25. The student rating system provides better information for counseling instructors than a traditional system.

| Strongly Agree | Agree | Neither Agree nor Disagree | Disagree | Disagree Strongly | Does Not Apply |

26. The student rating system is a better way of measuring college teaching than the traditional method.

| Strongly Agree | Agree | Neither Agree nor Disagree | Disagree | Disagree Strongly | Does Not Apply |

27. The student rating system is a more accurate reflection of teaching skills than the traditional system.

| Strongly Agree | Agree | Neither Agree nor Disagree | Disagree | Disagree Strongly | Does Not Apply |

28. The student rating system will be more helpful in making tenure decisions regarding teaching than the traditional system.

| Strongly Agree | Agree | Neither Agree nor Disagree | Disagree | Disagree Strongly | Does Not Apply |

29. Overall, the student rating system is superior to a traditional system.

| Strongly Agree | Agree | Neither Agree nor Disagree | Disagree | Disagree Strongly | Does Not Apply |

APPENDIX E: FEEDBACK EVALUATION QUESTIONNAIRE

This third version of the questionnaire was sent to all faculty who were evaluated more than once.

This questionnaire is designed to evaluate Phase 1 of the CVM teaching evaluation system, i.e., the student rating system. Please note that we are referring to the student rating system, not the newly proposed peer evaluation system. This questionnaire has two purposes: (1) to assess your overall responses to the student rating system, and (2) to determine what factors influence the use of the student rating system feedback to improve teaching effectiveness.

Because some of our analyses require the use of your actual average overall effectiveness and percentage of maximum scores, we have included your name on this questionnaire. Please be assured that only one individual on the research team will see your responses to these items and will never reveal your answers to anyone.

Name:

PART I.   BACKGROUND INFORMATION

1. Which of the following statements best describes your level of participation in the development of the student rating system? Please check all statements that apply to you.

   _____ I was a member of the Teaching Excellence Committee during the development of this rating system.

   _____ I was on the committee that developed the contingencies in my department.

   _____ I provided input at departmental meetings when modifications of the system were discussed.

_____ I attended at least one departmental meeting when the system was reviewed.

_____ I attended at least one of the collegewide presentations regarding the system.

_____ I was aware that a system was being developed, but I was not involved in any way in its development or approval.

_____ I was unaware that this system was being developed.

_____ I was not at Texas A&M when the system was being developed.

2. Have you been evaluated by the student rating system?

_____ Yes, I have been evaluated at least once.

_____ No, I have not been evaluated by the student rating system.

3. On average, what has your Percentage of Maximum score from the student rating system been?

_____ Below 50 percent.

_____ Between 50 percent and 59 percent.

_____ Between 60 percent and 69 percent.

_____ Between 70 percent and 79 percent.

_____ Between 80 percent and 89 percent.

_____ 90 percent or above.

_____ I have not been evaluated.

4. Which of the following statements best reflects how consistent your student ratings were with your expectations?

_____ On average, my ratings were lower than I expected.

_____ On average, my ratings were at the level I expected.

_____ On average, my ratings were higher than I expected.

5. In which department is your primary appointment?

PART II.   GENERAL SYSTEM EVALUATION

This section of the questionnaire is designed to evaluate your reactions to the Phase 1 *student rating system*. The "Does Not Apply" response is to be used with any question for which you have no opinion or have had no experience.

Satisfaction with the Phase I System

The next four questions ask about your satisfaction with the student rating system. Some of the questions ask about your satisfaction with the *design* of the system (e.g., the items on the student rating form, the contingencies, and the feedback reports); some ask about your satisfaction with the *implementation* of the student rating system (e.g., the scheduling of the evaluations, decisions regarding who will be evaluated and how often, the speed with which feedback is received, etc.); finally, some ask about your satisfaction with *how the data from the system have been (or will be) used* by either departmental or college administrators. Please think carefully about your level of satisfaction with each of these different components and then answer the following questions.

6. In general, I am satisfied with the design of the student rating system (e.g., items on the student rating form, the contingencies, and the feedback reports).

Strongly Agree	Agree	Neither Agree nor Disagree	Disagree	Disagree Strongly	Does Not Apply

7. In general, I am satisfied with the implementation of the student rating system (e.g., scheduling of the evaluations, decisions regarding who will be evaluated and how often, the speed with which feedback is received, etc.).

Strongly Agree	Agree	Neither Agree nor Disagree	Disagree	Disagree Strongly	Does Not Apply

8. In general, I am satisfied with how the administration in my department uses the data from the student rating system.

Strongly Agree	Agree	Neither Agree nor Disagree	Disagree	Disagree Strongly	Does Not Apply

9. In general, I expect I will be satisfied with how the College Administration (i.e., the Deans and Associate Deans) will use the data from the student rating system.

Strongly Agree	Agree	Neither Agree nor Disagree	Disagree	Disagree Strongly	Does Not Apply

Satisfaction with the Overall Teacher Evaluation System

10. If peer evaluations (with the option of direct or videotaped classroom observation) are added to the student evaluation system, I will be satisfied with the combined overall teaching evaluation system.

Strongly Agree	Agree	Neither Agree nor Disagree	Disagree	Disagree Strongly	Does Not Apply

System Validity

11. In general, I believe the student rating system is valid.

Strongly Agree	Agree	Neither Agree nor Disagree	Disagree	Disagree Strongly	Does Not Apply

12. The student rating system includes all the important aspects of classroom teaching that students are able to observe.

Strongly Agree	Agree	Neither Agree nor Disagree	Disagree	Disagree Strongly	Does Not Apply

Cost-Effectiveness and Usefulness of the System

13. The student rating system has produced results that have been useful in *helping me improve* my teaching performance.

Strongly Agree	Agree	Neither Agree nor Disagree	Disagree	Disagree Strongly	Does Not Apply

14. The student rating system produces results that are useful in *helping the administrators in my department evaluate* the quality of teaching.

Strongly Agree	Agree	Neither Agree nor Disagree	Disagree	Disagree Strongly	Does Not Apply

15. The student rating system produces results that are useful in *helping the College administrators evaluate* the quality of teaching at the CVM.

| Strongly Agree | Agree | Neither Agree nor Disagree | Disagree | Disagree Strongly | Does Not Apply |

16. The student rating system provides benefits that outweigh the costs (e.g., time, energy, effort, etc.) of using it.

| Strongly Agree | Agree | Neither Agree nor Disagree | Disagree | Disagree Strongly | Does Not Apply |

Participation in System Development

17. I was given as much opportunity as I wanted to participate in the development of the student rating system.

| Strongly Agree | Agree | Neither Agree nor Disagree | Disagree | Disagree Strongly | Does Not Apply |

Underlying Factors That Contribute to System Effectiveness

18. The student rating system has helped faculty understand what is perceived in their departments as good teaching.

| Strongly Agree | Agree | Neither Agree nor Disagree | Disagree | Disagree Strongly | Does Not Apply |

19. The student rating system has motivated faculty to make changes in the way they teach their classes.

| Strongly Agree | Agree | Neither Agree nor Disagree | Disagree | Disagree Strongly | Does Not Apply |

20. The feedback from the student rating system shows faculty what they need to change to improve their teaching.

| Strongly Agree | Agree | Neither Agree nor Disagree | Disagree | Disagree Strongly | Does Not Apply |

PART III.   EVALUATION OF FEEDBACK EFFECTS

This section of the questionnaire is designed to determine what factors influence the use of system feedback to improve teaching effectiveness. Because you have been evaluated more than once by the student rating system, we are interested in your experience with the system and how you have used the feedback.

Trustworthiness of the Source of the Feedback

21. Student ratings should be part of a comprehensive teacher evaluation system.

Strongly Agree	Agree	Neither Agree nor Disagree	Disagree	Disagree Strongly	Does Not Apply

22. The students here are able to rate accurately my classroom teaching performance.

Strongly Agree	Agree	Neither Agree nor Disagree	Disagree	Disagree Strongly	Does Not Apply

Organizational Support for the System

23. My Department Head appears to support the student rating system.

Strongly Agree	Agree	Neither Agree \nor Disagree	Disagree	Disagree Strongly	Does Not Apply

24. College Administration appears to support the student rating system.

Strongly Agree	Agree	Neither Agree nor Disagree	Disagree	Disagree Strongly	Does Not Apply

25. I expect that the results of the student rating system will be used in making promotion and tenure decisions.

Strongly Agree	Agree	Neither Agree nor Disagree	Disagree	Disagree Strongly	Does Not Apply

26. I expect that instructors who are rated highly by the student rating system are more likely to be rewarded (e.g., receive teaching awards, promotion, tenure, merit increases, etc.) for their teaching.

Strongly Agree	Agree	Neither Agree nor Disagree	Disagree	Disagree Strongly	Does Not Apply

Utilization of the Feedback Provided

27. Faculty are offered assistance in improving any teaching deficiencies they may have.

Strongly Agree	Agree	Neither Agree nor Disagree	Disagree	Disagree Strongly	Does Not Apply

28. Resources are available to faculty to help them improve their teaching.

Strongly Agree	Agree	Neither Agree nor Disagree	Disagree	Disagree Strongly	Does Not Apply

REFERENCES

Abbott, R. D., and others. (1990). The student perspective of collecting student opinions. *Journal of Educational Psychology, 82*(2), 201–206.

Abrami, P. C., D'Apollonia, S., & Cohen, P. (1990). Validity of student ratings of instruction: What we know and what we do not. *Journal of Educational Psychology, 82*(2), 219–231.

Abrami, P. C., Leventhal, L., & Kickens, W. J. (1981). Multidimensionality of student ratings of instruction. *Instructional Evaluation, 6*(1), 12–17.

Albanese, M. A., Schuldt, S. S., & Case, D. E. (1991). The validity of lecturer ratings by students and trained observers. *Academic Medicine, 66*(1), 26–28.

Aleamoni, L. M. (1974). *The usefulness of student evaluations in improving college teaching.* Urbana-Champaign: Office of Instructional Resources, Measurement and Research Division, University of Illinois.

Aleamoni, L. M. (1981). Student ratings of instruction. In J. Millman (Ed.), *Handbook of teacher evaluation* (pp. 110–145). Thousand Oaks, CA: Sage.

Aleamoni, L. M. (1987). Concluding comments. In L. M. Aleamoni (Ed.), *Techniques for evaluating and improving instruction.* New Directions for Higher Education, no. 31. San Francisco: Jossey-Bass.

Allen, M. J., & Yen, W. M. (1979). *Introduction to measurement theory.* Pacific Grove, CA: Brooks/Cole.

Alluisi, E. A., & Megis, D. K. (1983). Potentials for productivity enhancement from psychology research and development. *American Psychologist, 38*(4), 487–493.

Ammons, R. B. (1956). Effects of knowledge of performance: A survey and tentative theoretical formulation. *Journal of General Psychology, 54,* 279–299.

Annett, J. (1969). *Feedback and human behavior.* New York: Penguin.

Astin, A. W., & Lee, C.B.T. (1966). Current practices in the evaluation and training of college teachers. *Educational Record, 47,* 361–375.

Basow, S. A., & Howe, K. G. (1987). Evaluations of college professors: Effects of professors' sex-type and sex, and students' sex. *Psychological Reports, 60*(20), 671–678.

Bass, B. M., Cascio, W. F., & O'Connor, E. J. (1974). Magnitude estimations of expressions of frequency and amount. *Journal of Applied Psychology, 59,* 313–320.

Bilodeau, E. A., & Bilodeau, I. M. (1961). Motor-skills learning. *Annual Review of Psychology, 12,* 243–280.

Blackburn, R. T., & Clark, M. J. (1975). An assessment of faculty performance: Some correlations between administrators, colleagues, students, and self-ratings. *Sociology of Education, 48,* 242–256.

Brandenburg, D. C., Slindle, J. A., & Batista, E. E. (1977). Student ratings of instruction: Validity and normative interpretations. *Journal of Research in Higher Education, 7,* 67–78.

Braskamp, L. A., Brandenburg, D. C., & Ory, J. C. (1984). *Evaluating teaching effectiveness: A practical guide.* Thousand Oaks, CA: Sage.

Braskamp, L. A., & Caulley, D. (1978). *Student rating and instructor self-ratings and their relationship to student achievement.* Urbana-Champaign: Office of Instructional Resources, Measurement and Research Division, University of Illinois.

Braskamp, L. A., Caulley, D., & Costin, F. (1979). Student ratings and instructor self-ratings and their relationship to student achievement. *American Educational Research Journal, 16,* 295–306.

Brock, S. (1978). *Measuring faculty advisor effectiveness.* Manhattan: Center for Faculty Evaluation and Development, Kansas State University.

Brown, D. L. (1976). Faculty ratings and student grades: A university-wide multiple regression analysis. *Journal of Educational Psychology, 68,* 573–578.

Brown, D. L. (1983). *Principles of educational and psychological testing* (3rd ed.). Austin, TX: Holt, Rinehart and Winston.

Burton, D. (1975). Student ratings: An information source for decision making. In G. R. Cope (Ed.), *Information for decisions in postsecondary education.* Proceedings of the Annual Forum (pp. 83–86). St. Louis, MO: Association for Institutional Research.

Campbell, J. P. (1977). On the nature of organizational effectiveness. In P. S. Goodman & J. M. Pennings (Eds.), *New perspectives in organizational effectiveness* (pp. 13–55). San Francisco: Jossey-Bass.

Campbell, J. P., & Pritchard, R. D. (1976). Motivation theory in organizational and industrial psychology. In M. D. Dunnette (Ed.), *Handbook of industrial and organizational psychology* (pp. 63–130). Skokie, IL: Rand McNally.

Canelos, J. (1985). Teaching and course evaluation procedures: A literature review of current research. *Journal of Instructional Psychology, 12*(4), 187–195.

Carmines, E. G., & Zeller, R. A. (1979). Reliability and validity assessment. In J. L. Sullivan (Ed.), *Quantitative applications in the social sciences.* Thousand Oaks, CA: Sage.

Cascio, W. F. (1987). *Applied psychology in personnel management.* Englewood Cliffs, NJ: Prentice Hall.

Cashin, W. E. (1988). *Student ratings of teaching: A summary of research*

(IDEA Paper No. 20). Manhattan: Center for Faculty Evaluation and Development, Kansas State University.

Cashin, W. E. (1989). *Defining and evaluating college teaching* (IDEA Paper No. 21). Manhattan: Center for Faculty Evaluation and Development, Kansas State University.

Cashin, W. E. (1990). *Student ratings of teaching: Recommendations for use* (IDEA Paper No. 22). Manhattan: Center for Faculty Evaluation and Development, Kansas State University.

Cashin, W. E., & Clegg, V. L. (1987). *Are student ratings of different academic fields different?* Paper presented at the annual meeting of the American Educational Research Association, Chicago.

Cashin, W. E., & Downey, R. G. (1992). Using global student rating items for summative evaluation. *Journal of Educational Psychology, 84*(4), 563–572.

Cashin, W. E., Noma, A., & Hana, G. S. (1987). *Comparative data by academic field* (IDEA Tech. Rep. No. 6). Manhattan: Center for Faculty Evaluation and Development, Kansas State University.

Cashin, W. E., & Slawson, H. M. (1977). *Description of database 1976–1977* (IDEA Tech. Rep. No. 2). Manhattan: Center for Faculty Evaluation and Development, Kansas State University.

Cawunder, P., & Tasker, J. B. (1981). Students' ratings of teacher effectiveness: What are the criteria? *Journal of Veterinary Medicine Education, 8*, 21–22.

Centra, J. A. (1972). *Two studies of the utility of student ratings for improving teaching* (SIR Rep. No. 2). Princeton, NJ: Educational Testing Service.

Centra, J. A. (1973a). Self ratings of college teachers: A comparison with student ratings. *Journal of Educational Measurement, 10*(4), 287–295.

Centra, J. A. (1973b). *Two studies on the utility of student ratings for instructional improvement: I. The effectiveness of student feedback in modifying college instruction. II. Self-ratings of college teachers: A comparison with student ratings* (SIR Rep. No. 2). Princeton, NJ: Educational Testing Service.

Centra, J. A. (1975). Colleagues as raters of classroom instruction. *Journal of Higher Education, 46*, 327–337.

Centra, J. A. (1977). *How universities evaluate faculty performance: A survey of department heads* (Rep. GREB No. 75–5bR). Princeton, NJ: Educational Testing Service.

Centra, J. A. (1979). *Determining faculty effectiveness: Assessing teaching, research, and service for personnel decisions and improvements.* San Francisco: Jossey-Bass.

Centra, J. A. (1980). *Determining faculty effectiveness.* San Francisco: Jossey-Bass.

Centra, J. A., & Creech, F. R. (1976). *The relationship between student, teacher, and course characteristics and student ratings of teacher effec-*

tiveness (Project Rep. No. 76–1). Princeton, NJ: Educational Testing Service.

Cheong, G.S.C. (1979). Student achievement as a measure of teaching effectiveness. *Journal of College Science Teaching, 14*(16), 471–474.

Cliff, N. (1959). Adverbs as multipliers. *Psychological Review, 66,* 27–44.

Coburn, L. (1984). *Student evaluation of teacher performance.* ERIC Clearinghouse on Tests, Measurement, and Evaluation, Princeton, NJ.

Cohen, J. (1977). *Statistical power analysis for the behavioral sciences* (Rev. ed.). Orlando, FL: Academic Press.

Cohen, J. (1994). The earth is round (p < .05). *American Psychologist, 49*(12), 997–1003.

Cohen, P. A. (1980). Effectiveness of student-rating feedback for improving college instruction: A meta-analysis of findings. *Research in Higher Education, 13*(4), 321–341.

Cohen, P. A. (1981). Student ratings of instruction and student achievement: A meta-analysis of multisection validity studies. *Review of Educational Research, 51,* 281–309.

Cohen, P. A. (1982). Meta-analyses of validity studies. *Teaching of Psychology, 9*(2), 78–82.

Cohen, P. A., & McKeachie, W. J. (1980). The role of colleagues in the evaluation of college teaching. *Improving College and University Teaching, 28,* 147–154.

Cornwall, C. D. (1974). Statistical treatment of data from student teaching evaluation questionnaires. *Journal of Chemical Education, 51,* 155–160.

Costin, F. (1968). A graduate course in the teaching of psychology: Description and evaluation. *Journal of Teacher Education, 19,* 425–432.

Cronbach, L. J., & Meehl, P. E. (1955). Construct validity in psychological tests. *Psychological Bulletin, 52,* 281–302.

Cusella, L. P. (1987). Feedback, motivation and performance. In F. M. Jablin, L. L. Putnam, K. H. Roberts, & L. W. Porter (Eds.), *Handbook of organizational communication: An interdisciplinary perspective* (pp. 624–678). Thousand Oaks, CA: Sage.

Dickinson, D. J. (1990). Relationship between ratings of teacher performance and student learning. *Contemporary Educational Psychology, 15,* 142–151.

Divoky, J. J., & Rothermel, M. A. (1988). Student perceptions of the relative importance of dimensions of teaching performance across type of class. *Educational Research Quarterly, 12*(3), 40–45.

Doyle, K. O. (1975). *Student evaluation of instruction.* Lexington, MA: Heath.

Doyle, K. O. (1983). *Evaluating teaching.* San Francisco: Lexington Books.

Doyle, K. O., & Crichton, L. I. (1978). Student, peer, and self evaluations of college instructors. *Journal of Educational Psychology, 70,* 815–826.

Doyle, K. O., & Webber, P. L. (1978). *Self-ratings of college instruction.* Minneapolis: Measurement Service Center, University of Minnesota.

Doyle, K. O., & Whitely, S. E. (1974). Student ratings as criteria for effective college teaching. *American Educational Research Journal, 2,* 259–274.

Drucker, A. J., & Remmers, H. H. (1951). Do alumni and students differ in their attitudes toward instructors? *Journal of Educational Psychology, 42,* 129–143.

Duerr, E. C. (1974). The effect of misdirected incentives on employee behavior. *Personnel Journal, 53*(2), 890–893.

Duncan, A. J., & Biddle, B. J. (1974). *The study of teaching.* Austin, TX: Holt, Rinehart and Winston.

Dunkin, M. J., & Barnes, J. (1986). Research on teaching in higher education. In M. C. Wittrock (Ed.), *Handbook of research on teaching* (3rd ed., pp. 754–777). Old Tappan, NJ: Macmillan.

Earley, P. C., Connolly, T., & Ekegren, G. (1989). Goals, strategy development, and task performance: Some limits on the efficacy of goal setting. *Journal of Applied Psychology, 74,* 24–33.

Edgerton, R., Hutchings, P., & Quinlan, K. (1991). *The teaching portfolio capturing the scholarship in teaching.* Washington, DC: American Association for Higher Education.

Feldman, K. A. (1976a). Grades and college students' evaluations of their courses and teachers. *Research in Higher Education, 4,* 69–111.

Feldman, K. A. (1976b). The superior college teacher from the students' view. *Research in Higher Education, 5,* 243–288.

Feldman, K. A. (1977). Consistency and variability among college students in rating their teachers and courses: A review and analysis. *Research in Higher Education, 6,* 223–274.

Feldman, K. A. (1978). Course characteristics and college students' ratings of their teachers: What we know and what we don't know. *Research in Higher Education, 9,* 199–242.

Feldman, K. A. (1979). The significance of circumstances for college students' ratings of their teachers and courses. *Research in Higher Education, 10,* 149–172.

Feldman, K. A. (1983). The seniority and instructional experience of college teachers as related to the evaluations they receive from their students. *Research in Higher Education, 18,* 3–124.

Feldman, K. A. (1984). Class size and college students' evaluations of teachers and courses: A closer look. *Research in Higher Education, 21,* 45–116.

Feldman, K. A. (1989). The association between student ratings of specific instructional dimensions and student achievement: Refining and extending the synthesis of data from multisection validity studies. *Research in Higher Education, 30,* 583–645.

Follman, J., & Merica, J. A. (1973). *Student achievement and self, peer and supervisor ratings of teacher effectiveness.* Unpublished manuscript, University of Florida, Tampa.

French-Lazovich, G. (1981). Peer review: Documentary evidence in the evaluation of teaching. In J. Millman (Ed.), *Handbook of teacher evaluation* (pp. 73–89). Thousand Oaks, CA: Sage.

Frey, P. W., Leonard, D. W., & Beatty, W. W. (1975). Student ratings of instruction: Validation research. *American Educational Research Journal, 12,* 327–336.

Gage, N. L. (1958). *Ends and means in appraising college training.* Paper presented at the Conference on Appraisal of Teaching in Large Universities, Ann Arbor, Michigan.

Gigliotti, R. J., & Buchtel, F. S. (1990). Attributional bias and course evaluations. *Journal of Educational Psychology, 82*(2), 341–351.

Gillmore, G. M. (1975). *Statistical analysis of data from the first year of use of the student rating forms of the University of Washington Instructional Assessment System.* EAC Report 76–9. Seattle, WA: Educational Assessment Center, University of Washington.

Gillmore, G. M., & Naccarato, R. W. (1975). *The effects of factors outside the instructors' control on student ratings of instruction.* Seattle: Educational Assessment Center, University of Washington.

Goodman, M. J. (1990). The review of tenured faculty. *Journal of Higher Education, 61*(4), 408–424.

Gravetter, F. J., & Wallnau, L. B. (1988). *Statistics for the behavioral sciences* (3rd ed.). Minneapolis: West Publishing.

Guion, R. M. (1965). *Personnel testing.* New York: McGraw-Hill.

Guthrie, E. R. (1954). *The evaluation of teaching: A progress report.* Seattle: University of Washington Press.

Guzzo, R. A., Jette, R. D., & Katzell, R. A. (1985). The effects of psychologically based intervention programs of worker productivity: A meta-analysis. *Personnel Psychology, 38,* 275–291.

Hanges, P. J., Schneider, B., & Niles, K. (1990). Stability of performance: An interactionist perspective. *Journal of Applied Psychology, 75*(6), 658–667.

Harris, E. L. (1982). Student ratings of faculty performance: Should departmental committees construct the instruments? *Journal of Educational Research, 76*(2), 100–106.

Heiman, G. W. (1992). *Basic statistics for the behavioral sciences.* Boston: Houghton Mifflin.

Hildebrand, M., Wilson, R. C., & Dienst, E. R. (1971). *Evaluating university teaching.* Berkeley: Center for Research and Development in Higher Education, University of California.

Hines, C. V., Cruickshank, D. R., & Kennedy, J. J. (1982). *Measures of teacher clarity and their relationships to student achievement and satisfaction.* Paper presented at the annual meeting of the American Educational Research Association, New York.

Hoover, K. H. (1980). *College teaching today: A handbook for postsecondary instruction.* Needham Heights, MA: Allyn & Bacon.

Horner, K. L., Murray, H. G., & Rushton, J. P. (1989). Relation between aging and rated teaching effectiveness of academic psychologists. *Psychology and Aging, 4*(2), 226–229.

Howard, G. S., Conway, C. G., & Maxwell, S. E. (1985). Construct validity of measures of college teaching effectiveness. *Journal of Educational Psychology, 77,* 187–196.

Howard, G. S., & Maxwell, S. E. (1980). The correlation between student satisfaction and grades: A case of mistaken causation? *Journal of Educational Psychology, 72,* 810–820.

Howard, G. S., & Maxwell, S. E. (1982). Do grades contaminate student evaluations of instruction? *Research in Higher Education, 16,* 175–188.

Hunter, J. E., & Schmidt, F. L. (1990). *Methods of meta-analysis: Correcting error and bias in research findings.* Thousand Oaks, CA: Sage.

Ilgen, D. R., Fisher, C. D., & Taylor, M. S. (1979). Consequences of individual feedback on behavior in organizations. *Journal of Applied Psychology, 64,* 349–371.

Keppel, G. (1991). *Design and analysis: A researcher's handbook* (3rd ed.). Englewood Cliffs, NJ: Prentice Hall.

Kluger, A. N., & DeNisi, A. (1996). The effects of feedback interventions on performance: A historical review, a meta-analysis, and a preliminary feedback intervention theory. *Psychological Bulletin, 119*(2), 254–284.

Knapper, C. K., Geis, G. L., Pascal, C. E., & Shore, B. M. (1977). *If teaching is important.* Ottawa, Canada: Clarke, Irwin.

Kottke, J. L. (1984). Assessing instructor performance: A classroom project for an industrial/organizational psychology class. *Teaching of Psychology, 11*(4), 231–232.

Kremer, J. F. (1990). Construct validity of multiple measures in teaching, research, and service and reliability of peer ratings. *Journal of Educational Psychology, 82*(2), 213–218.

Kulik, J. A., & McKeachie, W. J. (1975). The evaluation of teachers in higher education. In F. N. Kerlinger (Ed.), *Review of research in education* (Vol. 3, pp. 210–240). Itasca, IL: Peacock.

Land, M. L. (1979). Low-inference variables of teacher clarity: Effects on student concept learning. *Journal of Educational Psychology, 71,* 795–799.

Land, M. L., & Combs, A. (1981). *Teacher clarity, student instructional ratings, and student performance.* Paper presented at the annual meeting of the American Educational Research Association, Los Angeles.

Landy, F. J., & Farr, J. L. (1980). Performance rating. *Psychological Bulletin, 87,* 72–107.

L'Hommedieu, R., Menges, R. J., & Brinko, K. T. (1990). Methodological explanations for the modest effects of feedback from student ratings. *Journal of Educational Psychology, 82,* 232–241.

Lunney, G. H. (1974). *Attitudes of senior students from a small liberal arts college concerning faculty and course evaluations: Some possible explanations of evaluation results* (Research Rep. No. 32). Danville: Office of Institutional Research, Centre College of Kentucky.

Mahoney, T. A. (1988). Productivity defined: The relativity of efficiency, effectiveness, and change. In J. C. Campbell and R. J. Campbell (Eds.), *Productivity in organizations* (pp. 13–38). San Francisco: Jossey-Bass.

Mali, P. (1978). *Improving total productivity.* New York: Wiley.

Marsh, H. W. (1982). The use of path analysis to estimate teacher and course effects in student ratings of instructional effectiveness. *Applied Psychological Measurement, 6,* 47–59.

Marsh, H. W. (1983). Multidimensional ratings of teaching effectiveness by students from different academic settings and their relation to student/course/instructor characteristics. *Journal of Educational Psychology, 75,* 150–166.

Marsh, H. W. (1984). Students' evaluations of university teaching: Dimensionality, reliability, validity, potential biases, and utility. *Journal of Educational Psychology, 76,* 707–754.

Marsh, H. W. (1986). Applicability paradigm: Students' evaluations of teaching effectiveness in different countries. *Journal of Educational Psychology, 78,* 465–473.

Marsh, H. W. (1987). Students' evaluations of university teaching: Research findings, methodological issues, and directions for future research. *International Journal of Educational Research, 11,* 253–388.

Marsh, H. W. (1994). Weighting for the right criteria in the Instructional Development and Effectiveness Assessment (IDEA) system: Global and specific ratings of teaching effectiveness and their relation to course objectives. *Journal of Educational Psychology, 86*(4) 631–648.

Marsh, H. W., & Cooper, T. (1981). Prior subject interest, students' evaluation, and instructional effectiveness. *Multivariate Behavioral Research, 16,* 82–104.

Marsh, H. W., Fleiner, H., & Thomas, C. S. (1975). Validity and usefulness of student evaluations of instructional quality. *Journal of Educational Psychology, 67,* 833–839.

Marsh, H. W., & Overall, J. U. (1979a). Long-term stability of students' evaluations: A note on Feldman's "Consistency and variability among college students in rating their teachers and courses." *Research in Higher Education, 10,* 139–147.

Marsh, H. W., & Overall, J. U. (1979b). *Validity of students' evaluations of teaching: A comparison with instructor self evaluations by teaching assistants, undergraduate faculty, and graduate faculty.* Paper presented at the annual meeting of the American Educational Research Association, San Francisco.

Marsh, H. W., & Overall, J. U. (1980). Validity of students' evaluations of teaching effectiveness: Cognitive and affective criteria. *Journal of Educational Psychology, 72,* 468–475.

Marsh, H. W., & Overall, J. U. (1981). The relative influence of course level, course type, and instructor on students' evaluations of college teaching. *American Educational Research Association Journal, 18*(11), 103–112.

Marsh, H. W., Overall, J. U., & Kessler, S. P. (1979). Validity of student evaluations of instructional effectiveness: A comparison of faculty self-evaluations and evaluations by their students. *Journal of Educational Psychology, 71,* 149–160.

Marsh, H. W., Overall, J. U., & Thomas, C. S. (1976). *The relationship between students' evaluations of instruction and expected grades.* Paper presented at the annual meeting of the American Educational Research Association, San Francisco.

Marsh, H. W., & Roche, L. (1993). The use of students' evaluation and an individually structured intervention to enhance university teaching effectiveness. *American Educational Research Journal, 30*(1), 217–251.

Maslow, A. H., & Zimmerman, W. (1956). College teaching ability, scholarly activity, and personality. *Journal of Educational Psychology, 47,* 185–189.

McKeachie, W. J. (1979). Student ratings of faculty: A reprise. *Academe: Bulletin of the AAUP, 65*(6), 384–397.

Menges, R. J. (1973). The new reporters: Students rate instruction. In C. R. Pace (Ed.), *Evaluating learning and teaching.* New Directions for Higher Education, no. 4. San Francisco: Jossey-Bass.

Menges, R. J., & Brinko, K. T. (1986). *Effects of student evaluation feedback: A meta-analysis of higher education research.* Paper presented at the annual meeting of the American Educational Research Association, San Francisco, Apr. 16–20.

Miller, R. I. (1972). *Evaluating faculty performance.* San Francisco: Jossey-Bass.

Miller, R. I. (1974). *Developing programs for faculty evaluation: A sourcebook for higher education.* San Francisco: Jossey-Bass.

Miller, S. (1987). Student rating scales for tenure and promotion. *Improving College and University Teaching, 32*(2), 87–90.

Mirus, R. (1973). Some implications of student evaluations of teachers. *Journal of Economic Education, 5,* 35–37.

Moritsch, B. G., & Suter, W. N. (1988). Correlates of halo error in teacher evaluation. *Educational Research Quarterly, 12*(3), 29–34.

Morsh, J. E., Burgess, G. G., & Smith, P. N. (1956). Student achievement as a measure of instructional effectiveness. *Journal of Educational Psychology, 47,* 79–88.

Morsh, J. E., & Wilder, E. W. (1954). *Identifying the effective instructor: A review of quantitative studies, 1900–1952* (AFPTRC Research Bulletin). San Antonio, TX: Air Force Personnel and Training Research Center, Lackland AFB.

Murray, H. G. (1976). *How do good teachers teach? An observational study of the classroom teaching behaviors of social science professors receiving low, medium, and high teacher ratings.* Paper presented at the annual meeting of the Canadian Psychological Association.

Murray, H. G. (1983). Low inference classroom teaching behaviors and student ratings of college teaching effectiveness. *Journal of Educational Psychology, 71,* 856–865.

Nadler, D. A. (1979). The effects of feedback on task group behavior: A review of the experimental research. *Organizational Behavior and Human Performance, 23,* 309–338.

Nagle, B. F. (1953). Criterion development. *Personnel Psychology, 6,* 271–288.

O'Hanlon, J., & Mortensen, L. (1980). Making teacher evaluation work. *Journal of Higher Education, 51,* 664–672.

Ory, J. C. (1980). The influence of students' affective entry on overall ratings. *Educational Psychology Measurement, 42,* 767–775.

Overall, J. U., & Marsh, H. W. (1980). Students' evaluations of instruction: A longitudinal study of their stability. *Journal of Educational Psychology, 72,* 321–325.

Pambookian, H. S. (1973). The effect of feedback from students to college instructors on their teaching behavior (Doctoral dissertation, University of Michigan, 1973). *Dissertation Abstracts International, 33*(9–A): 4950.

Pambookian, H. S. (1974). Internal level of student evaluation of instruction as a source of instructor change after feedback. *Journal of Educational Psychology, 66,* 52–56.

Peeples, D. E. (1978). Measure for productivity. *Datamation, 24*(5), 222–230.

Pohlman, J. T. (1972). *Summary of research on the relationship between student characteristics and student evaluations of instruction at Southern Illinois University, Carbondale* (Tech. Rep. 1, 1–72). Carbondale: Counseling and Testing Center, Southern Illinois University.

Pritchard, R. D. (1990). *Measuring and improving organizational productivity: A practical guide.* New York: Praeger.

Pritchard, R. D. (Ed.). (1995). *Productivity measurement and improvement: Organizational case studies.* New York: Praeger.

Pritchard, R. D., & Montagno, R. V. (1978). *The effects of specific versus non-specific, and absolute versus comparative feedback on performance and satisfaction* (Air Force Human Resources Laboratory Technical Report, AFHRL–TR–78–12, pp. 1–57).

Pritchard, R. D., Montagno, R. V., & Moore, J. R. (1978). *Enhancing productivity through feedback and job design* (Air Force Human Resources Laboratory Technical Report, AFHRL–TR–78–44, pp. 1–45).

Pritchard, R. D., & Roth, P. J. (1991). Accounting for non-linear utility functions in composite measures of productivity and performance. *Organizational Behavior and Human Decision Processes, 50*(2), 341–359.

Pritchard, R. D., and others. (1988). The effects of feedback, goal setting, and incentives on organizational productivity. *Journal of Applied Psychology Monograph Series, 73*(2), 337–358.

Pritchard, R. D., and others. (1989). The evaluation of an integrated approach to measuring organizational productivity. *Personnel Psychology, 42*(1), 69–115.

Przygodda, M. (1994). *Die forderung der effektivitat in arbeitsgruppen: Eine evaluation des managementsystems PPM.* (The advancement of the effectiveness in work groups: An evaluation of the management system PPM). Published doctoral dissertation. Aachen: Shaker-Verlag.

Rabalais, M. J. (1977). *The relationship between number of graduate semester hours, years of teaching experience, and student evaluations of overall rating of instructors for a selected sample of junior college faculty.* Paper presented at the annual conference of the Southwest Region of the American Educational Research Association Special Interest Group in Community College Research, New Orleans, July 19–20, 1977.

Ree, M. J., Carretta, T. R., & Earles, J. A. (1997). *When the criterion doesn't matter and other consequences of Wilks' theorem.* Unpublished paper, Armstrong Laboratory Human Resources Directorate, Brooks AFB, TX.

Remmers, H. H. (Ed.) (1950). *Studies in college and university staff evaluation.* Lafayette, IN: Division of Educational References, Purdue University.

Root, A. R. (1931). Student ratings of teachers. *Journal of Higher Education, 2*, 311–315.

Rotton, J. (1990). Research productivity, course load, and ratings of instructors. *Perceptual and Motor Skills, 71*(3), 1388.

Runco, M. A., & Thurston, B. J. (1987). Students' ratings of college teaching: A social validation. *Teaching of Psychology, 14*(2), 89–91.

Sawyer, J. (1966). Measurement and prediction, clinical and statistical. *Psychological Bulletin, 66*, 178–200.

Sawyer, J. E., Pritchard, R. D., & Hedley-Goode, A. (1991). *Comparison of non-linear ProMES versus linear procedures for obtaining composite measures in performance appraisal.* Unpublished manuscript, Department of Psychology, Texas A&M University.

Schmidt, F. L. (1992). What do data really mean? Research findings, meta-analysis, and cumulative knowledge in psychology. *American Psychologist, 47*(10), 1173–1181.

Schmidt, F. L., & Kaplan, L. B. (1971). Composite versus multiple criteria: A review and resolution of the controversy. *Personnel Psychology, 24*, 429–439.

Seashore, S. E. (1972). *The measurement of organizational effectiveness.* Paper presented at the University of Minnesota, Minneapolis.

Seldin, P. O. (1978). *Survey of current faculty evaluation procedures.* Report presented at the Fourth International Conference on Improving University Teaching sponsored by the University of Maryland.

Seldin, P. O. (1980). *Successful faculty evaluation programs: A practical guide to improve faculty performance and promotion/tenure decisions.* Crugers, NY: Coventry Press.

Seldin, P. O. (1984). *Changing practices in faculty evaluation: A critical assessment and recommendations for improvement.* San Francisco: Jossey-Bass.

Seldin, P. O. (1989). Using student feedback to improve teaching. In A. F. Lucas (Ed.), *The departmental chairperson's role in enhancing college teaching.* New Directions for Teaching and Learning, no. 37. San Francisco: Jossey-Bass.

Seldin, P. O. (1990). Academic environments and teacher effectiveness. In P. O. Seldin (Ed.), *How administrators can improve teaching: Moving from talk to action in higher education* (pp. 3–22). San Francisco: Jossey-Bass.

Seldin, P. O. (1991). *The teaching portfolio: A practical guide to improved performance and promotion/tenure decisions.* Bolton, MA: Anker.

Shapiro, E. G. (1990). Effect of instructor and class characteristics on students' class evaluations. *Research in Higher Education, 31*(2), 135–148.

Shaw, M. E., & Wright, J. M. (1967). *Scales for the measurement of attitudes.* New York: McGraw-Hill.

Shetty, Y. K., & Buehler, V. M. (1985). *Productivity through people: Practices of well-managed companies.* Westport, CT: Quorum Books.

Shingles, R. D. (1977). Use of regression to correct for student biases. *American Educational Research Journal, 14*(4), 459–470.

Spector, P. E. (1976). Choosing response categories for summated rating scales. *Journal of Applied Psychology, 61,* 374–375.

Spencer, R. E. (1968). *The Illinois course evaluation questionnaire: Manual of interpretation* (Rev. ed., Research Rep. No. 270). Urbana-Champaign: Office of Instructional Resources, Measurement and Research Division, University of Illinois.

Spencer, R. E., & Aleamoni, L. M. (1970). A student course evaluation questionnaire. *Journal of Educational Measurement, 7,* 209–210.

Stein, J. M. (1986). Public employee productivity: Can outcomes be validly measured at the jurisdictional level? *Public Personnel Management, 15*(2), 111–117.

Stevens, J. J. (1987). Using student ratings to improve instruction. In L. M. Aleamoni (Ed.), *Techniques for evaluating and improving instruction.* New Directions for Teaching and Learning, no. 31. San Francisco: Jossey-Bass.

Stumpf, S. A., Freedman, R. D., & Aguanno, J. C. (1979). A path analysis of factors often found to be related to student ratings of teaching effectiveness. *Research in Higher Education, 11,* 111–123.

Tatro, C. (1995). Gender effects on student evaluations of faculty. *Journal of Research and Development in Education, 28*(3), 169–173.

Tuttle, T. C. (1981). Productivity measurement methods: Classification, critique, and implications for the Air Force (AFHRL Tech. Rep. 81–9). Brooks AFB, TX: Manpower and Personnel Division, Air Force Human Resources Laboratory.

Tuttle, T. C., & Weaver, C. N. (1986). *Methodology for generating efficiency and effectiveness measures (MGEEM): A guide for commanders, managers, and supervisors* (AFHRL Tech. Rep. 86–26). Brooks AFB, TX: Manpower and Personnel Division, Air Force Human Resources Laboratory.

Walden, J.W.H. (1909). *Universities of ancient Greece.* New York: Scribner.

Ward, M. D., Clark, D. C., & Harrison, G. V. (1981). *The observer effect in classroom visitation.* Paper presented at the annual meeting of the American Educational Research Association, Los Angeles.

Watson, M. D. (1993). *The development and evaluation of a new approach to student ratings of teaching.* Unpublished doctoral dissertation, Texas A&M University.

Webb, W. B., & Nolan, C. Y. (1955). Student, supervisor, and self-ratings of instructional proficiency. *Journal of Educational Psychology, 46,* 42–46.

Weiss, C. H. (1984). Increasing the likelihood of influencing decisions. In L. Rutman (Ed.), *Evaluating research methods: A basic guide* (2nd ed.). Thousand Oaks: Sage.

Werdell, P. R. (1967). *Course and teacher evaluation* (2nd ed.). Washington, DC: United States National Student Association.

Wilke, S. S. (1970). The effects of feedback, guessing, and anticipation rate upon verbal discrimination learning. *Psychological Record, 46,* 171–178.

Wilks, S. S. (1938). Weighting systems for linear functions of correlated variables when there is no dependent variable. *Psychometrika, 3*(1), 23–40.

Wortruba, T. R., & Wright, P. L. (1975). How to develop a teacher-rating instrument: A research approach. *Journal of Higher Education, 46,* 653–663.

INDEX